Guidance and Couselling in Education

Guidance and Couselling in Education

A Modern Perspective

Rashmi Agrawal

SHIPRA

₹1500; US$ 50
ISBN: 978-93-91978-14-3

2023
First Published in India

Guidance and Couselling in Education: A Modern Perspective

Published by:
SHIPRA PUBLICATIONS
LG 18-19, Pankaj Central Market
I.P. Ext., Patparganj, Delhi 110092, India
Tel.: +91 11 2223 5152/6152; 96500 28065
E-mail: info@shiprapublication.com
www.shiprapublication.com

Preface

The worlds of learning and work have been enlarging and becoming more complex constantly. New vocations, educational streams as well as personal problems have emerged leading to necessity of guidance and counselling with new perspective. Activity-based learning emphasized in the National Education Policy 2020, the emergence of e-learning in various fields, and the sea change in the technology and its applications have increased the demand for guidance and counselling in recent years several fold. The processes of guidance and counselling also require innovations to reach to the last mile. For instance, while the spread of mobiles has brought about ease of communication even in situations that inhibited personal contact between the counsellor and client, as it happened during the recent pandemic times, the rapid expansion that is taking place in internet access and use has made the job of all the actors in the counselling process easy and difficult at the same time. On top of these phenomena, the emergence of Artificial Intelligence (AI) and machine learning has opened immense possibilities for an intelligent user of the technological advances in understanding the career options available, identify what is most suitable, and learn about what needs to be done to access such opportunities. Shifting sands have made the counselling profession a more essential and at the same time more challenging.

The present book looks at various facets of guidance and counselling. It starts with a quick review of National Education Policy 2020 and the changing need for and role of guidance. The first Chapter discusses the concept, objectives, and scope of guidance with special reference to it in difficult situations like Covid-19. The second Chapter describes sociological, economic psychological and philosophical foundations of guidance. Need of guidance is at various educational levels; it could be foundational level, preparatory and middle or secondary level. Therefore, Chapter three elaborates the functions of guidance at various educational levels.

Guidance can be for educational and or vocational needs as well as for personal-social needs. Chapters four and five provide details about the varying types of guidance explaining the concepts, objectives, and functions of guidance at each level. Guidance is provided through various services such as orientation services, individual and group guidance services, placement services and so on. Chapter six provides a bird's eye view of these services. The chapter also illustrates Cumulative Record Card and its need.

Individual guidance or counselling is extremely important as it focuses on specific needs of the individual and is commonly needed. Chapter seven details the concept, objectives and various types of individual counselling that includes directive-nondirective counselling, eclectic counselling, cognitive therapies, and case study approach to counselling. The chapter explains the process of each type of counselling with examples for better understanding and self-learning.

The next Chapter eighth relates to group guidance programme which could be imparted to large number of persons at a time. It explains the concept of group guidance, its objectives, and its process. Chapter nine elucidates as to how to identify various problems of the students, the role of various guidance workers, and internal and outside resources available to guidance personnel, while Chapter ten describes various techniques of group guidance which could be used as per need by various guidance personnel. Some of the techniques explained are group discussions, career exhibitions and conferences, talks, field visits, film shows and so on. Each technique has been explained with detailed examples.

Self- concept is a perception one has about him or herself. A self-concept includes self-image, attitudes, self -esteem etc. which are important in the process of education and guidance. While explaining self-concept theories in Chapter eleven, the role of guidance in developing a healthy and positive self-concept in individual has been high-lighted. A positive self-concept also relates to one's creativity. How to encourage creativity in children has been described in Chapter twelve along with role of guidance in developing the same.

Mental health is a very important issue to be tackled by counselling. It has become even more important as the spread of Covid-19 left more and more people suffering with mental health issues. Chapters thirteen and fourteen deal with the issues of mental disorders and mental health as well as various types of children with special needs respectively. There could be mentally retarded children, children who are differently abled, gifted children and so on. Their needs differ but they are to be mainstreamed. The role of guidance becomes very important in identifying needs of such children and guiding them appropriately.

Guidance services are based on the assessment of each individual—the abilities, intelligence, aptitudes, personality characteristics, interests, thinking and beliefs. These can be assessed by using various appraisal techniques. Chapters fifteen, sixteen and seventeen relate to these issues. While Chapter fifteen discusses psychological tests for assessment in general, and various characteristics of a good test, Chapters sixteen and seventeen dwell on intelligence, aptitude, interest tests and personality tests respectively with detailed examples and samples. These chapters also mention about emotional intelligence and its importance in life. Guidance and counselling are also possible in certain cases using other techniques of assessment and without using psychological tests. These techniques have been detailed in Chapter eighteen. These include self-reporting, observational and socio metric techniques.

Guidance is not complete till the guidance personnel maintain adequate information and guidance record. How to collect and maintain the information and other records have been elaborated in Chapter nineteen. The chapter also discusses about the authenticity and sources of information. Both primary and secondary sources are discussed.

For making the guidance effective and relevant for all the students, a proper place is needed. There should also be a well-designed guidance program for the year. Need for Career Resource Center, an indicative action plan and how to evaluate the guidance program have been detailed in Chapter twenty.

As mentioned earlier, use of technology is becoming a way of life. How technology can be used in guidance and counselling with special reference to new education policy, technology driven activities, online interviews etc. find a mention in Chapter twenty-one. This chapter specifically mentions about use of artificial intelligence in guidance and argues if robots will replace the guidance worker and will it be pragmatic?

Equally important is the Chapter twenty-two which brings out challenges and emerging trends in guidance and counselling relating to old age, gender imbalance, inclusivity, impact of pandemics, internet and social network addictions etc. and how it is leading to changing role and skills of a counsellor.

'Be your own employer and give employment to others' is the present-day demand. The last Chapter discusses the traits that are needed to be an entrepreneur and what choices are available if one wants to embark on own startup for a career.

The author's earlier works in the field in different forms have been widely used by various stakeholders like teachers, counsellors, learners etc. and also got accepted as self-learning material in open distance learning.

In writing this book, I have used material from various sources or referred to the works of various authors. It is mentioned here that only those materials, samples etc. have been drawn upon that are available in public domain. I am grateful to the authors and publishers and other resources from where materials have been referred or used to enrich this volume for its readers. I would also like to thank all those who had faith in me and shared their problems. While giving examples, all names have been changed to maintain the ethics of the profession and privacy of individuals.

The words like 'he' 'his' are used not to focus upon any gender. These should be treated as gender neutral.

Mr. D. Kumar, CEO, Shipra Publications, is at the back of this venture. I am grateful to him for always encouraging me. I hope this book would be useful to teachers, teacher-educators, pre-service teachers, parents and counselling professionals.

Suggestions are welcome.

Dr. Rashmi Agrawal

Contents

List of Illustrations

Tables

Figures

1

National Education Policy 2020 and Role of Guidance and Counselling

Introduction

Sustainable Development Goal (SDG) 4 of the 2030 Agenda relates to "ensure inclusive and equitable quality education and promote lifelong learning opportunities for all" by 2030. The government of India has endorsed SDGs in 2015 and working in the direction of achieving these. The global knowledge, learning and skill landscape is changing fast and calls for multidisciplinary learning. Education system needs critical thinking and problem-solving approach. 'Pedagogy must evolve to make education more experiential, holistic, integrated, inquiry-driven, discovery-oriented, learner-centred, discussion-based, flexible, and, of course, enjoyable.' (New Education Policy 2020). This National Education Policy 2020 is addressing the overall developmental agenda.

The New Education Policy was approved in India from July, 2020 which will be implemented in a phased manner. India needed revamping of education system in the light of the new knowledge that is emerging making some of the historical knowledge obsolete and irrelevant. Speaking at the World Education Summit organised in November 2017, Dr Rajendra Pratap Gupta, Member, National Education Policy Committee, Ministry of Human Resource Development, Government of India indicated towards complete transformation of the education system. He was of the view that economic growth without improvement in education and health cannot facilitate development.

The process of learning has also become important in this context. The transformation of education system is also needed due to technological revolution which brought change in employment system as well. With various scientific and technological advances, such as the availability of big data, machine learning, and artificial intelligence, transformation of jobs from unskilled jobs to skilled ones or captured by machines opened up new vistas of employment and in turn need for capacity development. New skilled labour is also needed in other disciplines as well, like—agriculture, climate science, and social science. To meet the demands for employment markets, capacity development in digitisation, automation and other tech related areas became imperative.

It is always desired to review country's policies from time to time giving due weightage to various national and international developments and demands. The first National Education Policy (NEP) came into being after independence in 1968. This was revised in 1992 after a gap of 18 years. It was high time to have a relook at the education policy as 25 years have passed since the education policy was revised.

Indicative Features

The new education policy focusses upon various important features such as Incorporating processes to be in sync with the global trends, demand -based skill training to enhance employability and use of technology for enhancing learning outcomes.

The new NEP 2020 is approved after due consultations with various stakeholders as well as feedback from various corners. Under this NEP, the format of 10 + 2 system has been abolished. Now it is divided into 5+ 3+ 3+ 4 system. 5 donates to preschool, 3 relates to 6 to 8 Mid School, again 3 is 8 to 11 High School, and 4 is 12 onwards Graduation. This shows that degree courses will be of four years.

To develop skills in the young, vocational courses are to be introduced at 6th standard onwards. From 8th to 11th, students can choose subjects instead of studying all the subjects. All graduation course are to have major and minor courses. In this system even science students can opt for Physics as main and Music as another subject. Various permutation combinations are available in the system as per aptitude and interest of the learner. Rules and regulations and grading system will be similar in all Universities may be Government, Private, Open, Deemed, or Vocational. New Basic learning program will be created by government for parents to teach children up to 3 years in home and for preschool 3 to 6.

There is also provision for multiple entry and exit from any course and credit system for graduation. For each year student are to get some credits which s/he can utilize if s/he takes break in course and come back again to complete the course. All schools' exams will be semester wise twice a year. The syllabus will have drastic changes to focus upon developing core knowledge of any subject. The theoretical knowledge will be combined with hands on sessions, practical and application of knowledge and learning. For any graduation course, if student completes only one year, s/he will get a basic certificate, if s/he completes two years then s/he will get diploma certificate and if s/he completes full course then s/ he will get degree certificate. Thus, students can utilise each year's of knowledge and are to get certificates accordingly.

Under this National Education Policy, attention is given on activity-based learning. Other features are E-courses in eight regional languages, modification in education for the differently abled and promotion of technology in education. It is also noteworthy that medium of education should be made in mother tongue till 5th standard as it is believed that a child learns much better in mother tongue than in any other language. The aim of the new education policy is to boost the abilities of every student with conceptual understanding, creativity and promotion of critical thinking. Under the new policy, there will be an option to run open distance learning and online programs as well.

National Education Policy 2020 and Guidance

Do education and guidance mean the same process or are they different? The answer to this depends on the meanings one attaches to education and guidance. The concept of guidance is easier of the two; it involves advice given to individuals to enable them to make decisions on various aspects of life including choice of career, choice of subjects for studies, managing stress anxiety etc. Guidance relates to what a person wants to do in life; how best that can be achieved; what would be the result of his/her action; what are the alternative courses of action and their relative merits, etc.?

In this context guidance and education have a strong connect. The connect has become stronger than earlier in the light of the NEP as it has special emphasis on the development of the creative potential of each and all from the very beginning a child starts education. The education has to develop cognitive abilities like critical thinking and problem solving and also social, ethical, and emotional capacities. How this can be done comes under the purview of Guidance.

While education relates to holistic development of a child, guidance helps the person in self-understanding. Education is a macro intervention while guidance is a part of the whole programme. Thus, guidance meets various requirements of education system, implementors, parents and students. A pre -planned and well thought out guidance program helps at every step of education

Concept of Guidance

Today's world is a fast changing. Due to massive industrialization, technological upgradation and globalisation, distances are rapidly shrinking. People are no longer contented to be confined to one locality or even one country. Tremendous opportunities for education, technical knowledge and vocations are available to each and all according to one's own abilities and choices. But how would one know where the same are available, whether one is suited to a particular opportunity, or a particular opportunity suits him and how to approach to avail of the opportunity? There are other situations in which similar questions arise. A person is doing a business. He meets with heavy losses in the venture. He does not know where to go and how to deal with the situation? A girl wants to join fine arts but her family is insisting that she goes in for a course in Law. In another situation a person is over- worked. He is frustrated. He has started taking drugs. Yet another situation could be in which an individual is not able to concentrate on his studies due to various family, personal or emotional problems. The answers to all such and similar questions lie in the concept of guidance.

A.J. Jones (1934), focusing upon individual stated "Guidance involves personal help given by someone... It does not solve problems for the individual but helps him to solve them. The focus of guidance is the individual, not the problem, its purpose is to promote the growth of the individual in self- direction."

Ruth Strang, defining guidance, emphasised it as a "process of helping every individual, through his own efforts, to discover and develop his potentialities for his personal happiness and social usefulness."

Crow and Crow's definition of guidance also indicated as to who should provide guidance. In their opinion "Guidance is assistance made available by personally qualified and adequately trained men or women to an individual of any age to help him manage his own life activities, develop his own point of view, make his own decisions and carry his own burdens."

Humpureys and Traxler, emphasised the concept of guidance as a continuous process, and said, "At any level, guidance implies that the individual attains self-direction ...Guidance of the younger or less mature individual, of course, calls for closer direction than does guidance of the older or more mature individual. The term guidance, moreover, aptly applies to working with an individual all along the lines from early childhood into adulthood." This definition also indicates the extent to which direction may be given by the guidance worker to the client at various levels of life span.

Mathewson's definition of guidance refers to the developmental aspect of guidance: "Guidance is a continuous and pervasive process as a favourable directional influence upon appropriate social behaviour, personal effectiveness in every day affairs, academic competence and progress and assimilation of right values and attitudes." In his opinion, guidance is not only remedial, but is developmental as well.

It may be noted that all the definitions agree that the person who is providing guidance does not take any decisions for the person who seeks guidance. The guidance worker has only to assist the guidance seeker in taking his own decisions.

Guidance is a continuous process of helping the individual develop to a maximum of his capacity in the direction most beneficial to himself and to society.

The definitions given above brings out some basic components of guidance that can be seen in Figure 1.1.

Need for Guidance

Guidance is needed at every stage of a person's life. But the question is why a person needs guidance at all? Here are some examples which would highlight the need for guidance:

Sir C.V. Raman, the well-known scientist, started his career in the field of audits and accounts and then switched over to physics. Thus, he had ultimately chosen the career through trial and error in which he attained great heights. Such trials and errors could waste a lot of time, energy and money. To avoid this, guidance is necessary at a proper stage.

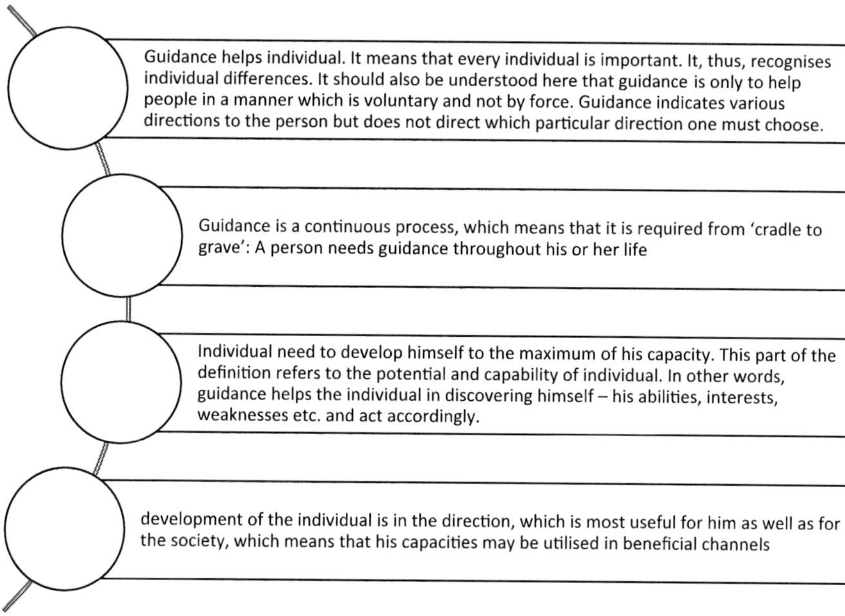

Figure 1.1: *Summary of definition of Guidance*

Tarun's friend joined MBBS course. He thought that 'since his friend is going to become a doctor, I should also be the same.' So he also appeared for the entrance exam and got through. After one year of the course, when he was sent for practical to a hospital and saw a dead body with blood all over, he fainted and dropped forever the idea of becoming a doctor. He was in the lurch again with all confusion as to what to do? If he could analyse his personality earlier with the help of guidance this situation could have been avoided. Guidance helps in choosing a career according to one's potential and personality

Sumit passed his graduation in general subjects with good grades. Due to family constraints he wanted to take up a job. When he started trying for a job in the job-market there were no takers for him, and there was 'no vacancy' for him everywhere as he had no technical qualification. Proper guidance in time would have enabled him to know the demand for various skills in the market and to pursue a course with job potential.

Joint family system in India, like most other countries, is cracking up. Earlier the seniors in the family used to be there as a support system for the younger ones, guiding them in times of crisis. Now with nuclear families, guidance from professionals is required as a support system.

With the rapid diversification in the educational streams, the technical arenas, and the world of work, it is almost impossible for a person without a professional level guidance, to acquire and understand the vast information about various aspects of careers, and then make a choice from the available alternatives.

In a school system, there are children with extra-ordinary talents and, on the other hand, there are children who are slow achievers. Both types of groups of children need extra and special care. A teacher in the classroom should know their special needs. Specialised guidance services can help to tackle such problems.

At school or college levels there could be several other problems such as adjustment with school, teachers or peers, maintenance of proper discipline, family problems that may be affecting an individual's psycho-social development. All such problems require guidance at proper time.

In the area of work, people face problems of inadequate communication skills, lack of team spirit, job stress, non-adjustment with the type, process or duration of work, non-adjustment with the work environment, low salaries etc. Guidance is needed to help people in all such situations.

There can be social needs also. Individuals are supposed to develop right kinds of attitudes towards themselves, family and society. They should know their social responsibilities and should develop desirable habits. There could also be a mismatch between individual aspirations and social demands that may create frustration and tensions. At family level there could be sibling rivalry. Appropriate guidance helps the individuals in dealing with all such issues.

Most youngsters in school left to themselves would aspire to become engineers or doctors. But the society needs people in a variety of occupations. Economic development programmes require engineers, craftsmen, social scientists, administrators and so on. It is not in the interest of the society or government or even the individuals that the educational system over-produces manpower in one field while there are shortages in the others. Guidance can help in channeling youth into different vocations required by society.

In the modern-day world, increasing competition between employers due to globalisation and economic liberalisation is often leading to reduction in workforce in the firms. The workers thus retrenched, many of whom are in their middle ages and possess skills/experience no longer needed, would need help and guidance in learning new skills and finding alternative avenues of jobs/ self-employment.

Some of us are good in technical fields. However, for success in life, it is not enough to possess expertise in a particular field. In these days, multiple skills are increasingly becoming the need of the hour. Moreover, soft skills – communication skills, inter- personal relations, ability to work in a team, decision-making, etc. have become more essential. Development of one's personality to acquire the soft skills requires guidance services.

Guidance also deals with personal – emotional problems. To quote a few, such problems could be lack of decision-making abilities, lack of leadership qualities, shyness, extreme aggression or sensitivity, lack of self-confidence or high self-esteem, inability to cope with emotional stress, etc.

Taking into account the above and similar issues, the need for guidance can be divided in four verticals:

Table 1.1: *Need for Guidance - Four Verticals (Indicative list)*

Educational Needs	*Vocational Needs*	*Personal Needs*	*Social Needs*
Choice of education streams- to have right education for self	Choice of vocations	Overall dev. of the individual	Planning development and utilisation of manpower
Choice of training / vocational courses	Matching of self with employment needs	Facing new challenges	Bringing weaker sections to main stream
Self- assessment and matching with the courses	Vocational development	Coping with problems	Encourage women to enter into labour market
Academic development and Learning skills	Self-employment motivation	Better adjustment with self and environment	Develop desirable behaviour in people
Time Management	Adjustment in employment life	Understand, accept and realisation of self	Development of individual to develop the society.
Dealing and accepting handicaps and problem areas	Minimize wastage of time and energy in choice of career	Right attitudes towards self, work and society	
Adjustments with school environment	Mid- career retirement planning	Development of soft skills	Eradication of evils like child labour, drug abuse
Overall academic growth	Change of occupation	Development of emotional intelligence	Development of Social intelligence
	Career development	Adequate use of leisure time	

Objectives of Guidance

- To help in accepting ones strengths and weaknesses, personality, interests, aptitudes, attitudes etc.
- Develop one's potential to the maximum through assisting him in exploring his self as well as the environment.
- Provide a wide choice and opportunities available for him and pre-requisites for availing such opportunities.
- Help in making own decisions in the light of relative advantages and disadvantages of different alternatives to choose from.

- Help in preparing an action plan for following up his decisions with appropriate action.
- Help make adjustment in new life situations.
- Make one accept the responsibility for his own decisions.
- Enable to accept the failures and success and move forward with Them.
- Help in making further decisions in the light of success and failures, if required.
- Help in facing the challenges of life and manage tensions by realising and accepting the facts.
- Enable the individual to learn the life skill techniques to cope with the problems of daily life and be useful to the society.
- Help in solving social and personal problems and be able to adjust with oneself and the environment.
- Help in overall holistic development to have purposeful, productive and happy life.

Principles of Guidance

- Guidance serves developmental and adjustment needs of all.
  - The guidance worker has to be impartial and unbiased to be a role model.
  - Trained personnel should provide guidance services.
- Guidance services should be well planned.
  - Guidance should be need-based, and according to the specific individual/target groups and environment. No uniform guidance programme can be implemented universally.
- Guidance recognises individual's rights, capabilities and weaknesses to help one taking decisions.
  - Guidance relates to every aspect of life and needs cooperation among all.
  - Orientation of teachers, principals, community agencies and other support services are necessary to make the guidance programme effective.
- It should focus on the overall development of the individual.
- Individual differences are recognised in guidance.
- Guidance helps one in making decisions oneself but does not force a decision. Thus it develops insight in the individual.

Scope of Guidance

Initially guidance started with the concept of vocational guidance, which aimed at helping the students in their educational and vocational planning. Such guidance had relevance primarily to school settings and perhaps at the entry stages of employment. This had a very narrow scope. But as the societies developed and expanded many more situations other than vocational issues cropped up where the need for professional guidance emerged, and its scope expanded vertically and horizontally. Its responsibility now, is not restricted only to making a choice of career but also how to adjust in it, to excel in a job, and to attain maximum levels of job satisfaction and job success, and to meet with the changing demands of the work situation? Lifestyles have to be adjusted according to the needs of the ever-changing demands of the occupations. For example, the rapidly growing phenomenon of Business Process Outsourcing in many spheres has resulted in many workers staying in offices and away from home at nights, causing stresses in the family life. Continuous upgradation of skills possessed is required to keep pace with changing technologies. On the other hand, complexities of life are increasing. Be it the financial matters, competition, adjustments at home with marital life, adjustments with children, coping with retirement blues, maintaining status in the society, contributing to the society and the nation, developing social skills—in all these spheres guidance is increasingly finding relevance.

Culture and traditions are fast changing. As society opens up so are the problems. There are problems relating to sexual development. Parents are still shy in discussing and dealing with the sex related problems of children. Adolescence brings with it a whole gamut of problems – smoking, alcoholism, drug addiction is influencing the young minds. Parents as well as individuals need help on all these issues. It may be said that scope of guidance is extremely large and sky is the limit.

Covid -19 has also created a new set of problems. Various measures like on-line education, lockdowns, stay home etc have become new normal in which adjustment of children is becoming very difficult. Staying at home increasing boredom and frustration among children due to lack of face-to-face interactions. The scope of guidance has increased manifolds.

2

Foundations of Guidance

Guidance is a commonly used word and is used in terms of informal guidance and also as formal guidance. Two friends discussing over some issue where some kind of advice takes place is also guidance. Advice from elders, parents and teachers is also termed as guidance. These are some examples of informal guidance. But as discussed elsewhere, there is a constantly growing need for imparting professional guidance – a need that emerged due to changes in the socio-economic, cultural and psychosocial fabric of the societies. In the past, a person's vocation, behaviour, education, and almost every aspect of life used to be predetermined by the social group to which he belonged. A certain level of education, certain areas of vocation and certain pattern of social behaviour was automatically associated with a social group. There was no place for guidance to enable a choice between alternatives. A fisherman could never imagine that his son would not be able to join him in the occupation of fishing as he was scared of water or a doctor could not think of his daughter wanting to be a musician as she had talent in the field of fine arts. As the times changed, these things came into focus. Gradually 'individual' became important. How did the term guidance emerge and what is its base? How is it associated with socio-psychological changes in the society? The concept of professional and formal guidance rests on sociological, economics, psychological and philosophical foundations.

(a) Sociological Foundation

(i) Individual Worth

The sociological basis of guidance is an outcome of the realization and acceptance of the individual worth, his needs and problems. Society is made of the individuals and development of a society can take place only if all the individuals get opportunity to develop themselves. When equal opportunities are not provided to each and all for development to their full potential, dissatisfaction and discontent emerges and evolution of civilization gets hampered.

(ii) Human Beings as a Resource

No two persons are same but at the same time everyone is endowed with some or the other talent which need to be identified and facilitated to be developed. If that is not done, people would be a liability on the nations than being an asset. The importance of human beings as resources for a country has to be realized and an atmosphere has to be provided where each one can develop his abilities and potentials to the maximum. The socially useful population becomes an important resource for any nation. This concept is also the foundation of guidance, as guidance can develop people as a resource.

(iii) Demands of the Society from the People

Society collectively needs and demands from its people positive attitudes, desirable behaviours, sense of responsibility towards the society, and ability to cope with the changing expectations of today's world. Today's world is fast changing and society's demands are becoming complex. Maintaining unity among people, facing the global challenges and technological development, surviving in and other evils like fighting terrorism, drug addiction, surviving in environment of competition in the world of work and complexities of daily life are to be achieved with harmony, life skills techniques and a positive approach. Guidance addresses these situations.

The complexities of modern life have made life simplistic on one hand and have created manifold problems on the other. The individual is confused. Opportunities are vast but the competition is tough. What to do and what not to do – individual remains in a dilemma. How to deal with peers, teachers, parents, neighbours etc. are some of the areas and social issues where guidance is relevant.

(iv) Individuals with Special Needs

In every society there are people who require extra attention and care. There are old people, there are infants, there are people with some handicap, some are specially gifted children, some belong to single parenthood, and some children are coming from problem and or violent homes. Obviously their needs for assistance differ and society cannot afford to ignore their needs. Professional guidance services can deal with such people with special needs.

(v) Women and Their Problems

Women constitute about half of the total population. Overcoming the social handicaps they faced in the past, they not only are joining diverse educational streams but also diverse occupational fields. A number of problems are emerging with this changed scenario of rising participation of women in economic activities. Women performing the dual roles of looking after the home and children, and work outside the home, face a lot of strain and stress and need assistance. Moreover, in the modern labour market, where the presence of women is increasingly conspicuous – new relationships, new adjustments, new needs, new societal expectations have emerged. Guidance plays a special role in keeping societal harmony and progress in the right direction.

(b) Economic Foundation

(i) Specialisation and Multi-skilling

Another issue that makes guidance relevant is the demand for specialized skills and even multiple skills in the society. There are fields, which require specialization for doing a particular activity. For example, in the profession of medicine one doctor specializes in giving anesthesia to the patients during the course of operations, the other is ENT specialist and so on.. In some areas of work there is a demand for multi-skilled people. This is, in fact, the trend in recent times. For example, a person who is handling photocopying work, should also be able to handle phones, PBX, Fax and other electronic equipments in an office and almost everyone needs skills in using computers apart from the skills in his own specialized field. New occupational areas are also emerging like herbal plantations, biotechnology etc. that require trained people. Who can do what, is the basic question. How to match occupations with people? Guidance can address these and other related issues.

(ii) Placements

There may be people possessing requisite skills, as well as demand for such skills. Even then, there can sometimes be constraints in the labour market that prevent the coming together of this demand and supply skills. Imagine a situation where a girl is trained on how to grow herbal plantations, which can generally be grown in hilly areas. The girl, however, has her family in the plains. She cannot move out from her native place. Now what about her getting a placement? In another situation, there may be persons with skills and no demand for them. A person for example, has skill in providing training in yoga but there are no vacancies. There can be numerous situations relating to trained manpower. Everyone has his choices and preferences for a job, job area and job activity. Getting placement according to that preference is a challenge. How to get it? How to know about it? How can one get a right placement or how a job can get the right person? If these issues are handled properly, individuals can get job satisfaction and if individuals can succeed in their respective jobs, ultimately the society succeeds.

(iii) Utilisation of Manpower

The State formulates programmes for the development of economy. A variety of skills are required to man these programmes and at different places. The State also makes arrangements for the development of such skills. However, proper utilization of the trained manpower for purposes for which it is meant can be a difficult task as the choice is in the hands of the individuals trained. An example is the need of doctors in rural areas. There may be enough doctors but they do not go to rural areas. Another example is the need for the people to join the armed forces. Guidance would enable channeling these human resources into areas where they are required.

(iv) Job Losses

For a variety of reasons people lose their jobs after holding them for quite a long period. With changing technology and competition, the employer may not need the skills possessed by his workers. Or he may relocate his industry to some other place or even close it leading to job losses. Such retrenchments lead to economic discomfort as well as emotional tensions. Guidance can play a vital role in helping the retrenched workers to acquire alternative skills, move to alternative places of employment or seek fresh jobs.

During COVID 19 a number of organisations got closed and people lost their jobs leading to frustrations and tensions. The world is also witnessing economic slow down and even big companies like Google are reducing their manpower. Sudden loss of income creates several problems at individual as well as family level. Guidance is extremely necessary in such contexts.

(c) Psychological Bases of Guidance

It has been seen, while discussing the sociological bases of guidance, that the focus is on individuals – their development in relation to the society. The psychological foundation of guidance is similarly important which emphasises the individual's abilities, interest and aptitudes, differences between one individual and the other, differences within the individual in relation to traits and skills, the personality characteristics and his adjustments with himself and environment.

(i) Individual Differences

People differ in their physical characteristics. The height, weight, the structure, the face, etc. make one person different from the other. People also differ in their mental capabilities. Abilities vary, attitudes, interests and aptitudes differ and so do the personalities. It is common experience that some children are very sharp in doing the calculations or playing with the numbers, while others are good in painting or music and some others in doing the mechanical repairing etc. Personality-wise, some people are fond of making friends, while some want to be aloof, some are outspoken while some are shy. Besides, they also differ in emotional maturity and emotional adjustments. The children of same age may show different degrees of emotional maturity in the similar situations. Of the two children who fail in the examination in the same standard, one may remain calm and quiet and may analyse his reason for failure and decide to try again with more positive attitude, while the other child may burst into tears, may get bouts of depression, may think that he can never succeed.

Such differences are measurable and individuals who need help can be identified and counseled appropriately.

(ii) Differences Within

Individuals differ from one another in many ways. But the differences within the individual can also be seen and measured. These differences within the individual are in terms of various traits. One individual may get 100 per cent marks in science subjects, but only 40 per cent in languages. Or he may be good in climbing a hill but not well in swimming. Guidance can help in identifying individual's strengths and weaknesses. Strengths may be developed to their maximum while weaknesses may be overcome through proper guidance upto a certain extent. Teachers and parents can also be helped in dealing with strengths and weaknesses of the individual. Guidance provides an insight to understand the nature of the individual in a better way. The patterns of one's traits may be matched with the requirements of the trait patterns of different occupations.

The matching of the two to a greater extent may result in greater satisfaction and happiness for the individual.

(iii) Personality Characteristics

Personality of an individual is another psychological base for guidance. Personality is combination of both physical and mental characteristics. Problem in one area may lead to problems in the other. If a person is not physically fit or remains sick, his behaviour would be different. He may show irritation, anger, frustration etc. On the other hand if a person is healthy, he would be energetic and show happy attitudes and behaviours. In the same situations, two individuals may show different behaviours. During the examinations some children are extremely anxious while some are calm. The guidance programme has to take the individual as a whole and identify specific personality characteristics that may help in understanding the individual and helping him to choose the right direction or modify behaviour as and when needed through intervention. Here the psychology of individual adjustment should be looked into. How a person would behave or adjust with the situations depends upon his perception of self. In order to modify the behaviour, the change in self-concept is essential. Think about a person who thinks that he can not do good in public speaking, he would like to avoid such situations where he is supposed to speak before people. To alter this situation, he has to analyse his problem, think that he can do it. Guidance worker can help in modifications of behaviours through various techniques.

This psychological understanding of a person is the foundation of guidance process.

(d) Philosophical Bases of Guidance

(i) The Indian Culture and Indian Constitution: The Indian culture is based on the principles of *Vasudheva Kutumbkum* which means that the whole earth is one home and all should live as if they belong to the same family. That is possible only when the values of unity, equality and respect for each other are imbibed in the daily living. There should not be any discrimination on the basis of the caste, creed and religion. Dignity of the human beings should be valued. The Indian Constitution embodies these values of respect, equality and dignity of the citizen and seeks to assure to all.

(a) Justice – social, economic and political
(b) Liberty – of thought, expression, belief, faith and worship
(c) Equality – of status and of opportunity and to promote among all feeling of fraternity while assuring the dignity of the individual.

This philosophy of human dignity and equality is the foundation of guidance, where each individual is important.

(ii) The Goals of Life: The Indian philosophy is based on the concept that the ultimate aim of life is self-understanding, self-acceptance and self-realization. The role a 'guru' or the 'guide' in this process of self-realization of the individual is well recognized. Guidance helps in attaining self-realization sooner than later.

3

Guidance at Various Levels of Education

Guidance at Foundational Level

The foundational level of education consists of two stages one from the ages of 3 to 6 years which will be covered by Aanganwadi or pre -school or Balvatika system and the other from 6 to 8 years relating to class 1 and 2. The early childhood care and education lays the foundation of learning. It is envisaged in the NEP that cumulative brain development occurs prior to the age of 6 therefore at this stage therefore, education needs to be a 'flexible, multi-faceted, multi-level, play-based, activity-based, and inquiry-based learning, comprising of alphabets, languages, numbers, counting, colours, shapes, indoor and outdoor play, puzzles and logical thinking, problem-solving, drawing, painting and other visual art, craft, drama and puppetry, music and movement. It also includes a focus on developing social capacities, sensitivity, good behaviour, courtesy, ethics, personal and public cleanliness, teamwork, and cooperation. The overall aim of ECCE will be to attain optimal outcomes in the domains of: physical and motor development, cognitive development, socio-emotional-ethical development, cultural/artistic development, and the development of communication and early language, literacy, and numeracy' (NEP 2020). After this pre-school child has to move to school for class 1 and 2.

At this level guidance has to play an immense role as a child goes from home environment to outside environment for learning. Each child needs individual attention for physical, mental and emotional development. School counsellors need to work along with preschools and other early schools to help teachers in understanding the children and their needs. Guidance worker needs to identify each child's strengths and weaknesses, developmental potential and help teachers making children participatory in school activities. The guidance unit need to be equipped with diagnostic and post-diagnostic processes. The units should have performance and functional behaviour assessment; bottlenecks and constraints that hinder natural development and prepare a well-planned strategy to cope these hinderances. For instance, there could be learning difficulties in a single or multiple subjects' area, lack of adjustment with the school environment, lack of interest in school activities, dominance of some children over others and so on. This is the time when specific talents of a child need to be identified.

Guidance at Preparatory and Middle Level

In the NEP, classes 3-5 from the ages of 8-10 are designated as preparatory school while from 6-8 from ages 11-14 are middle level education. The

Preparatory Stage education will be based on activity-based learning similar to that of the Foundational Stage. But at this stage small and simple text books will be introduced. The education at this stage will be more formal but interaction based. The Middle Stage will be building on the 'pedagogical and curricular style of the Preparatory Stage, but with the introduction of subject teachers for learning and discussion of the more abstract concepts in each subject that students will be ready for at this stage across the sciences, mathematics, arts, social sciences, and humanities. Experiential learning within each subject, and explorations of relations among different subjects, will be encouraged and emphasized despite the introduction of more specialized subjects and subject teachers.' (NEP, 2020)

At these levels it is important to inculcate in the students the basic values and ethics of the work including dignity of labour, importance of systematic and planned work, need for working in groups, taking advantage of others' experiences, develop good entrepreneur skills and also provide the orientation towards various jobs.

The emphasis of guidance would be on various activities that would help in learning. At present, schools are one teacher classes, where the teacher has more interaction with each individual student. The classes are relatively smaller and visits of parents are frequent at this level. The developmental needs of the child are most important. Maslow's Hierarchy Theory emphasises the developmental process up to self-actualisation and both teacher and counsellor have to support this developmental process. The purpose of the guidance at these levels is

- To help the child to make school progress appropriate to his age
- To help the child in adjusting himself to the school environment basically this is the level where transition from interactive to formal education takes place. At this stage, the child learns to discipline himself. The new relationships other than the child-parent relationship emerge. New relationships are with other children of the class, with teachers and other members of the school
- To help the child in managing his emotions in the new environment and new relationships

Here the objectives of the guidance are more towards personality development, developing good habits in the children, helping the child in exploring his talents and creativity. At this stage, guidance can provide the students an exposure to wide variety of activities, new learning situations and meeting the developmental needs of the children. Education and guidance go hand-in-hand at this stage.

Guidance at Secondary Level

Special problems occur during secondary level of schooling, as children are in the adolescent age. This age group is 14-18 and the children are in 9th to

12th standards. The Secondary Stage will thus comprise of four years of multidisciplinary study, 'building on the subject-oriented pedagogical and curricular style of the Middle Stage, but with greater depth, greater critical thinking, greater attention to life aspirations, and greater flexibility and student choice of subjects. In particular students would continue to have the option of exiting after Grade 10, NEP and re-entering in the next phase to pursue vocational or any other courses available in Grades 11- 12, including at a more specialized school, if so desired'.

This stage is a critical stage as at this stage, the child is neither a small child nor a grown-up. It is a very delicate stage where lot of physical and mental changes takes place. The behaviour of adolescents becomes unpredictable and uncontrollable. This is the age when parents complain about the children saying 'they do not listen', while children say 'parents do not understand'. This may be called a transitional period between childhood and adulthood. The children start dreaming about their future and want some kind of independence and freedom. They want to choose their own lifestyles. Their friends are more important than their family members and they want to establish their own identity.

At this age, the following problems may occur, which require the attention from the guidance worker:

- Adjustment with the family members and new roles in the family as well as outside
- Problems relating to academics and learning
- The emotional changes and emotional instability, physical development and physical needs
- Problems relating to career management
- Unrealistic choices and aspirations
- New interests and curiosities. Children have to come up with multi-disciplinary approach integrating various interests like art integration, sports integration, emotional balance, physical development and so on.

Here the responsibility of guidance worker is to help the child in developing socially desirable behaviours, to help in discovering his new self, to help him in coping with anxieties and help in developing productive habits. Individual guidance is as important as the group guidance at this stage. The child comes in contact with a number of teachers at this level. The activities of guidance may include orientation to various courses available, improvement in adjustment and social relationships, self- understanding and acceptance, looking for appropriate occupation. The guidance worker should also help the child in assessing his academic performance and the problems therein. A comprehensive guidance programme may be worked out in consultation with the teachers and principal. The guidance worker may also use the relevant psychological tests at this and earlier stage. At secondary school stage it is important to provide information about various careers, information about the student himself and about opportunities available to pursue a career. Those who go for higher studies, vocational guidance does not end. Career options at various educational levels, information about vocational assistance and avenues for a higher study, etc., are imparted.

Specific Functions of Guidance at Various Levels

- Administer relevant psychological tests and help children in understanding themselves at appropriate stage. Help them in accepting their strengths and limitations
- Provide information about options available about various educational vocational courses and their suitability.
- Information about tentative job openings through various educational and vocational streams
- Orient them towards the status of employment, current and future trends, requirements of skills.
- Help in dealing with their problems relating to development
- Help in assessing their academic personal and social performance and their capabilities of improving
- Help in choosing hobbies and leisure time activities to enhance creativity and critical thinking
- Assist in making adjustments with self, home, peers and the school.
- Assist in developing communication skills, self-direction skills and decision-making skills.
- Assist potential dropouts and children with specific needs.

Guidance program which includes educational, vocational and professional guidance should be integrated at various levels of education. They are also interdependent. All the objectives of guidance elaborated earlier assume importance. Students have a number of options. These options are going for higher studies, taking up some technical courses, preparing for competitive examinations, looking for various job opportunities on regular basis as well as on part time basis, exploring the institutions for further education suiting their finances, etc. This is a transitional period because after school they will move to college or school to world of work. They have to move out from structured and disciplined system of school education to a relatively free and independent atmosphere. While in school the progress of the students is monitored, at college level the individuals are responsible for their own performance. They are also considered as grownups and different kind of behaviours in adjustments are expected from them. Professional assistance is especially important at this stage. The guidance worker should provide information about a wide range of educational, vocational and technical courses, list of institutions about the availability of these courses, their eligibility conditions, their preparations on one hand, the specific attitudes, aptitudes and personality characteristics of each individual on the other. Guidance should also provide a wide range of

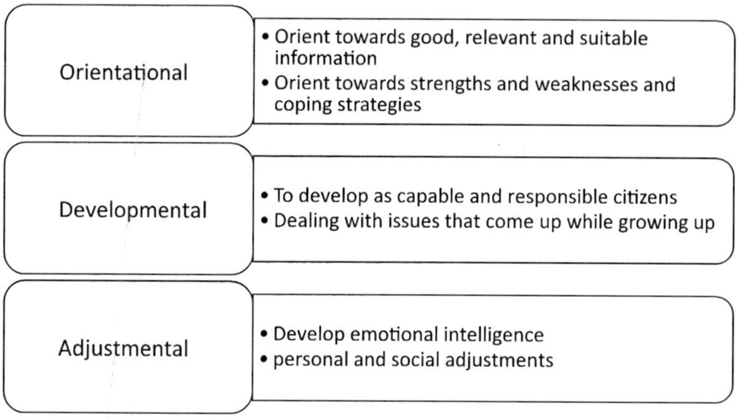

Figure 3.1: *Functions of Guidance in School at a Glance*

information about the occupational fields available for students, the eligibility conditions, the entry, the remuneration and perks, progress in an occupation and information about the way of life that would be available with the choice of an occupational field. For example, if a student is opting for a medical occupation, he should be guided about the life style of a doctor. There are no time limits for work in this profession and he may have to visit the patients even during the nights. On the other hand, a teacher's profession may be according to the school timings. The counsellor has to collect and collate the information about various educational courses and vocational opportunities. The collection, compilation and dissemination of information is a technical task which should be done by the counsellor in an authentic manner and the information should be updated from time to time. The counsellor has to be vigilant about the changes in the job market and should be able to guide the students accordingly. In the light of changing scenario of school system due to Covid, there is a need to look at the system of providing guidance also. Possibilities need to be explored to provide on-line guidance services.

4

Types of Guidance

The word 'guidance' symbolises the general process in which an individual unable to solve a problem or make a decision by himself receives assistance and advice from another person. The type of advice and assistance needed would vary from situation to situation. While some may need such guidance to take up a particular educational stream or vocational field, others may have to be guided in personal problems like marital life and health, and yet others in matters concerning the society, like good citizenship, community service, etc.

Myers has classified guidance into eight types with the same perspective:

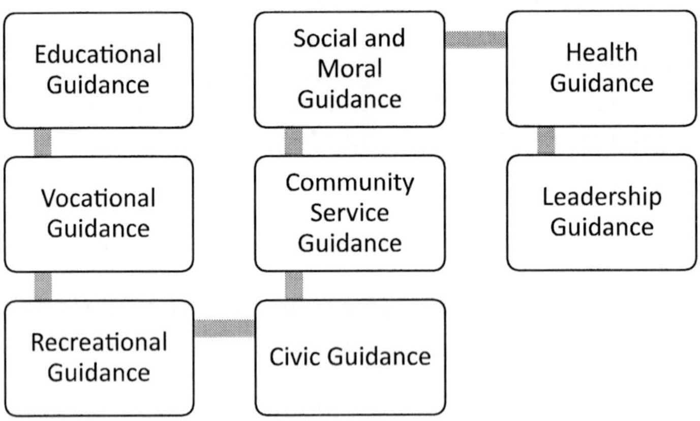

Figure 4.1: *Types of Guidance Services*

Keeping the problems in the various spheres of life in focus, guidance, for practical purposes, may be broadly classified as Educational Guidance, Vocational Guidance and Personal Guidance. Guidance relating to health, recreation etc. may be treated as parts of personal guidance. In this broad framework, the Educational and Vocational Guidance is being discussed in this chapter. Since the personal and social guidance is assuming large focus in recent years, this would be detailed in the next chapter.

Educational Guidance

In the modern days a wider choice of educational streams is available for the children than before. Earlier, there were only a few subjects which everybody had to study. Now each subject has various branches, which are not known to all the students. Students also have their own choices. In earlier times, if a father was in business his child used to be in the same profession. Same was the case of doctors and lawyers. But in the changed scenario, it is not necessary for the children to follow their parent's footsteps. They have varying interests and their cultural backgrounds and traditions differ. They need to know which stream should be suitable for them according to their background and traditions. Education is also seen to be related to vocational choice and planning a career. In the vocational choice it is also imperative that people should know which educational streams are in demand for future vocations. Life is becoming complex and people have to adapt to a new life style, to the new technology and to ever changing market demands. Students may also face some other problems like under achievement, lack of concentration, lack of motivation for studies, etc. All such situations show the need for educational guidance. The number of institutions providing education in the same field has also increased along with the increase in the number of children going to school from all strata of the society. These institutions differ in the levels of prestige attached to them, in the quality of education they offer, in the cost of learning in them, the procedures for gaining admission into them and eligibility conditions. One needs to know about all these aspects before choosing an institution.

Thus, educational guidance meets the requirements of problems relating to education in the school. These could be choice of subjects, low academic achievements, lack of concentration in the classroom activities, etc. According to Myers "Educational guidance is a process concerned with bringing about between an individual pupil with his distinctive characteristics on the one hand, and differing groups of opportunities and requirements on the other, a favourable setting for the individual's development or education. If there is a single group of opportunities and requirements, as is the case with a fixed curriculum, the problem is simply one of the education by the best methods possible in a setting already determined and not of educational guidance." According to Jones, "Educational guidance is the assistance given to the pupils in their choices and adjustments with relation to schools, curriculums, courses and school life." In the opinion of Traxler, "Guidance enables each individual to understand his abilities, interests and personality traits, to develop them, to relate them to his life goals and finally to reach a state of complete and mature self-guidance as desirable citizen of a democratic social order. Guidance is thus vitally related to every aspect of the school, the curriculum, the methods of instruction, the supervision of instruction, disciplinary procedure, attendance, problems of scheduling, the extra-curricular, the health and physical fitness programme, and home and community relations." Tolbert defines educational guidance as "the total programme or all the activities and services engaged in by an educational institution that are primarily aimed at assisting an individual to make and carry out adequate plans and to achieve satisfactory adjustment in all aspects of his daily life".

The above definitions not only define educational guidance but also indicate some of the problems that the student may face during their stay in the schools. The definitions also reflect the need for educational guidance from kindergarten stage to higher levels.

Objectives of Educational Guidance

- To help the student to achieve in adjusting himself to the school environment, the peer group and the school curriculum
- To assess the individuals through psychological tests and other non-testing techniques
- To assess the needs of the individuals for educational guidance
- To prepare a plan for rendering guidance services according to the needs
- To set up a career resource center in the school
- To help students to make a choice of subjects which may be most suitable to them according to their interests, aptitudes and personality
- To provide information regarding the courses and institutions available for higher level schooling or training
- To provide detailed information about the eligibility criteria about various courses and training programmes
- To provide information about the finances which are required for opting a particular course
- To help in monitoring the academic progress
- To help in choosing the leisure time activity according to his interest and resources
- To help in developing good study habits
- To monitor academic achievements of students and identify high and low achievers and help teachers in dealing with such students
- To assist the students with special needs
- To help parents to deal with their children specially with special needs

Principles of Educational Guidance

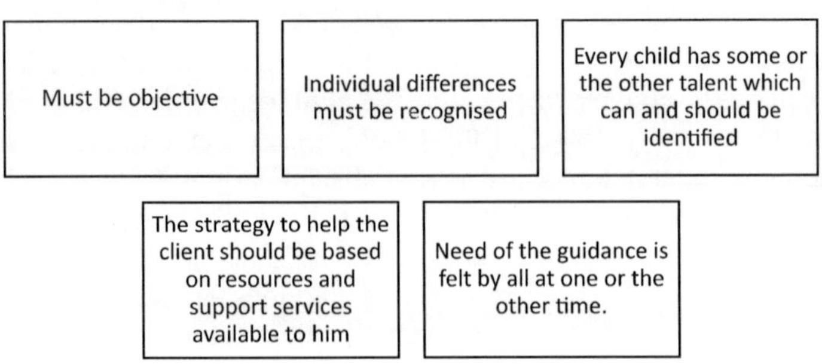

Figure 4.2: *Principles of Educational Guidance*

Functions of Educational Guidance

The broad functions of educational guidance would include collection of information about various educational opportunities (their location, costs, requirements, careers, etc.) on the one hand and about the students (scholastic achievements, family backgrounds, health and financial status, etc.) on the other; preparation of education guidance material and formation of profiles; providing orientation about guidance services to parents, teachers and students; dissemination of educational information through mass media, organising class talks, etc.; administration of psychological tests; identify children requiring special guidance such as low achievers, and interacting with children, their parents and teachers to discuss their educational problems.

The specific functions of educational guidance professional are:

- To provide orientation about guidance services to students, teachers, parents and community
- To collect and disseminate educational information useful for the students
- To arrange group guidance as well as individual guidance activities
- To help the individual in selection of educational streams suitable to his aptitudes and interests, personality and intelligence
- To help the individual in improving the academic achievements
- To help the child in modifying the study habits if required
- To help the child in making proper use of library
- To improve the motivation of the students in the school curriculum and activities
- Help students in preparing for competitive entrance exams.
- To identify the weak areas of the individual and help him in overcoming those
- To assess the individuals through psychological tests and other non-testing techniques
- To assess the needs of the individuals for educational guidance
- To assist children with handicaps
- To help the students in dealing with failures
- To arrange special guidance services for gifted, slow learners and children coming from backward areas
- To discuss with the teachers and parents about the problems of the child to solve them
- Prepare Cumulative Record Card

These are some of the activities a guidance worker can organise in a school. Many of these activities can also be taken up outside the school environments.

It is important to mention here that due to COVID -19 situations many of these services can not be organised as schools are closed during such crisis situations. It is necessary to provide educational guidance services online. This aspect will be discussed later in the book.

Vocational Guidance

With a variety of educational streams as well as occupational opportunities available to the students, it is not always possible for them to match their abilities with the demands of occupations. For making a right vocational choice, information relating to various occupations is necessary in relation to one's achievements, abilities, aptitudes and interests.

National Vocational Guidance Association defined (1924) the concept of vocational guidance as "the giving of information, experience, and advice in regard to choosing an occupation, preparing for it, entering it, and progressing in it." The definition places emphasis on giving information, experience and advice. Another Committee of the Association revised (1937) the definition as "Vocational guidance is the process of assisting the individual to choose an occupation, prepare for it, enter upon and progress in it. It is concerned primarily with helping individuals make decisions and choices involved in planning a future and building a career." The revised definition, indicates a shift from 'giving advice' to 'assisting the individual to make a choice' on his own. Super in 1949 defined the concept as "... help people make good vocational adjustments and to facilitate the smooth functioning of the social economy through the effective use of manpower." He was of the view that every individual is endowed with some or the other abilities and if one could identify those abilities, he would be able to adopt himself in different situation and activities. In his words "Vocational guidance is, therefore, a dual process of helping the individual to understand and accept himself, and of helping him to understand and adjust to society; it is both psychological and socio-economic."

Thus, vocational guidance is not only achievement but also adjustment. The definition stood revised as follows:

> "Vocational guidance is the process of helping a person to develop and accept an integrated and adequate picture of himself and his role in the world of work, to test this concept against reality, and to convert it into a reality, with satisfaction to himself and benefit to society."

Myers defined the concept in the following manner:

> "Vocational guidance is fundamentally an effort to conserve the priceless native capacities of youth and the costly training provided for youth in the schools. It seeks to conserve these richest of all human resources by aiding the individual to invest and use them where they will bring greatest satisfaction and success to himself and greatest benefit to society."

All these definitions, thus, emphasise the development of the individuals to the maximum extent to be successful in their chosen occupations to be satisfied and be useful to the society.

Objectives of Vocational Guidance

Jones has identified the following as the specific aims of vocational guidance:

1. To assist the student to acquire knowledge of the characteristics and functions, the duties and rewards of the group of occupations within which will probably lies his choice.
2. To enable him to find what general and specific abilities, skills, etc., are required for the group of occupations under consideration and what the qualifications of age, preparation, sex, etc., for entering them are.
3. To provide opportunity for experiences in school (try-out courses) and out of school (after-school and vocation jobs) which may give such information about conditions of work as may assist the individual to discover his own abilities and help in the development of wider interest.
4. To help the individual realise that all honest labour is worthwhile and that the most important bases for choice of an occupation are:
   (i) the special service that the individual can render to society,
   (ii) personal satisfaction in the occupation, and
   (iii) aptitude for the work required.
5. To assist the individual to acquire a technique of analysis of occupational information and to develop the habit of analysing such information before making a final choice.
6. To assist the individual to secure such information about himself— his abilities, general and specific, his interests and his powers as he may need for a wise choice.
7. To assist economically handicapped children above the compulsory attendance age to secure financial assistance through public or private funds, scholarships or other means so that they may have opportunities for further education in accordance with their vocational plans.
8. To assist the students to secure knowledge of the facilities offered by various educational institutions for vocational training and the requirements for admission to them, the length of training offered and the cost of attendance.
9. To help the worker to adjust himself to the occupation in which he is engaged; to assist him to understand his relationships to workers in his own related occupations and to society as a whole.
10. To enable the student to secure reliable information about the risk of alluring short cuts to fortune.

The recommendations of Education Commission set up by Government of India in 1964 indicated the aims and scope of educational vocational guidance emphasising to widen the scope of these services. These recommendations suggested the following:

(i) The aim of guidance is not just to help the students in making a right choice for a vocation but the focus should be on the overall development of the child so that he could make a good citizen of the country.

(ii) Guidance should start at primary level and continue thereafter at all stages of primary education. Help may be provided to students in solving their learning difficulties, in developing their academic excellence, and helping the students who are thinking dropping out the school systems, to develop study habits.

(iii) The purpose of guidance at secondary level should be to identify the capabilities, potentials, limitations and strengths of the individuals and help them in making realistic vocational choices.

(iv) Students who are hyperactive need extra attention. Their potentials can be developed through advising them to take up extra-curricular activities, providing specialised courses according to their talent to channelise their energies and potentials. They may be helped in a number of creative ways. On the other hand, there may be low achievers and slow learners. Help should be provided to these children to get adjusted in the normal school and, if there is a need, they should be referred to the special agencies. Special classes may be arranged for slow learners so that they could cope with the normal school programme.

(v) Children join the school stream from various strata of society. They may belong to weaker sections; they may belong to various cultures; they may be first-generation learners who have no orientation of education at home. Adjustment in the schools may be a great difficulty and they could also be potential dropouts. Such students have to be identified and provided counselling.

(vi) Guidance has a different role at college level. There is a problem of transition from school to college. Some students have to join the co-education system for the first time, which may bring in another set of problems to them. There is a future problem of lack of jobs staring at them. At this stage, it is extremely important to help them in dealing with their problems of all kinds—educational, vocational and personal. They should also be guided about the adjustment needed in the job market and how to deal with it. They should be acquainted with the process of obtaining and filling up the forms and of interviews. Information may also be provided to college students about apprenticeship, training, competitive examinations and scholarships available in the country and abroad for higher education, etc.

The vocational guidance has become more relevant in the light of the new structure suggested in NEP 2020 which emphasises on the spread of vocational education in India as less than 5% of the Indian workforce in the age group of 19–24 received formal vocational education as compared to the countries such as the USA the number is 52%, in Germany 75%, and South Korea it is as high as 96%. One of the primary reasons for the small numbers of students receiving vocational education is the fact that vocational education has in the past focused largely on Grades 11–12 and on dropouts in Grade 8 and upwards. Moreover, students passing out from Grades 11–12 with vocational subjects did not have further openings. Vocational education is perceived to be inferior to mainstream education. The new policy aims to overcome the social status hierarchy associated with vocational education and requires integration of vocational education programmes into mainstream education in all education institutions in a phased manner. Beginning with vocational exposure at early ages in middle and secondary school, quality vocational education will be integrated smoothly into higher education. Guidance would help internalizing the dignity of labour and importance of various vocations involving Indian arts and artisanship from the very beginning.

Specific Need for Vocational Guidance

1. *Matching individuals and demands of skills in jobs*: It is an established fact that people differ from one another in their abilities, skills and personalities. A person can be skilled in doing clerical work, which is a desk job, while the other may be good in outdoor activities like jobs relating to public dealing. People with physical strength may be suitable for security-related occupations and so on. While, thus, on the one hand, people differ in their abilities, on the other hand different jobs demand different skills. Matching of individual skills with the skills demanded by the occupations calls for vocational guidance services.
2. *Assessment of Individual*: How would one know about himself? A person may have interest in music but may not be that talented to take it as a career. What are the capabilities a person has and what are his limitations? These are to be analysed with the help of a professional guidance worker to assist the individual in assessing himself and accordingly choose the right kind of career.
3. *World of Work*: The world of work is expanding. Jobs are available at national and international levels, through direct advertisement, through contacts, through outsourcing. What is the whole range of occupations? What options one has with him? How to choose from several alternatives? How to know about the details about the occupations? What are the terms and conditions? How the life would be after choo-sing a particular occupation? All these and many more issues are addressed by vocational guidance.
4. *Minimise the Mismatch*: People choose occupations often by chance or whatever is available or due to influence of parents and friends. At a later stage when they do not succeed in these jobs, they feel that the choice did not match with their capabilities. Many people in this situation either

remain dissatisfied throughout life or leave the jobs for better options. Vocational guidance at a proper time may help in reducing such mismatch and also the wastage of time, money, energy and other resources.

5. *Maximum Utilisation of Human Resource*: Manpower can be developed as a resource with proper and timely guidance. Once developed such resources need to be properly utilised. The skills of each individual may be identified and opportunities may be explored for their proper nurture. Productivity can be increased with development and utilisation of human resources. It can be a boon for the employers, society and the nation.
6. *Dealing with failures:* The present age is one of competition. It is a kind of the 'survival of the fittest' situation. Even after putting in all the effort needed to reach one's goals, failures are bound to occur. Entry into an occupation, even when a person is suitable, may present a number of barriers. These can be failures in the entry examinations, failures in competing with others in settling down in an occupation and failures in getting promotions. In dealing with failures in the occupational fields, the role of vocational guidance cannot be ignored. The role of vocational guidance is not only restricted to one's entry into the occupation but is also to help the individual in making useful contributions and to excel in life through continuous exploration and development.

Functions of Vocational Guidance Programme

1. Assessment of the individual in terms of his academic achievements, intelligence, aptitudes, interests, attitudes, personality characteristics, hobbies, habits, health and limitations.
2. Assessment of individual's immediate environment such as background of family, financial resources, expectations of the family, support systems, pressures and stresses.
3. Assessment of occupational fields – jobs available in the local area and outside, demands of skills, emerging fields of occupations, entry demands, nature and conditions of work, collection, compilation and dissemination of information.
4. Assessing suitability of the individual to the demands of the job market and vice-a-versa.
5. Helping the individual in preparing for entry into the job-market.
6. To help in appreciating dignity of labour
7. Facilitating setting up self-employment ventures if the individual so desires.
8. Counselling for adjustments in the job.
9. Follow up services – taking feedback from the clients to further help them as well as modify the programme.

What types of problems one may face and how a professional guidance worker could identify these have been discussed later in the book.

5

Personal and Social Guidance

Guidance movement started with vocational guidance and later it included educational guidance. But with the increase of complexities in life, the need for personal guidance has been growing. An example can be a student who is good in studies but cannot participate in extra-curricular activities; in the class, whenever he tries to speak (even when he knows the subject) he is not able to express himself well; he is suffering from lack of confidence due to which he is not able to utilise his capabilities. Another person who always thinks that he cannot do, although he is not lacking in capabilities and potentials; he has low levels of self-esteem. There is yet another student who is suffering from malnutrition and poor health, which is affecting his performance. All such types of cases require personal guidance. Individual belongs to society and society consists of individuals. On one hand, individual has to develop such skills that could contribute to the development of the society, while on the other hand, society should create an environment where the individual gets opportunity to utilise his competencies. Being a part of the society, people also have to learn coping strategies to tackle the problems they may face from time to time. Thus, personal guidance is basically concerned with the enhancement and development of life skills. A child experiences in the family, in the school and in the society; he learns from these experiences and personal and social development takes place. Personal guidance helps in the individual's development in a desired direction.

There is another aspect of social guidance. Some personal issues, when they start affecting the society, become social issues where necessity of social guidance emerges. For example, marriage is a personal issue. Who will marry whom, or if a divorce is needed, is somewhat a personal matter but marriages at early ages have negative implications for growth of healthy population, while a sharp increase in divorce rates may change the social fabric of the country, hinder the normal growth of the children, and single parenting may raise concerns for the society in terms of security, employment etc. Hence the need of social guidance, firstly to prevent such problems and secondly to deal with the problems if they emerge.

Social guidance is assuming greater importance in recent years due to various socio-economic, technological and cultural changes in the societies. Some social issues that are of immediate attention are female feticide, issue of maintaining harmony among various groups of people with varying traditions, religions and cultures, increasing rates of crimes specially against the vulnerable groups such as women, the elderly and children, health-related problems such as AIDS, empowerment of women, etc. On technological side children are getting addicted to technology like mobiles, computers, TV. This addiction keeping them away from physical activities and outdoor games affecting their physical and mental health negatively. Lack of social interaction also decreasing social and communication skills in them. Social guidance in such matters requires multi-faceted approach ranging from individual guidance to group guidance, from family guidance to community guidance and interventions at family, school, community as well as national levels.

Objectives

The objectives of personal and social guidance can be summarised as below:

- To help in developing personal and social competencies
- To make the children aware of the life skill techniques.
- To assist in learning and developing life skills
- To identify personal and social aspects that are hindering the normal development of the child
- To help the students in minimising the gaps between personal aspirations and social demands.
- To help in maximising personal and social success in life.
- To help the individual to develop to his fullest competencies and be a good citizen.
- To help the people to make up a harmonious society where everybody gets opportunities to excel and all enjoy living in that society.

The personal and social guidance includes the following broad areas:

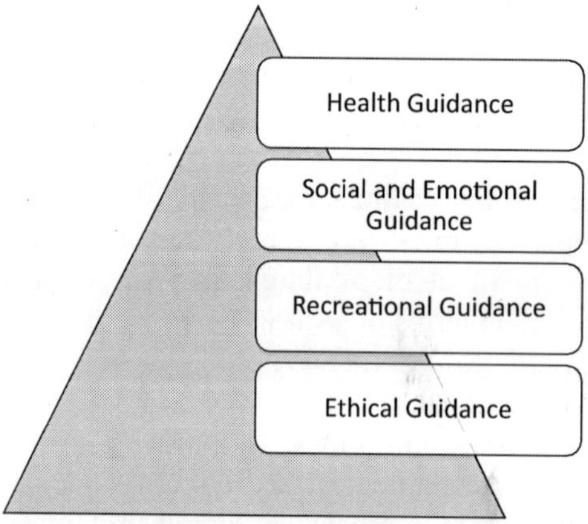

Figure 5.1: *Broad Areas of Personal Guidance*

Health Guidance

The need for health guidance starts at the nursery level of school. In developing countries like India, a large number of children suffer from malnutrition and other ailments. There are also issues of hygiene and sanitation. The guidance teacher should be able to identify such children who need health guidance and should refer them to the medical facilities available either in the school or outside. The parents should also be educated in such cases. Low school achievement may also be due to ill health. Abnormal behaviours of the children in the school should not be ignored as these may be associated with health problems.

Use of tobacco, alcohol and even other drugs is becoming more common in the schools, with many students getting tempted towards such intoxicants, which would affect their health. Sex related problems is another area which needs immediate attention. On one hand, due to curiosity, students are going for unsafe sex, and on the other some smaller students are forced into sex- related activities by anti-social elements. Awareness programs are to be organised on a massive scale. The role of guidance worker here is not only to refer the diseased person to the doctor but also to create awareness on how to prevent such occurrences.

Social and Emotional Guidance

As has been discussed elsewhere not only the joint family system is cracking up but there is also an increase in the number of single parent children due to the increase in divorces. There are also families with domestic violence which hampers the normal development of the children. They may suffer from irritability, high aggression, and sibling rivalry. Children with low self-esteem may indulge in frequent fighting with peer groups or they may face other adjustment problems with the school environment. To tackle such problems counselling is essential. Some other support services in the community may also be utilised for social guidance. These agencies can be Child Guidance Centres, special cells in the hospitals, etc.

Recreational Guidance

Present generation is 'do me' generation. Recreational facilities are now available on payment. The well-off students can buy such facilities, while the not so well-off persons can only aspire for them. In such circumstances they always impose demands on the parents. There are varieties of recreational facilities available within reach of most.

Recreation of modern-day children is getting restricted to watching television and playing games on computers. Consumerism is becoming an activity of recreation. Children keep an eye on changing fashions and go for buying whatever new comes to the market. Purchasing things is developing unhealthy competition among children. Junk foods are popular with the present day's generation. Children avoid playing with each other, socialising, and engaging in creative activity.

Recreational guidance can help a child in striking a balance between various activities. He can choose activities according to his interests, capacities and available opportunities. Playing games together with other children, creative activities along with others creates healthy competition and develops various mental faculties.

Ethical Guidance

Values and morals develop naturally with the process of growing up in the environment of the families and the schools, but due to several factors a need is being felt to include moral and value education at school level. Cultural invasion through mass media and liberal education have been upsetting the traditional ethical fabric of the society and new value systems and codes of conduct are evolving. There is also an increasing felt need to maintain harmony among the groups of students coming from various religious, ethical and cultural backgrounds. Hence, ethical guidance is important.

Guidance and Utilization of Human Resources

According to the Indian epic Ramayana, Hanuman had to be told by Jambavant of his strength and ability to jump across the ocean, before he could actually realize his prowess and cross the mighty ocean. Many times, people have their own innate abilities and unique styles of performing activities that are highly productive and satisfying but do not realize them and their own strengths unless advised by someone. Guidance helps them to discover themselves, to increase their understanding of their interests and strengths and motivate them to utilize their strengths best and overcome their weaknesses to move along on their path to progress.

Riwik's parents hoped that he would become an administrator and for that dream to be realized he had to put in hard and long hours of study. He was an obedient boy, went on working as his parents wanted and used to achieve a measure of success, even though he did not really enjoy the studies — until the school counsellor observed in him all the characteristics required to become an excellent cricketer. He contacted Riwik's parents, explained the boy's natural abilities and persuaded them to allow and encourage the child to spare some time for cricket. It was a momentous decision. The boy soon not only excelled in the game, but the pleasure he derived from the sport acted as an added incentive in pursuing his studies more enthusiastically. Similar instances of mismatch between natural talents and forced aspirations occur very often, for example in opting for studies in science when the child's *undiscovered* aptitude is for painting or music or for pursuing engineering when the *undiscovered* aptitude is for medicine. The situation is different here from one where the natural aptitudes and abilities of the person are *known* but for some reason or the other, they are ignored.

Discovery of unrealized talents calls for different guidance procedures. The guidance worker has to observe the person very closely in every activity he performs to identify his aptitudes and natural inclinations. Aptitude tests may be conducted or a variety of tasks may be given as assignments. Keen observations on seemingly insignificant points such as initiative with which the assignment is taken up, the promptness with which it is completed, the quality of work done and the interest displayed in doing it, all help in spotting over time the areas in which the person's interests and natural abilities lay. Discussions with the individual, his parents and peer groups would also contribute towards discovering the person's strengths and weaknesses. Through this process, the guidance counsellor helps the individual gradually to discover himself and his abilities so that he can make a right vocational choice, and excel in life.

A variety of tools can be used in this process of discovery. Some of them are:

- Myers Briggs Type Indicator (MBTI) assesses personality preferences and provides understanding of how the individual's personality type can help in career planning.
- Strong Interest Inventory matches the individual's reported interests, general occupational themes and basic interests.
- Values Driven Work Inventory assists in determining what the individual values in work environment, work tasks, and relationships in the work place.
- Strengths Finder assessment helps you to identify, develop, and apply talents to increase your success in academics, learning, leadership, careers, and relationships.
- Talent Discovery Guide is a helpful tool in discovering natural talents.
- Dependable Strength Articulation (DSA) process enables individuals to identify and articulate their core abilities, talents, positive traits, and skills -their primary dependable strengths.

More tools are discussed in details in chapters 15 to 18. Discovering the individual's natural talents or enabling the individual to realize such talent is not an end in itself. To take the process to its logical conclusion, the talent discovered has to be gradually nurtured into fruition. Guidance needs to be given on how to develop the talent and pursue activities that employ that talent to the individual's utmost satisfaction, so that the talent is properly utilized.

Population of the country can be a resource only when it is fully developed and nurtured according to the individual' abilities. National development also requires various types of skilled people. Demands of manpower at the national level can be met only when individual's talents are discovered, nurtured and matched with the national demands. Utilisation of skills is directly linked with individual's satisfaction and happiness on one hand and with national development on the other. Guidance services make this happen.

6

Essential Guidance Services

It has been seen that the guidance programme consists of educational guidance, vocational guidance and personal guidance. How this can be imparted? What should be the minimum basic services that should be included in a guidance programme. In the following paragraphs the essential services, which should be rendered through guidance, have been discussed. In its narrow view guidance is related to problem solving, while in its broader view guidance relates to the overall development of the child which is a continuous process.

The following are the general features of guidance:

- It is an organised programme which is offered by schools, universities, and other guidance personnel.
- It creates a sense of wellbeing and addresses to extra-instructional field of class-room instructions.
- It is both specialised and generalised service wherein teachers, parents, community personnel, psychologists, trained staff, principles all play an important role.
- Guidance services are meant for all and for all ages of people.
- Guidance is a continuous process.
- Guidance is directly and indirectly related to good citizen development concept and thus helps in nation building.

To address the above features of guidance, The following services should be included in a comprehensive guidance programme.

Orientation Services

Orientation of guidance services is extremely essential to make the programme relevant and effective. Guidance counsellor cannot work in isolation. He needs the cooperation from parents, teachers, principal, employers and the community. He has to utilise the various resources available in the area, which can provide technical and other inputs for a guidance programme. Guidance counsellors should discuss about the guidance services, their need and importance and how the others can be helpful in making the services a success. Similarly, the orientation of the target group (in case of school guidance programme, the target group would be students) is important as without the target group no programme can take place at all. Students are to be taken into confidence and the usefulness of the guidance services has to be explained. If a Career Resource Centre is in one school and the guidance counsellor has to cover other nearby schools also, he has to provide orientation services in all the schools. Many may think that once orientation has been given, it is the end of the orientation services. But that attitude is not correct. Orientation is also a continuous service. The newcomers in the school – be they the principal or teachers or students – would require orientation. Similarly, in the community also there would be new employers, new services, new people, and the counsellor has to keep track of all those and continue with the orientation services.

The orientation may be done through talks, discussions, narrating success stories of the guidance service, calling those students who were benefited with the guidance services earlier and requesting them to share their experiences with the newcomers, taking people to some established Career Resource Centres which are already imparting guidance services successfully, showing a film, etc. More than one technique may also be used for orientation services.

Individual Inventory Information Services

It is the responsibility of the guidance worker to maintain full record of each student such as student's background, qualifications, interests, habits, problems of adjustment, problems relating to study habits, achievements, and so on. The information should be updated as and when required. For organising this information, a Cumulative Record Card (CRC) may be maintained for each student. Such information would be useful in understanding the students, their environment, their growth and developmental processes. The information should be collected and verified from more than one source. Cumulative Record forms help in maintaining the facts about each individual over a period of time. These can be used in discussions with the teachers, parents, identifying the needs of the individuals, helping the students in educational- vocational guidance and making decisions. On the basis of this information, students may be helped for modifying their behaviours in desired directions. Employers can also be helped in knowing about the potentials of the students in various areas. Moreover, in case new guidance workers join they can have updated knowledge of each student by just seeing the CRC.

A format may be developed for each student for maintaining the information depending upon the level of the education a child is at.

Sample of Cumulative Record Form

I. *Personal Background*

- Name Age Gender
- Name of the father Occupation
- Name of the mother Occupation
- Address
- With whom the child is living and relationship

- Other family members with their age, gender, education and activity status

  Relationship Age Gender Education Activity Status
- Position among brothers/sisters 1 2 3 4 5 6 7 8 9
- Home Town: If left home-town why?

  Any information about family, the child may like to provide.

II. *School Background*
- Name of the School
- Class in which studying
- Subjects taken (when optional subjects are there)
- Schools earlier attended – name, period, class
- Why left earlier school
- Grades got in earlier school
- Any weak areas (subjects)
- Which subjects the student likes, which he/she does not
- Experience of the child with earlier school
- Friends in earlier schools
- Whether maintaining the relationship
- Attendance in the present school
- Performance in the academics/ co-curricular activities.

III. *Details of Performance in the School*

A. Academics: Performance Grades Problems

Foundational Level Preparatory Level Middle Level Secondary Level

B. Vocational: Performance Grades Problems

C. Experiential Learning and General Personality

IV. *Information about Health:*
- General Health Excellent Good Average Below average
- Hearing
- Sight
- Nutrition
- Any sickness
- Frequent fever or other ailments
- Any allergies
- Physical disability (if any)
- Any check-ups got done – when and what were the results?
- Any Other disease: Write details about since when, how why etc.

V. *Psychological Test Record*

What measured? How measured? Which Norms used for results?
1. Intelligence
2. Attitude
3. Interest
4. Aptitude
5. Personality

6. Achievement
7. Emotional Intelligence and Social Intelligence
8. Any other

VI. *Information collected through non-testing techniques like observations,* reporting from others, teachers, incidents, etc. Record here.

Technique used   Who reported   Information   Comments

G. Hobbies and Co-curricular Activities: Indicate in order of priority

- Sports & Games
- NCC
- Theatre
- Music
- Dance
- Fine Arts & Crafts
- Science activities
- Taking leadership roles like monitor of the class, organisation of functions
- Literature/Writing
- Social service
- Travel & tours
- Reading
- T.V. watching
- Mobile watching
- Leisure time activities
- Any other

VII. *General Information*

- Friends' circle
- Adjustment in the school
- Discipline in the school
- Behaviour with teachers/peers
- Regularity in home work
- Financial status
- Experience (if any)
- Membership of clubs
- Any other

VIII. *Problems*

- Problems Indicated – educational, vocational, personal
- Problems Identified – educational, vocational, personal (*State the problems in details)*
- Support system available
- Support system required.

IX. *Any other information/remarks counsellor may like to add*

(*Note*: This is only a sample of format, which may be amended as per need.)

Summary of Cumulative Record Card

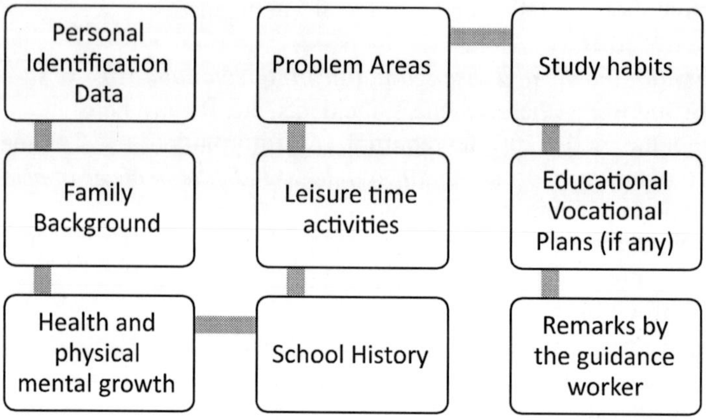

Figure 6.1: *Summary of Cumulative Record Card*

Here it is important to note that the information collected need to be updated periodically as soon as some change takes place. For instance, if a child goes to next class immediately information needs to be filled in CRC. The information to fill up the format has to be collected and compiled through various sources such as school records, teachers, the child himself, the report cards, psychological tests, etc. CRCs for each individual may be maintained on computers also these days.

Features of a Good Record Card

Hahn and Mc Clean has listed the following features of a good Cumulative Record Card:

1. A comprehensive and detailed system of cumulative personnel records is indispensable for the proper functioning of the modern school.
2. The most important purpose of personnel records is to improve the instruction and guidance of each individual pupil.
3. Records are needed that will be continuous over the whole school history from the kindergarten to the junior college, and that will follow the child from school to school.
4. The personnel records for all pupils should be readily accessible to the entire faculty of the school.
5. The record system should be simple enough and well enough organised so that the essential facts about any given pupil will be brought together on one central record card or set of cards in such a way that they may be grasped through a few moments of study by busy teachers and counsellors who are not highly trained in interpreting records.
6. An attempt should be made to keep the records high in reliability and comparability by basing them as far as possible on objective data.

7. The records should be uniform in type throughout all the schools of the local system.
8. The record system should provide for a minimum of repetition of items.
9. The building of personnel records system for a given school does not begin with a consideration of records themselves; it begins with a study of the nature and purposes of the school and of the pupil.
10. If a school adopts one comprehensive cumulative record form as its basic personnel record, it should not only plan this form with meticulous attention to detail, but it should also carefully plan the forms which are to be used in collecting data which will contribute to the main record.
11. A detailed manual of directions should accompany the personnel records for the guidance of persons filling out or using the forms.
12. There is a natural and logical relationship between the information on reports made to parents and the information recorded for purpose of permanent record; this relationship should be taken into account in planning both types of forms.
13. The system of personnel records must not be static; it must be revised frequently as a school's theory of education changes.
14. It is imperative that a system of personnel records be associated with a program of teacher education in the use of these records.

How to Use Cumulative Record Card (CRC)

- For using the CRC the person has to see the interrelationship of information. One should have an insight to understand the human behaviour.
- CRC provides a sound data base which can help in understanding the student, his academic performance, his family background, his behaviour, his assets, his relationship with others etc.
- It can help in diagnosing the problem and plan remedial measures.
- It can serve as an aid for parent-teacher counselling.
- On the basis of this data base, group and individual guidance activities can be planned.
- This can serve as a tool for discussions with the employers

Sometimes instead of maintaining CRC some guidance workers prefer to prepare an individual inventory and give it to the individual to fill up the same. Maintenance and use of Individual Inventory helps in identifying if a child requires any guidance or counselling to enable him to adjust suitably with him/herself, or with the external environment whether at home or in school or within the community at large. Such inventories are useful as tools in individual counselling and guidance by the counsellors or to the teachers in adjusting their teaching to suit the children's abilities. Maintenance of Individual Inventories requires collection of complete and detailed information about the individual child in all relevant respects. The information Inventory will differ with that of CRC as it is to be filled by the individual only.

Pupil Information Inventory *(A Sample)*

I. Personal and Family History

Full name .... Date of birth ....
Class .... Section ....
Father's name ....
His occupation ....
Mother's name...
Her occupation ....
Home address..
Number of brothers .... Sisters ....
Your position among them ....
Do any other relatives live in your home ? If so indicate below by a tick mark.
Grandparents .... Uncles .... Aunts.......................
Cousin .... Any other (Pl. mention)

II. Your Education

1. How many schools have you attended? List them below. Please also indicate why you left those?

Name of School	*No. of Years Attended*	*Reasons for Leaving*

2. Have you ever had to repeat a class? Yes .... No ....
3. What grade in class do you generally obtain? ....
4. Have you held any position of responsibility in school or class? Tick the items below.
   Class monitor .... Captain of team................................
   President or secretary of any association...............................
   Troop or patrol leader in N.C.C./A.C.C./or Scouts.................
   Any other position...
5. Name the school and subjects that

You like best	You like least
....	....
....	....
....	....

You find easy	You find hard
....	....
....	....
....	....

6. What kind of books do you like to read if you like reading..........
   ....
   ....
7. How many hours per week outside of class do you usually study ? Mention number below.
   At school ....
   At home..
8. Outside of school where do you generally study or do your home work ? Tick one or more items below :
   Room of my own...
   Share a room with brothers and sisters..
   Study in the drawing or dining room ....
   Any other place (Pl. mention ....
9. Is the place where you study
   Very quiet ....
   Usually quiet but sometime disturbed ....
   Noisy with many distractions ....
   Any other remarks ....
10. What do you plan to do when you leave school ?
    Go to work .... Take some technical training ....
    Go to college ....Other plans..................................

III. Your Interest

11. In what extra-curricular activities do you take part in your school or outside? Tick one or more items below.
    Sports .... Dramatics ....
    Music............................... Debates/Discussions............................
    Art.................................. Crafts..
    Dancing........................... Photography.......................................
    Any other (Pl. Mention)..
12. Are you a member of any club or organization outside school? If so, name them below.
    ....
    ....
13. In what kind of hobbies or games do you take part outside of school hours? Mention some.
    ....
    ....

IV. Your Vocational Plans

14. Mention one or more occupations that you think you would like to take up as your future career.

First choice	Second choice	Third choice
....	....	....
....	....	....
....	....	....

15. Have you had any job experience? Yes .... No...................
If yes Name of job .... What was the nature of work? ....
....
Did you like it?...
16. How long ago did you decide to enter the occupation which you have listed as your first choice?
17. Have you made any attempts to find out something about the occupation (or occupations) you have listed above? Tick one or more items below :
Read some books, pamphlets,
Talked to persons in that occupation ....
Talked to my teachers ....
Talked to friends ....
Visited place of work ....
18. What are some advantages of occupation you have given as your first choice?
....
19. What are some disadvantages? ....
....
20. Are there some obstacles which might prevent you from following this occupation? ....
....
21. Will the education you are getting help you in entering any of these occupations?...
....
....
22. Have you discussed your plans for your future education and career with your parents?...
....
23 How do they feel about these plans?...

V. Your Health

24. Have you had any serious illness? Yes .... No.................
How long ago?...
25. Do you have any problems or worries about your health? If so, mention them here...
....
....
26. Are you absent from school because of illness ? Tick one of the items below:
Frequently .... Seldom ....
Never ....

All the above information and updated from time to time providing latest observations on the child's progress.

Educational and Occupational Guidance Services

For planning and executing career plan, a student requires various types of information. The educational information may include the various choices and opportunities open to him at various levels, the procedure for admission, courses in the streams chosen and jobs available, types of abilities required for a particular educational stream and so on.

Occupational information that should be available with the guidance worker would be nature of work, places of work, skills required, training and experience required, places of training, demand for the jobs, career development opportunities, working conditions, pay scales, etc.

Educational and occupation information services under a guidance programme are useful not only for students but also for parents, teachers and employers. The information is vast and cannot be circumscribed. If the information is available at one place all the needy may refer it for planning and development purposes. Students would know what skills are to be developed for a particular job and from where, parents may be able to advise the children about advantages, disadvantages of particular jobs and employers would be able to match their requirements with the skills of the students. Students would know what new skills are emerging in the market.

For collecting the information, a counsellor must know the sources of information. He should be able to disseminate the information properly through various techniques and means. He should also understand the importance of career information in a guidance programme. He should not give any information if he is not certain about its correctness.

For knowing the job opportunities, skills in demand, the emerging areas, he should conduct a small survey of the area to have first-hand information. Many opportunities for salary/wage employment may not be available. In that case, he should explore the possibilities of self-employment ventures and their linkages with markets and consumers. The present age is of creating online facilities. Guidance workers should be equipped with such facilities and abilities to use technology for collection and disseminating information.

Group Guidance Services

Under these services a number of activities may be organised to deal with the common problems of the students. Group guidance is less time consuming than dealing with the problems of the students individually. The various techniques used for group guidance and objectives of group guidance services have been discussed later. It is important to note here that these days group guidance is provided using computer and other on -line resources through zoom meetings, Skype etc.

Counselling Services

Under the group guidance services, students who require individual attention may be identified. The school guidance programme should be able to cater to the needs of individuals, as this is most important. Counselling services are, generally, for those who are under-achievers, whose academic performance declines; late comers; absentees; needing extra attention for academic achievements; dropouts from the school; have sudden problems at family front; are not able to adjust with the school environment, have adjustment problems with some teachers or classmates; who are shy; show attention getting behaviours; first generation learners; show problem behaviours or have unrealistic aspirations. On the other side those with high IQs and extra ordinary abilities also need counselling to channelise their energies and capabilities.

Counselling can be done only when the client has full trust in the counsellor, who should be a well-trained person. Maintaining confidentiality is the basic principle of counselling. Counselling is a time-consuming process. Timings for counselling should be chosen keeping in mind the school's academic time table so that student may not miss his classes. The place of counselling should be calm and quiet, and one where the client would feel relaxed. More details about counselling will be discussed in later chapters.

Support Services

Besides the above basic services, the guidance worker should be able to map the resources outside school and agencies that can help in organising guidance activities in the school. The other agencies, such as employment exchanges, the employers, the banks, may provide a lot of information input to the guidance worker. Some students may need special services in respect of health problems and others may need welfare services. A guidance worker should collect information of the institutions offering such help. The guidance worker should also have a good rapport with fellow teachers, the principals and other authorities by explaining the purpose of guidance programme so that he could get the information from the respective teachers from time to time about the students.

The guidance worker should also know the support system of individuals. In case of need he should discuss the problem of the child with family members and friends. If a child has some health problems, he should be helped by referring him to the appropriate place.

Placement Services

Of late placement services are getting importance as a part of guidance programme. Placement in jobs has become a technical affair and it is the responsibility of institutions to help the students to get a right placement. Employers also need a suitable person to carry out the work. Counsellor's role in providing the placement services is not only to help the students in getting prepared, filling up the application form, preparing Curriculum Vitae, and preparing for interviews, but also to list the agencies that help in placement and also keep liaison with the employers to get the information about the types of jobs available with them, their requirements, and emerging avenues of employment. Information regarding part-time jobs, summer jobs, details of getting registration in the employment exchange, vacancy analysis, details of financial assistance available to the persons who want to start their own work, future expected vacancies, developmental plans of the area which would require manpower, new and emerging industries, etc. has to be kept easily accessible with the guidance counsellor.

The placement services are not restricted to helping a student in getting a job but in the words of Stoops and Wahlquist:

> "The placement service should follow up placement to help students improve their services and to gain satisfaction on the job. In this sense, placement service begins with proper training and continues as long as the school can help the worker advance and readjust while working."

The counsellor should maintain sample formats of applications. Project profiles and area skill survey reports should be shared with the students. Mock sessions may be had to prepare the students for interviews. Visits to employment exchange and placement services may be arranged. For interaction with employers and credit institutions *Rozgar Melas* where employers and students could discuss with each other needs to be organised. Students should also be prepared to give on-line interviews.

Follow-up Services

Students have been helped in the school by the guidance counsellor but to what extent? What is the progress? A follow-up programme should be put in place. The basic aim of the follow-up services is to ensure that the beneficiary has settled and adjusted well in his chosen area of work or educational stream and in life. Let us look at some examples. A child has been helped in choosing the subjects. But is he finding any difficulty during the studies? Does the child needs further help? Or, in case of the students who have left the school, it would be of interest to know as to how well they are doing in their post-school activities. Suppose somebody has started a self-employment venture. Follow-up is necessary to see whether one is able to sell his product in the market? Does he require further financial assistance or any further technical help? In dealing with personal problems of the students, after termination of the counselling sessions, the counsellor should see whether the client is able to cope up with new and emerging situation? Whether new developments require any modifications in the plans the students have made for themselves? What help is required to the students who are dropping out from the school. These are some of the questions the guidance personnel have to address themselves.

Evaluation Services

Any guidance programme should include evaluation as an integral part of the programme. The evaluation may be concurrent or after one year or two years

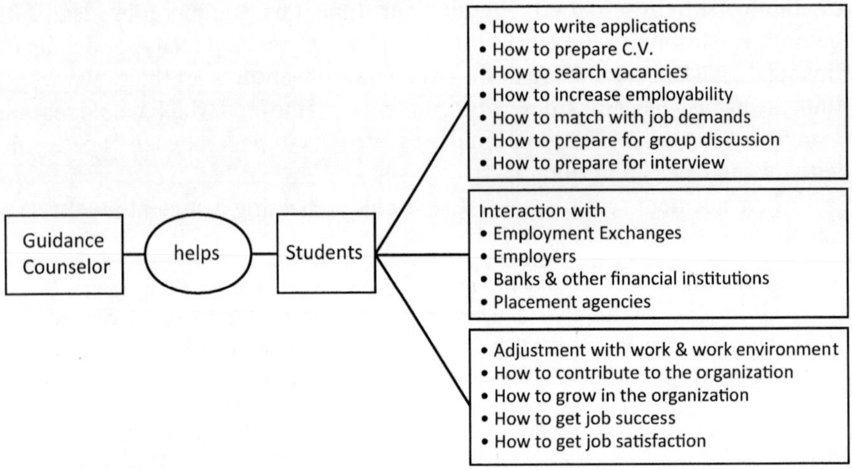

Figure 6.2: *Placement Services to be given by Guidance Worker*

as per plan. It may be conducted by the counsellor, by a Guidance Committee or by an outside agency but the activity should be included in the schedule. Follow-up services also provide some kind of evaluation of the programme. The success of the programme can only be ascertained through evaluation. Evaluation can show whether the guidance is meeting the needs of the students or not, and what modifications are required to make it more effective.

7

Individual Guidance and Counselling

Individual Guidance is also termed as **counselling** which has been defined as "face to face relationship in which growth takes place.' The underlying idea behind the counselling is that it is one to one interaction between an individual facing certain problems which he cannot cope up with by himself and a professional counsellor is needed who is ready to help the individual to come out of his problems. The individual guidance is focused upon the problems and needs of the client. According to the Committee on Definition of American Psychological Association counselling means "to help individuals towards overcoming obstacles to their personal growth, wherever these may be encountered and towards achieving optimum development of their personal resources." The definition shows that through counselling the behaviours of the client are expected to be modified in order to maximize personal development. The goal of counselling is self-understanding, self- acceptance and finally to achieve self-realisation.

Smith (1955) has defined counselling as "essentially a process in which the counsellor assists the counselee to make interpretations of facts relating to a choice, plan or adjustment which he needs to make." Williamson & Foley (1949) said that "Counselling has been defined as a face-to-face situation in which, by reason of training, skill or confidence vested in him by the other, one person helps the second person to face, perceive, clarify, solve and resolve adjustment problems."

The above definitions describe that the counsellor knows better than the client and he has to counsel the client, *i.e.,* it is more counsellor-centred. Contrarily, the theorists who believe that client has to be helped in understanding himself to make his own choices, propagate for client-cantered approach. Wrenn (1951) following this approach of counselling stated that "counselling is a personal and dynamic relationship between two people who approach a mutually defined problem with mutual consideration for each other to the end that the younger, or less mature, or more troubled of the two is aided to a self-determined resolution of his problem". The definition does not indicate the dominant role of the counsellor.

Blackham (1977) said that "Counselling is a unique helping relationship in which the client is provided the opportunity to learn, feel, think, experience and change in ways that he or she thinks is desirable." Here the dominance of the client may be observed.

Tolbert's definition (1972) about counselling is commonly used. According to him, counselling is a "personal, face to face relationship between two people, in which the counsellor, by means of the relationship and his special competencies, provides a learning situation in which the counselee, a normal sort of person, is helped to know himself and his present and possible future situations so that he can make use of characteristics and potentialities in a way that is both satisfying to himself and beneficial to society, and further, can learn how to solve future problems and meet future needs."

Myers says "Counselling implies a relationship between two individuals in which one give a certain kind of assistance to the other."

Arbuckle (1905) defining the concept said "Counselling is helping a person to come to see who he really is, what he has and does not have; what he can do easily, what he can do with difficulty and what he probably cannot do at all...(It) is a close sharing of a human relationship with one who has for him a high regard; one who can offer him unconditional acceptance, but one who has no guarantees, no answers."

Any definition can be followed but basically counselling is a professional relationship between the counsellor and the client which helps in mutual growth and understanding. The focus is on client's problems.

Objectives

The objectives of the individual guidance (counselling) are to make the person

(a) understand once own problems clearly
(b) realise what he is able to do and what he should do that means to accept his abilities and weaknesses
(c) Develop insight and understanding in relation to self and environment, opportunities open to improve in respect to his potentials and goals he has chosen.
(d) Decide a course of action by making his own decisions.

Features of Counselling

- Counselling is a professional service, which is imparted by a professional counsellor who is properly trained to handle various kinds of situations.
- Problems and needs of the individuals are important.
- Counselling helps the client make his own decisions during the process of counselling. The counsellor is not supposed to make decisions for the client. Counsellor may provide various types of information so that the client could get insight to take a decision
- It is more focused on one-to-one relationship even when the participants are involved with group counselling programmes. They are generally some or the other time approach for individual counselling because it is personal and more confidential
- The individual counselling is more about personal problems.

Types of Counselling

Counselling methods vary according to the needs of the individual. Basically, it is a voluntary process from the side of the individual, which provides a structured learning situation. Various approaches are followed according to the process involved in the method of counselling. On this basis counselling has been classified as Directive Counselling, Non-Directive Counselling and Eclectic Counselling.

The contextual method of classification classified counselling as cognitive therapies and behaviour therapies. All these have been detailed in the following pages.

Directive Counselling

In this type of approach counsellor plays an important role. A major goal is to replace the emotional behaviour of the individual with deliberate rationale behaviour. Although he/she avoids dictatorial advice. This approach is also known as counsellor-centred. Under this process the counsellor plans the counselling process, the work is to analyse the problem, identify the triggers, identify the exact nature of problem and provide various options. Williamson was a great profounder of this kind of approach as he stated that this approach is good to address the problems relating to educational and vocational adjustment. This type of counselling is a concept, where educational and vocational guidance relate to the personality dynamics and interpersonal relationship. This type of counselling is more useful where the individual wants information and advice for choice of a career. This approach does not focus its attention on personality development as such.

Steps of Directive Counselling

Williamson has given six steps of directive counselling:

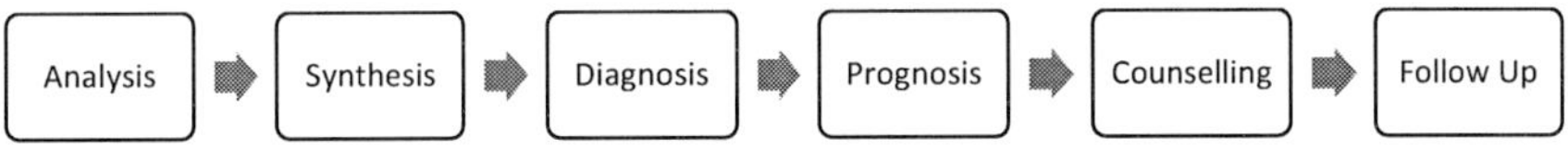

Figure 7.1: *Steps of Directive Counselling*

1. Analysis: It includes collection of information about the individual which can be collected through structured interviews, psychological case history methods, interaction with family members, friends, etc.
2. Synthesis: After collection of lot of data the information is organised in the logical manner to analyse the individual in terms of his qualifications, assets, potentials, liabilities, adjustment, cultural background, habits, etc.
3. Diagnosis: The diagnosis consists of the interpretation of the data in relation to the nature of problem, the causes of problems.
4. *Prognosis*: Under this step a prediction is made about the future development of the problem

5. Counselling: The counselling here is to bring about adjustment and re-adjustment to the individual in relation to his problem. Attitudes and interests of the individual are considered during the counselling. It emphasises the individual to develop life cycle where an effort in the positive direction could lead to success and the success in turn could lead to further efforts and motivation.
6. Follow up: The sixth step in directive counselling is follow up which is extremely important. An individual may be able to solve immediate problem through counselling but new problems may occur or the original problem may re-occur. Follow up with the client is extremely necessary. The role of counsellor is important as he has to make the individual understand and accept his strength and also his weaknesses and faults.

This technique is considered as a most economic approach and also important for student counselling because it is less time consuming and students who lack experience are easily influenced by the counsellor's experience and specialised knowledge. The students feel that the counsellor is superior in knowledge and therefore a professional relationship takes place. The relationship is the base of this kind of approach. A submissive and highly emotionalised counselling of student can cultivate self-confidence in the individual. A relationship is based on dignity to help the student to reach his goal.

Example of Directive Counseling and Reporting

Identification Data:

Name of the Client	-	Ajay Kumar
Father's Name	-	Shri A.P. Saxena (Not alive)
Gardian's Occupation	-	Assit Editor General Office
Class & Section	-	IX B
Name of the School	-	Boys Higher Sec. School
Date of birth	-	6-1-63

Statement of the Problem: Client has some vocational problem. He wants to go to I.I.T. & he wants information about it.

Family Background: The client is living with his uncle. His father is dead. His family is living with some other relation. He is having two brothers and three sisters. One brother is elder to him and he is studying in IX class. Others are younger to him.

His uncle has two sons and one daughter. All are elder to the client. His elder son is Engineer at Faridabad and younger is also serving as an Assistant. Uncle's daughter is studying in B.A. Final. Client is quite happy with the uncle's family.

Father: His father was a store keeper. He was suffering from cancer. He was a smoker. He sends the client to his brother's house before his death. Client has no domestic problem.

Physical Health of the Client: Client is very active and smart. He is very talkative and quick responder. Physically he is very normal. He takes part in school's activities.

Educational Information: He is a good student of the class. Since his childhood he is getting good marks and making a position in the class. He likes his studies. He likes the science subjects. He has some difficulty with History but he is not at all worried about it. He wants to improve his studies. He takes a great interest in his studies. He wants to study further.

Interests & Hobbies: He takes interest in playing Cricket and Hockey. He also has interest in reading some good books from which he can improve his knowledge. He takes interest in learning new things.

Test Reports:

Group Tests:

1. According to Standard Progressive Matrices client's IQ is 27 – Stanine V & he comes under average category.
2. In the Verbal Ability Test he has a score of 27 which comes under VII Stanine & above average category.
3. In the Mechanical aptitude test client's weighted score is 0 and he is low in this ability and have I Stanine. It shows that client's mechanical aptitude is low.
4. According to interest record client has VII Stanine in Social area. In clerical and outdoor he is average.

Individual Test Report: According to Bhatia Battery Client has an IQ of 97 which comes under the category of average. He has a Pd. of 105 which is known as average performance.

Teacher's Opinion: Teacher's opinion is very good for the client. Everybody loves him. He is known as a good and active student of the school. As teacher States – "He is naughty but lovely." He is very small looking boy and lovely. He is intelligent also. He gives all school work in time so everybody likes him.

Achievement Test Report:

Subjects	*Total*	*Maximum Marks*
English	65	100
Hindi	58	100
Math	96	100
S. Studies	67	100
Science	70	100
Craft	62	100
Physical Education	55	100

☞ *Counseling Interviews*

Ist Interview:

It was very easy to establish rapport with the client. Client voluntarily came to discuss his problem. After some general talk such as "How are you going on with your studies", "What are your hobbies", "How are you preparing for your exams."

Then when counselor asked his future plans he was looking very enthusiastic and he answered.

Client – Actually I want to be an Engineer because I am keenly interested in this field. I want to join I.I.T. Can you help me in this field? Can you provide me some information about I.I.T. and other alternatives?

Couns – It is good that you are thinking about your future. I will try to give you some information regarding I.I.T. But why you want to go to this field.

Client – I have a high interest in science. My uncle's son is an Engineer. So my uncle says to me that I should be an Engineer. And secondly when my father died he told me "It is my desire, you try to be an Engineer" so I regard my father and I am motivated and I want to go to this field.

Couns – So how many marks you are getting in Science?

Client – I am getting 70 per cent But I know I should get more. I should study more. I used to study from 7.30 to 11 in the night and in the morning also I study but I am getting low marks in science.

Couns – So what can you do for it?

Client – Now I will give more time to science subjects. I am trying to get some good magazines concerned with science. I can solve some of my problems with my brother.

Couns – So it is all right. You are thinking seriously about your studies and you know how should you improve your studies. So come next time I will give you information about I.I.T.

IInd Interview

Next Thursday client came

Client – Today can I know something about I.I.T. What type of courses are available there & how can I get admission there?

Couns – Yh. There are following Engg. courses. These are in

1. Chemical Engg.
2. Civil Engg.
3. Electrical Engg.
4. Mechanical Engg.
5. Textile Engg.
6. Computers

You can take admission in any one of these. They provide B. Tech. degree. Course is of five years. You can get admission through Joint Entrance Examination. Qualification should be a pass in the +2 examination of a Central or State Board of Secondary Education or Pre-University or Pre-Degree examination, Indian School Certificates or any equivalent examination is necessary. At this stage the counselor provided the prospectus of courses and other material relating to IIT courses and entrance examination

Client – What are the physical standards needed?

Couns – No special physical standard is needed but as Engg. Profession demands good physique and stamina, the candidate should not suffer from any organic defect and is physically fit to bear the strain of the course and later of the professional life.

Client – When the examination would be?

Couns – Examination medium is English and Admission notices are published as advertisement in the national dailies some time in December, January every year.

Client – From where I can get the form?

Couns – From the I.I.T's.

Client – What about the expenditure?

Couns – Counsellor gave the information about expenditure.

Client – What about the scholarships?

Couns – Yh. Scholarships are given according to merit basis after entrance examination. Loans are also available for education

Client – What else I can do if I am not able to get admission in I.IT.'s

Couns – You can go to Engg. Colleges such as Rurkee, Ranchi, Kanpur etc. In some colleges the selection is on merit basis and in some colleges there is an entrance examination. You can apply for that after +2 stage. Other than Engg. Courses there are options for pure sciences. You can do B.Sc. then M.Sc. in any specialized field from any university and then you can do some job of such as research work in various research laboratories/institutes or you can be a science teacher. There are good future prospects in it. After M.Sc. you can do Ph.D. & chances of going abroad are very good. Anything else if you want to ask me?

Client – No that is all right. I will try my best to do it thank you very much. If I am in need of some other information from where I can get?

Coun. First you choose from the options and make up your mind, detailed information for each option is available with me. You can refer to the career literature which is available in the center

Client – Thank you very much.

Counselor-Thank you and you are most welcome any time you like.

Counselor's Comments and Suggestions

As the client was in need of some information regarding his vocation, counselor provided that to the best of his knowledge. Client wanted to select a direction and the counselor helped him in choosing that. Counselor gave some alternatives in the same line so that client may be able to select a vocation according to his choice and can choose a career if he is not able to go to IIT.

During the counseling, counselor tried to explore the reason his choice of vocation. Why is he motivated towards this job? Is his selection worthy and genuine?

Follow up: Follow up was not needed in this case immediately because this time client was in IX class. The problem was connected with his vocational career and just now he is studying.

Non-directive Counselling

While Directive Counselling involves a counsellor-centred approach, Non-Directive Counselling is client-centred counselling. Rogers was the pioneer of this kind of technique. It is assumed in this approach that the individual is capable of making decisions, once his emotions and tensions are released. He can think in a positive direction and can help himself to come out of his problems. The counsellor's role is of that of a listener and facilitator. Psychological tests are not essential in this kind of technique. Rogers was of the view that people are self-directed. They need only a congenial atmosphere where they can explore themselves. Counsellor does not provide analytical input to the client and only empathises with the client and responds only to the feelings and emotions. This type of counselling is more useful in the case of personal and emotional problems.

By providing this theoretical base Rogers explained how the change takes place in the client. He said that the individual has personal anxiety or is in distress. The Counsellor relates himself with the problems of the client and pays positive regard to him. An empathetic relationship takes place where counsellor keeps himself in the place of the client and plays the role of a 'facilitator' or 'reflector'. In this approach it is assumed that each individual is basically good and has capability to develop his insight.

Steps in Non-directive Counselling

Rogers gave the following steps in the process of non-directive counselling.

1. The individual comes for help. He has taken a tentative step.
2. The helping situation is usually defined.He is made aware at once that the counsellor does not have the answers; the client is merely helped to work out his own answers.
3. The counsellor encourages free expression of feelings in regard to the problem. He tries to keep from blocking (and even encourages) the flow of hostility and anxiety, the feelings of concern and of guilt, and the indecisions that come out freely if we have succeeded in making the client feel that the hour is his to use as he wishes. The counsellor does not attempt to persuade the client that he is wrong or that he is right. He accepts him as he is. He merely tries to encourage free expression.
4. The counsellor accepts, recognises, and clarifies those negative feelings. The counsellor must respond to the feelings of the client, not to the intellectual context of what the person is saying, not to the rightness or wrongness of the position or belief taken by the client. He tries to verbalise it and clarify it without undue sympathy.
5. When the individual's negative feelings have been quite fully expressed, they are followed by the faint and tentative expressions of the positive impulses that make for growth. This is one of the most certain and predictable aspects of the whole process.
6. The counsellor accepts and recognises the positive feelings which are expressed in the same manner in which he has accepted and recognised in the same manner in which he has accepted and recognised the negative feeling. They are not accepted with approval or blame.
7. This results in an understanding of and insight into the self and an acceptance of the self. This provides a basis on which the individual can go ahead to new levels of integration.
8. A clarification of possible decisions, possible courses of action.
9. The initiation by the individual of minute, but highly significant, positive actions. The client is not urged; he still is merely accepted and encouraged.
10. A development of further insight, a more complete and accurate understanding. This is a further element of growth.
11. Increasingly integrated positive action.
12. A feeling of increased independence, of decreasing need for help. (The relationship must terminate.)

Example of Non-Directive Counseling

Identification Data:

Name of the Client - Mahinder

Father's Name - Shri Guru Vachan

Father's Occupation - Lift Operator
Client's Class & Section - IX
Name of the School - Govt. Co-Educational School
Date of birth - 20-9-60
Age - 16 years 6 months

Statement of the Problem:

1. He is weak in English & Mathematics – Educational problem.
2. Adjustment problem – The client is not able to adjust with the teachers.

Family Background:

Client has two brothers, one is elder to him. This elder brother is a writer. He used to write poems and stories. Client has one younger brother who is studying in VIII class in the same school. He has no real sister. There is a cousin sister who stayed with client's family. His father was a lift operator and just now as he stated in his last interview, he has retired and is doing agricultural work. Client's mother is a housewife. Because his father has retired client wants to support his family by joining some night school so that he may be able to do some job. His mother and brothers are going with the father and he himself stayed with his sister because he thinks he will get some good job over here. His sister is working in some office.

Physical Health of the Client: Physically the client is quite normal. He takes active part in school's activities. He was the monitor of his class as it was observed he is good at administration.

Educational Information: Client is interested in his studies. Since his childhood he likes photography and now at this stage when he is in class IX, he has taken photography as a subject. He likes this subject very much. As he stated he was normal with his studies. While at school every teacher used to like him. Since his childhood he is weak in Maths and English. He was weak in Maths so he doesn't like it. Whenever he is not able to solve any problem, he skips it. He doesn't try further. He says, 'when I am not able to solve the previous question how I can be successful in this'. He doesn't pay any extra attention to Maths. He is weak in English also but even then, he likes it. He takes much interest in other subjects such as Hindi.

Interest & Hobbies: Client takes interest in music. He plays on instruments such as Tabla or Drum. He has learnt this from his father. He father is a musician and he uses to go to some musical sittings. Client also wants to learn some specific instrument in music and he wants to develop his hobby of music.

Sports: He likes cricket very much. Whenever he gets time he used to play cricket with some of his good friends. Client also feels pleasure in seeing new places.

Test Reports:

Group Tests:

1. Standard Progressive Matrices: According to this group test, client has an average IQ.
2. In the verbal ability test client's score is 33. He comes under VIII Stanine, and he is above average in this category.
3. According to the Interest Record he is getting VII Stanine in artistic field. He is above average in this interest area. In some fields such as clerical and outdoor fields he is average.

Individual Testing: According to *C.I.E.* Individual scale of Intelligence client's IQ is 83.33 and he is slightly below average according to the IQ's categories.

Bhatia Battery Individual Test Report:

The client has an IQ of 86 and his PQ is 96. According to this report client's IQ comes under slightly below average and according to PQ he is average person.

Achievement Test Report:

Subjects	*Evaluation* I	II	III	*Total*
1. English	09	04	10	23
2. Hindi	20	15	13	48
3. Maths	20	02	16	38
4. Social Studies	20	14	12	48
5. Science	11	13	16	40
6. Craft	256	21	12	48
7. Physical Education	08	11	A	19

Teacher's Opinion: Teacher's opinion about the client is not very good. They think him as an aggressive boy. Principal and other teachers referred his case for his adjustment problem. The client voluntarily came for his educational problems.

Teachers don't complain anything about his studies. They only stated – "He is very disobedient and doesn't listen to anybody."

General Opinion: As it is observed that client is very open. There was no difficulty in establishing the rapport with the client. During the tests, he was taking interest in the activity.

☞ *Counseling Interviews*

Ist Interview: The first interview was, in reality, an initial interview. As stated earlier, it was very easy to establish rapport with the client. He was feeling friendly with the counselor. A good relationship was established during the test administration. Therefore, it was very easy to talk with the client in first interview. After some general talk such as, "What are your hobbies"? "How did you like the tests which have been administered to you" and some other questions about his family, the client was feeling relaxed and then he stated his problem. The client so opened up with the counselor that he himself stated his adjustment problem also. But in this initial interview counselor didn't talk anything about his adjustment problem. He overlooked the client's statement and tried to lay emphasis mainly upon the educational problem.

Client stated – "I am weak in Maths and English. Main problem is with Maths. I can't understand anything in this subject.

Counselor asked him to come next time so that he may discuss his problem.

2nd Interview:

Couns – How many marks are you getting in maths?

Client – Only 38 out of 100.

Couns – What are the things you are not able to understand in maths?

Client – You see, I can't understand anything. I am weak in maths from the very beginning.

Couns – Why are you weak in maths from very beginning? Can you think of any reason? Were you not paying much attention or anything else?

Client – Yes. This was the reason. Now I pay more attention. In the beginning I was not paying any attention. Wherever I could not solve any question I skipped it because I got puzzled. In the beginning, I always used to get 0 marks but now I get some marks.

Couns – So you are understanding what should you do?

Client – Yes… I am …. but ….

Couns – How much time do you give to your studies?

Client – Not much, only 2 hours in the night from 9 to 11.

Couns – You study two hours in the night. How do you plan it? For how much time do you study maths?

Client – I study maths for one-hour daily, half an hour English and rest half an hour science. Other subjects I feel very easy and I study other subjects very little.

Couns – Do you study in the morning?

Client – No, I don't, because I wake up in the morning at 9.

Couns – What you can do for it?

Client – Now I have taken an alarm piece and I try to wake up early in the morning.

Couns – What are the courses in the maths?

Client – Algebra, Geometry and Trigonometry I can't understand a word of it.

Couns – What is the thing? Do you think teacher is not good or you don't concentrate?

Client – No, teacher is quite nice but actually I don't pay much attention because I have no interest

Couns – But you know, you have to study all subjects upto 10th standard and Maths is a very scoring subject.

Client – That is right but what can I do? Can you tell me?

Couns – Yes. You come next time. I will think over your problem, you should also think and then we will try to find a solution for your problem.

3rd Interview:

Next Thursday the client came. After some general talk we started –

Client – Yes, can you tell me something to solve my problem?

Couns – You see, as you have stated previously, it seems that you have no interest in Mathematics because you are not able to understand it.

Client – ….. Yes, that's right.

Couns – And you were not paying any attention in the beginning, therefore you are not able to understand it.

Client – Yes. When I don't know about previous things, how can I understand further?

Couns – You can tell your problem to the teacher.

Client – Till now I never went to him, but if you say so, I will go.

Couns – No, you should not go just because I am saying so you. You should think about it yourself, whether to go or not. Is there any other person in your house who can teach you?

Client – No, there is non but I will go to my teacher personally.

Couns – And, what is your problem in English

Client – I can't understand grammar. My teacher says you have to study new grammar. I don't know even what parts of speech are. I don't know the difference between a noun and pronoun.

Couns – What about other students?

Client – Nobody understands.

Couns – You haven't studied it in class VIII?

Client – No, there was no grammar in VIII class. When we ask the teacher, he says 'you are so foolish that you don't know even these things'.

Couns – You can study in groups in the class.

Client – There is too much noise in the class. There is no study-room, and they don't allow us to sit in the library. They think we are cutting our classes.

Couns – You can study in any class where there is no lecture going on.

Client – Then other boys disturb us. They laugh at us.

Couns – So it means you are afraid of them.

Client – Yes

Couns – Why?

Client – Because, if friends insult me, I feel bad.

Couns – Do you think it insulting if you are studying.

Client – .... No .... that is not the thing. But when they want me and I am studying, then they say 'Oh you have to top'-or something like that.

Couns – But you can also tell them that you have to study. If they say, 'you leave studies' will you leave?

Client – No, I will not. How it can be?

Couns – So, you can tell them that at this time you have to study and at this time you can or you can complain to your teachers.

Client – They don't do anything.

Couns – Then, what do you think, what can be done? It is a problem, but studies are more important. Are they not?

Client – That's right. Now, I have to make my timetable. Now I won't talk with anybody. There is only one friend of mine. I uses to study with him. We solve our problems with the help of each another.

Couns – Yes. You can do like this. Everybody can't understand everything, and you can solve your problems with the help of each other. Tell me one thing what do you want to be in future?

Client – There are some family problems with me. I have to join some night school. To support my family, I want to take up some job. I am having photography in my work experience; I want to have my own shop.

Couns – How has your interest in photography developed?

Client – Since my childhood I have interest in photography. Some relations were having cameras with them. I wanted to know about it. When I asked something about photography, they told "you are a child, when you grow up, you will be able to understand it". Now when I came in IX class, I took photography as a subject.

Couns – Do you have any friend or somebody or relation with whom you want to open your shop?

Client – Yes, a friend of mine is interested in photography, but he doesn't know about it. I am teaching him and then we have decided that we will contribute fifty-fifty and open a shop.

Couns – Do you want to open your shop after completing your studies or, as you have stated, you will join some night school, and start your work right from now.

Client – Yes, I will do some other job, because we don't have so much money. I will save some money and then I will do my own work.

Couns – It is very good that you think in this way and want to do your work on your own. If you are not able to open your own shop, you can do some other job in photography. For example, you can be a photographer in any company, or advertising agencies or in some newspaper.

Client – That's all right.

Couns – Anything else you want to say?

Client – No. Now I don't have anything to say.

Couns – So, I think now you will study well. You are a good student.

Client – Yes, I will try my best. Now I can solve my problems. Thank you very much.

4th Interview:

Couns – Last time we were discussing about the problem of difficulties in your studies. Once you told me about your adjustment problem. Will you discuss it today?

Client – Yes, of course I will.

Couns – Then tell me what the matter is.

Client – You see, teachers used to harass me. Once the entire class was making noise. So the teacher punished the whole school and even those who were not at fault were all punished. Then there was my brother. He asked some teacher how to make me remember things. The teacher told him to cut my hairs. I felt very bad. It is a kind of comment on my Dharm. This was in class VIII. In class IX there was a boy. He commented "Hello Sardarji. Is it .. o'clock?" I felt very bad, and I slapped him. He went to the teacher. The teacher abused me and beat me. The boy is the same fellow who was talking against the teacher last year.

Couns – From the very beginning you had bad relations with the teachers.

Client – No. not so. When I was in class V, some incident took place. Some teacher told something nasty to my brother. These things I cannot tolerate. One day I want to some palmist. He told me "You could never tolerate injustice. You are very aggressive type. You will be just like Gandhiji, who could never tolerate injustice and started non-cooperative movement. You will also do like that.

Couns – Have you read anything about Gandhiji?

Client – Yes, I have. There was a book on Gandhiji, I have read that.

Couns – Do you think he was very aggressive?

Client – No, he was not. He was very calm and quiet. He was a very simple man. Whatever step he took he took it peacefully.

Couns – Yes, you are right. He never tried to win any injustice through anger. Is it not so?

Client – Yes.

Couns – He told that if anybody is angry, you can win him by love and not with anger. Now, take your fight with that boy. Actually, it may not be any comment. He is just like your friend. Friends can say anything. You see, when you like Gandhiji and you want to be like him, you study more about him then you can understand the real facts about him.

Client – Yes, I will study more.

Couns – You were a monitor of your class. I have seen that you were doing a good job in the class. You can enforce discipline in the class. But, do you feel you can control the people only with aggression?

Client – They don't understand the things otherwise. I can't do anything else.

Couns – No, you can. Why not? You see, if your parents always tell you, "You have to do like this, otherwise we will punish you," would you like it? Would you do the work by such type of threats or when they ask you to do the work with affection?

Client – Yes, I will not do by force.

Couns – Then.

Client – But when I was in class V there was a teacher of mine. He told me to beat the students if they are not controllable. So, I became hostile.

Couns – But hostile ones can be .... Is it not?

Client – Yes. It is but it cannot be in one moment. It will go gradually.

Couns – Will you try not to be hostile?

Client – Yes, I will. You see, every teacher used to like my brothers. They always tell me "you are so bad but your brothers are very simple". I also feel that I am not a good boy and my brothers are so good.

Couns – You don't want to be like your brothers?

Client – I want, but now it is not possible because now teachers could not forgive me.

Couns – Do you feel if someone has done something wrong, he can never be a good man.

Client – Some people think like that.

Couns – No, it is not. Suppose somebody has done some mistake, will you not forgive him if in future he realizes his mistake?

Client – Yes, I will.

Couns – Have you heard about Valmiki?

Client – No I haven't. You tell me.

Couns – Yes, I will. He was a dacoit. One day some saints came to him. Valmiki asked them to give him whatever things they had. The saints said that they would give but asked "you are committing sins to support your family. When you will be punished by God, will the members of your family help you or not?" Valmiki replied I don't know. They should support me. Valmiki went to his home and asked the members of his family. They told that they would not help him when God punished him. Since that very day Valmiki got reformed and became a very good man. So, don't you think a bad man too can be good some day?

Client – You are right. Actually, I am a weak person, so I was thinking like this. I was feeling that teachers would not change their opinion.

Couns – Now you understand you can be a good man through your behaviour. It is good that you should not tolerate injustice, but you should not be aggressive. You think yourself which is better?

Client – Now I will try my best to change myself. I will study some good books.

Follow up – The time was not much but in the limited time, counselor observed client takes interest in his studies. He has left the monitorship because of his studies. He is friendly to his classmates. He respects his teachers. His classmates also gave positive comments.

Counselor's Comments & Suggestions

If counselor was able to get more time, he could do much better. Problem was much lengthy it needs time. As counselor knew about the adjustment problem of the client, he observed that client couldn't listen anything against about his 'Dharm'. Counselor gave the example of Valmiki because counselor observed that he could be changed only through such example. For the study problems of the client counselor tried to open up the client and asked for suggestions as to what he could do to tackle the problem.

Counselling and Psychotherapy – Two Different Concepts

Sometimes the concepts of counselling and psychotherapy are misunderstood as one. But these two concepts are different. While counselling deals with normal people, psychotherapy deals with abnormal people. Another difference is that counselling relates to conscious mind, while psychotherapy relates to unconscious mind. Counselling is said to be focused on cognitive and rational behaviour whereas psychotherapy relates more to emotions and feelings. (Bordin)

Differences have also been observed in the ultimate aim of both. The aim of counselling is to help a person, the aim of psychotherapy is to change the personality of a person (Tyler 1961). Buchheimer and Balogh (1961) tried to differentiate the two concepts stating that counselling refers to individual's present and immediate awareness while therapy refers more to past experiences and symbolism.

On the other hand, Byrne (1963) sees the two concepts as having many similarities, except that the difference is in "degree to which psychotherapists uncover and work with hidden psychological dynamics because the individual seeking help reports a long-standing dissatisfaction with life, accompanied by long-standing ineffective or unwanted behaviours."

Table 7.1: *Comparative Analysis of Directive and Non-Directive Counselling*

Directive	*Non-Directive*
Economical	Time Consuming
Emphasis is on the problem	Emphasis on individual
Emphasis on the intellectual aspect	Emphasis on emotional aspect
Methodology is direct and persuasive	Methodology is indirect
Solves immediate problems	Deals with self-analysis and new problems of adjustment may be taken care of
Uses psychological assessment data	May not use psychological assessment
Counsellor plays active role	Counsellor plays passive role
Direct counselling sometimes may be done by supporting staff	A highly professional, competent and trained person with understanding of relationship skills is required
Help is offered by counsellor to take decisions	Client takes his own decisions
It is more information giving, rapport formation is not that significant	It is to develop self-insight and more towards solving the personal problems-rapport formation is essential.

Process of Counselling

It cannot be expected that a person would just come for counselling, would state his/her problem, that the counsellor would give a solution and the person would be happy that the problem is resolved. Counselling is a time-consuming process where trust building between the two is extremely essential. There are no readymade solutions. A long process is involved in the problem solving.

Brammer (1973) has pointed out four stages of the counselling process. These are: entry, clarification, planning and termination. Similarly, Blackham has identified the stages as problem identification and relationship establishment stage; exploration and analysis stage; and termination stage. Although the stages relating to identification and analysis of the problem as well as planning a solution are the most important where the actual work takes place, but the initial stage of rapport building and the last stage, *i.e.*, termination stage are extremely crucial and difficult. It is the responsibility of the counsellor to prepare an atmosphere where the client could feel relaxed and accepted. The client has to have faith in the counsellor to confide himself. This trust building takes time. It develops gradually in a friendly harmonious relationship. Non-verbal communication like shaking hands, smiles, eye contacts etc. play an important role. The counsellor should understand the importance of such clues.

Similarly, the termination stage is difficult because during the whole counselling process, even though the relationship between the client and counsellor is said to be professional, it is, in fact, extremely sensitive. Many a time; the client develops special affection for the counsellor, totally depends upon him and looks forward to continued relationship. At this stage the counsellor needs to be tactful. Gradually he should withdraw from the relationship of dependability. The counsellor should, however, welcome in case the client really needs some help.

Eclectic Counselling

This is the middle path between Direct and Non-direct approaches where both approaches are adopted simultaneously. There may be cases and situations where one approach exclusively may not help to reach the desired results. Hence a middle path, in which both the approaches can be combined under this technique as and when needed. Here the counsellor accepts that an individual can choose his goals but motivation on the part of the counsellor is essential so that the client may solve the problems. Counsellor takes an initiative in providing information and suggestions wherever he feels that these are necessary for the client to take the decisions. In cases where school environment or work environment is responsible for individual's problems, the counsellor, under this approach, tries to amend the environment with the help of other members of the school. Under this approach it is also believed that the present behaviour is influenced by past and, therefore, information about the client is collected from various sources. The counsellor also takes into account the support services available in the client's environment like family, community, friends' circle, and other agencies that can help the client in solving his problems and reaching the goal. In this eclectic counselling approach finding the solution to the problem is joint responsibility of the counsellor and the client.

Cognitive Therapies

Under the cognitive therapies, Rational-Emotive therapy by Albert Eliss (1950) and Cognitive Restructuring Therapy by Aaron Becks are the two important ones to mention. These are based on the concept that problems occur in people because of the distortions in the cognitive or the thought process.

While explaining the Rational-emotive therapy, Eliss considered that whenever the person has irrational thought, emotional problems emerge. The person starts feeling anger, anxiety, depression etc. People sometimes make illogical interpretations of the events; they compare themselves with others and develop self-defeating attitudes. This therapy helps in changing such thoughts and beliefs into rationality by challenging the irrational thoughts through arguments and rational interpretation of the situation.

Restructuring therapy also tries to change the client's negative self- images through restructuring their thoughts, but in this case the situation is not analysed in a more rational manner but the client is told of certain experiences that could disapprove the client's negative self-image. For example, if the client comes with an image 'He is no good and cannot do anything'; the counsellor has to talk with him about those activities where the client excelled earlier.

Behavioural Counselling

Behavioural counselling is based on social learning theory, which relate to process of changing the behaviours and how the learning takes place. The outer symptoms of behaviour are most important. It is believed that a person is not behaving properly because his learning is faulty. Re-learning has to take place and mal-adaptive learning has to be unlearned. These therapies concentrate on a person's present behaviour.

Various techniques are used to change the undesirable behaviour known as

1. Classical Conditioning and
2. Operant Conditioning.

Classical Conditioning

The following two techniques are used in Classical Conditioning:

Desensitisation: Joseph Walpe developed this technique in 1950. Desensitisation for a problem situation is conducted systematically under this technique. People are trained to relax in the situations that create anxiety. The process involves identifying the triggers that induce anxiety and their intensity. In the second step, the person is asked to relax physically and mentally. When a person is totally relaxed, he is asked to think about the triggers according to their intensity till he feels anxious. When the person is trained to be relaxed in such situations, which he imagines as anxiety situations, he is asked to face the real situation. This technique is effective in dealing with anxiety and phobias.

Aversive Conditioning: In this technique, the person is asked to feel discomfort with the behaviour he wants to change. For example, if a person wants to leave his habit of smoking, he is asked to feel that his mouth has a bad taste, he is not enjoying, and he is feeling physically uncomfortable while smoking. In this technique, some drugs are administered after which the person would develop such discomfort when he would smoke or drink. This technique is used generally to deal with the problems of smoking and alcoholism.

Operant Conditioning

These therapies are also known as behaviour modifications methods through providing positive reinforcements to encourage desired behaviour and to remove some existing stimuli to punish the undesirable behaviour. In other words, reinforces are used manipulatively to change the behaviour. The techniques used under this therapy are positive reinforcement, extinction, and punishment. In the positive reinforcement technique, some rewards are given for encouraging the desirable behaviours. When a child is rewarded for his desirable behaviour for example, by giving a toy and by giving the food he likes, he may get encouragement for his behaviour and would continue to act in the same manner. In extinction technique, when a child's behaviour is not liked, the reinforce to encourage that behaviour is eliminated. In cases where children cry for getting attention and parents immediately attend to the child when he cries, he develops crying as a behaviour. If such situations have to be dealt with, the parents are advised to heed to the child before crying and not to encourage crying by responding to it.

In punishment technique the child is punished for his undesirable behaviour. Modeling is also a technique for behaviour change. Successful stories of people and identification of children with their ideals is common for behaviour modifications. This also involves role-playing, in which people try to act in hypothetical situations. Once they are confident in such situations, they will be comfortable when placed in real life activities.

Group Therapy

In dealing with emotional problems of people, the concept of group therapy is a recent phenomenon. Problems such as alcoholism, smoking, introvertive behaviours etc. may be dealt collectively. The groups may be the families, the couples or the people having similar problems. For example, in marriage counselling, the therapists call both the husband and the wife. Group therapy provides a therapeutic effect. These days with mobile addiction problems in children group therapies can provide good results. It also encourages the group relationships and feeling of togetherness and support. Interaction with the group develops interpersonal skills. Suggestions come from various members and there is an opportunity to see how others are coping with the problems. For example, in case of alcoholism the people who want to get rid of this habit may come together, where they can discuss their problems, or a person who earlier had this problem and has been successful in coming out of it, may interact with the group and discuss the strategies to change the habit. These behaviour therapies have been criticised to be over simplistic and ignoring the individual's growth and development process.

Specific Skills Required in Counselling

One to one counselling is a specialised activity, which requires besides training, some special skills in the counsellor.

1. *Ethics*: The ethical attitudes of the counsellor matter most, as client is providing extremely personal information to the counsellor, in other words, the client is confiding in the counsellor, and the counsellor should have professional attitude and also some basic ethics that personal information should not be revealed to others and would not be used other than professional. The counsellor should also have respect and regards for the client for 'what he is'. The client's feelings should also be respected.: Counselling requires unconditional warmth towards the client. In a counselling process, counsellor should always be welcoming with a smiling face; he should not say "say it fast, I have to do some other work." He should not even give the non-verbal clues like seeing the watch many times. Client may feel that his is not wanted.
2. *Sensitivity and Empathy*: The counsellor should be sensitive towards the client's needs and problems. He should not pass remarks 'what you are wearing is not a proper dress' or 'I was told you are a mischievous boy'. Empathy is the competence of the counsellor to experience the client's experience. Rogers (1990) defined empathy as 'perceiving the internal frame of reference of another person'. Egan (1990) defined the concept of empathy as 'entering the private perceptual world of the client and being sensitive to his/her feelings, whether good or bad.' For example, if the client comes to the counsellor for confessing some act he is guilty of now, counsellor should not go into the value judgement about the act, expressing his feelings. He should not say, "What did you do? You should have not done it" but try to listen to the client patiently and help him to come out of his feeling of guilt. Such situations can be handled by

giving some examples, indicating that these things can and do happen. Self-disclosure also helps in dealing such situations.

3. *Communication and Listening*: Communicating through listening is most important in counselling. The counsellor should possess that intellectual competence to react verbally as well as non-verbally wherever required. Most of the problems of the clients are resolved only when the counsellor is a good listener and a good communicator. The expressions, the tone, the pitch, the body language, eye contact all are equally or even more important than words. If a client comes and counsellor says 'Hello, I am happy to see you' but the expressions of the counsellor do not reflect that happiness, the communication would not be effective. A small touch is better than thousand words to the crying.
4. *Giving Leads*: In communicating with the client, the counsellor makes use of statements called 'leads'. Such leads may be classified into the following categories of techniques.
   (a) Restatement: The counsellor attempts to convey his understanding of what the client communicated by repeating or rewording the client' s statement.
   (b) Questioning
   (c) Reflection of feeling: The counsellor seeks additional information from the client.
   The counsellor expresses understanding of the client's point of view and communicates that understanding.
   (d) *Reass*urance: The counsellor's statement serves as a reward or reinforcing agent. This technique is often used to support the client's exploration of ideas and feelings or test different behaviour.
   (e) *Interpretation:* The counsellor tries to explain the meaning of what the client stated.
   Example: The counsellor met the student for the first time. The student said: "The teacher asked me to see you, I do not know why. She says I should learn to stay awake in the class. I feel sleepy because I walk five kilometres to reach the school. Moreover, her lessons bore everyone."
   In response, the counsellor may say one of the following:
   i. "You were bored and felt sleepy in the class and the teacher asked you to leave the class". (Restatement)
   ii. "Why do you get bored in that teacher's class?" (Questioning)
   iii. "So, you felt bad when she asked you to go" (Reflection of feeling = Understanding)
   iv. "Do not worry! It should be possible to find a solution soon" (Reassurance = Supporting)
   v. "Do you think that you are making the teacher responsible for what a. happened?" (Interpretation)

Figure 7.2: *Five Basic Functions in Counselling*

Importance of Interview in Counselling

Interviews play an important role in counselling, be it directive, non- directive or eclectic. The process of interview changes according to the type of counselling. While in directive counselling, the counsellor can directly ask questions to get information from the client and can ask about his needs, in non-directive counselling, the role of the counsellor is to encourage the client to speak about himself. The counsellor has to be supportive and empathetic in his approach. Direct questions should be avoided. Silence and non-verbal clues are to be interpreted adequately. In general, according to Humphreys a counsellor has to perform five basic functions in an interview. These are:

1. *Rapport Formation*: To establish harmonious and congenial relationship with the client.
2. *To Secure Information*: Counsellor may seek information from the client during interview or can have the information from other sources like Cumulative Record Card, Anecdotal Records, School Records.
3. *To Impart Information:* During the interviews counsellor can impart the information to the client as per his need.
4. *To Motivate:* Motivation here is not forcing the client to do something but to help the counselee to understand and develop his motivational forces inside.
5. *To Help*: Under this function counsellor helps the counselee to make adjustments and have long-term planning.

For conducting an interview, counsellor should:

1. *Prepare*: Such as collection of information about the client from various sources; note down the gaps, fix up the appointment, see the physical settings, keep himself prepared to face the client.
2. *Create a Pleasant Atmosphere*: Counsellor should be able to create such a pleasant atmosphere that the client is ready to trust the counsellor and open up his feelings.
3. *Be a Good Listener*: The counsellor should have patience in dealing with the client. He should be a good listener and should not interrupt the client to cut his speech. He should not comment like 'I know this, go further'.
4. *Be Unbiased*: While interacting with teachers, or peers or parents about an individual, the counsellor should not form any opinion. He should meet with the client without any pre-conceived ideas.

5. *Be Accepting*: The counsellor should not pronounce value judgement. He should receive the client with open heart. He should accept him as 'what he is' and not as 'what he should be'.
6. *Be Aware of his Limitations*: The counsellor himself may not deal with all cases. He should take the help of others wherever required or he should be willing to refer the client to the appropriate agency wherever needed.
7. *Be Able to Maintain the Privacy*: Total privacy should be maintained during the interview process. The counsellor should ensure that others are not waiting in the queue. Counsellor should keep himself free from other activities.
8. *End the Interview on a Positive Note*: At the end of the interview session, counsellor should be positive. He should not be depressed or gloomy or leave the client in depressing mood.
9. *Interpret with Full Understanding*: Counsellor should be able to make interpretation from the discussions with counselling properly and with adequate understanding.
10. *Recording of Procedures*: Wherever client agrees, the interview may be recorded so that information and clues given by the client are not forgotten.

Process of Interviews in Counselling

1. *Rapport Formation*:
   - Have the interview where privacy can be maintained.
   - Welcome the client, with smile or a handshake or with pleasant greetings.
   - Make him/her sit comfortably and relax
   - So far as possible use only first name of the client. With this the client will get a feeling of intimacy.
   - Start with informal conversation like – How are you doing today, or how was your day today, or how you did in the class today, etc.
   - Use the native language of the client as far as possible.
   - Avoid interruptions created by other visitors, phone calls.
   - Listen attentively and slow empathy towards the problem of the client.
   - Patience is required in establishing rapport. Sometimes no words are required, only small gestures of affection like smile, welcoming attitude may help while with some clients, it may take a long time.

     In a case where student came with saying 'I want to commit suicide' the reply from the counsellor's we will talk it over, first let us have a cup of tea together; was enough to form the rapport.
   - Sincerity, non-judgmental attitude and friendly behaviour is essential.
2. *Client's Problem*:
   - In counselling, it is important to know how the client perceives his problems. Questions like 'you want to share something with me', or 'what would you like to talk with me?' may be the initial questions that may encourage the client to start talking.

- When the client narrates his problem, listen. With small words Oh! or O.K. or with some non-verbal gestures show that you are concerned with the problem of the client.
- When the client stops speaking questions like 'what your parents feel about this problem; or whether you have discussed it with any of your friends and relatives' may be asked to know how the client see others' advice.
- Thought Providing Clues:
  During counselling interview, the counsellor may raise certain questions and issues that may start thought provoking process in the client other than how he perceives himself or his problem.
  For example, with a totally negative self-image, the counsellor may ask the client what strengths he thinks he has or what good things happened in his life or count small achievements of the day or the week, etc.
- *Self-Understanding and Self-Realisation*: It is said that sharing the problem provides a kind of catharsis (release of tension) and client starts understanding the self in a positive manner. Factual data on the clients performance or the environment should be provided to the client so that he could start realising and accepting him self like 'you got good marks in Science', or 'you did extremely well in the annual function of the school.'
- *Information Providing*: Wherever necessary counsellor should provide the information to the client to facilitate his decision making, *e.g.,* where the client is confused in making a choice of career, or has no choice.
- *Motivation*: During the interview, motivate the client when he puts forth some idea towards the process of decision making in solving his problem like 'yes that's a good idea' or 'yes it would work out'
- *Self-insight or Change in behaviour*: When the client is able to get self-insight into the problem and says 'yes it can be done like this' or I will do this, counsellor should help the client in executing the idea with follow up.

Interview with the client may not be complete in one sitting. The whole process takes three or four interviews minimum.

Case Approach of Guidance

Case study approach is in a way an approach for individual guidance.

Meaning

Case study approach of guidance relates to analyse the personality and problems of a child from more than one perspective. In other words, it is an intensive analysis of various facets of the child's personality. The detailed analysis helps in understanding the child which is evidence based. Guidance can be provided on the basis of this understanding. Case studies are prepared for individuals and used in counselling.

Systematic Case Study: The Nature

Under this method, the major activity is to collate all the information collected from various sources and techniques. This can be the information from the school record, from achievement record of the students, the psychological tests, or information collected by teachers. All these collected bits of information may be systematically reviewed and analysed and prepared in the form of the case study. Allport says that "It provides a framework within which the psychologist can place all of his observations gathered by other methods; it is his final affirmation of the individuality and uniqueness of every personality. It is completely synthetic method; the only one that is spacious enough to embrace all assembled facts. Unskilfully used, it becomes a meaningless chronology, or a confusion of fact and fiction, of guesswork and misinterpretation. Properly used, it is the most revealing method of all."

For preparing the case study, some order of reporting may be prescribed, say, introduction, scores on achievement test, school progress, teacher's observations, learning defects, family history, social background, health background, scores on psychological tests, personal problems, pupil groups observations and the interpretation.

Case studies are important records in situations where individual counselling is required. They can serve as successful cases to be referred by other students. Case study record also indicates the gaps in information.

Steps of Case Study

Writing a case study is an art as well as a science as it has to collate both quantitative and qualitative information about a child. The case record has to be totally unbiased otherwise it would have its repercussions which may not be in the interest of the child.

In the words of Jane Warter, "Whether long or short, written in formal manner or in free description and narrative style, the case study should present as accurate and as objective an account and as complete and dynamic a picture as possible." The following steps are involved in preparing a case study:

1. *Identifying the Child*: It is impossible to prepare case records for each and every child in the school. Child has to be identified from the lot who needs special attention and counseling. So, the first steps is to identify the child for whom a case history has to be prepared.
2. *Identifying the Writer*: Everybody is not competent to write a case study. One should have writing skills, capabilities of collecting and collating information, ability to unbiased observation; the one who can help the confidentiality of information when needed and also the ability to analyse and interpret. The work can be done by guidance counsellor, a trained teacher, the psychologist or any other person who is fully trained.

3. *Purpose*: The objective of case study must be decided. It should be seen as to how the case record would help the child. Does he required any remedial help, counseling, guidance for future, discussions with his parents, etc.
4. *Data Collection*: Next step is to collect information about the identified child for whom the case history has to be prepared. Information can be available from cumulative Record Card, School records, with teachers, parents and peer group, friends or relatives, hospitals and other sources which are to be identified and tapped.
5. *Deciding Strategy of Data Collection*: One or more persons can collect the data. It should also be decided what information has to be collected.
6. *Preparing Outline*: For developing a case history, an outline should be prepared. Under these major heads data collected can be placed.
7. *Checking of Information*: Data collected should be scrutinised and checked using more than one source. Inaccuracies should be corrected.
8. *Analysis*: Analysis of information should be done on the basis of the objectives prepared for the case study.
9. *Interpretation and Recommendation*: This should be done with great care and recommendations should be referred to the concerned.
10. *Follow Up*: After counselling or referring the child to the concerned, follow up of the case should always be done and recorded.

Outline of the Case Study

Allport said case studies relate to present past and future in the following manner which can be kept in focus while preparing a case study.

Table 7.2: *Factors to Focus while preparing case history*

Present	*Past*	*Future*
1. Problem	History of Problem	Educational plans
2. Educational status	Educational History	
3. Intellectual Status	Intellectual Development	Prediction of ultimate level
4. Health and physical status	Health and physical History	Prediction of future health
5. Maturity level	Development History	
6. Personality	Personality Development	Vocational plans
7. Social relations	Social History	
8. Vocations	Vocational History	
9. Family relationships	Family History including home and neighbourhood	

A tentative outline for preparing a case study can be as follows:

- Identification Data: Name, address, class etc.
- Problem: Educational, vocational, personal (specific problem should be mentioned)

- Case referred/Identified by: Teachers, parents, peer groups or by the child himself.
- Family Background: Conditions, relationships, problems, discipline at home.
- School Record: Performance, problems.
- Health and Physique: Any illness, injuries etc.
- Interests and Hobbies, personalists Characteristics, Intelligence: can be measured through Aptitude Testing Programme. Vocational plans.
- Symptoms and problems stated by the person who referred the case.
- Interview record with the parents/child.
- Observations of the guidance worker
- Counselling and Outcome Summary: Recommendations.
- Follow up.

Example
Writing a Case Study

Problem: Child belongs to first generation learner's category and has problems in adjustment in the school.

Case Record: Name - Amita Kumari

Class A- III

Age 11

Family Background: Amita's parents are illiterate and are landless labourers. She is the eldest child in the family. She has three younger sisters and one brother. The brother is the youngest of them.

Economic Background of the family: Being landless labourers, the family lives hand to mouth. They hardly get meals a day. The family migrated from a remote village of Bihar to the town area where they work on someone else's farms or sometimes are engaged by some Transporter for loading unloading work. *Social background of the family*: The family belonged to Scheduled Tribe category. The village they were living in belonged to high castes. The family was working in the village on the farm of the Head of the Panchayat. They were paid a very meager wage or sometimes no wage at all. So they moved out of the village.

Educational background of the family: The family is illiterate. No body in the family got any education through generations. After migration from the remote village to a small town, they started to send their eldest child to school. Her younger sister who was 11 years' old looked after the other siblings while parents were at work.

Problem stated by the teacher: The case was referred to counsellor by the teacher stating that the girl was unable to concentrate in the class. She does not complete her home work. She forgets to bring the note book or the pencil or the text book to the school. If she is asked to prepare a model etc. she does not bring the material. Even after scolding the child, no improvement has taken place.

Interview with the Child and her problem: During the interviews with the child it was understood that the parents were sending the child to school for 'mid-day meal' scheme, as they were not able to feed all their children. She was unable to understand the study material, as there was nobody to help her at home. She used to get more tensed when scolded by the teacher in the presence of the other girls of her class. The other girls also teased her. She didn't want to continue with the school.

Interaction with Parents: In this case, interactions were had by counsellor with the parents, who told him that they were unable to meet the demands of the school to buy things for preparing charts, or raw-material for preparing models etc.

Counsellor's Observations:

- Neither the parents nor the child knew the importance of education.
- Financial problems of the child.
- Teacher was not able to understand the adjustment problems of the child and was unable to handle her with sensitivity.
- Child required remedial teaching.

Counselling and Outcome Summary: Counsellor discussed the case with the teacher and suggested as to how to be sensitive towards the child's problems. Remedial classes to help the child in doing homework etc. were arranged. Parents were counseled to understand the importance of education. Financial support for education was arranged from school's fund meant for poor children. Group activities were arranged so that the child could be friendly with other classmates.

Follow up: Follow up was done after 15 days. Teacher reported a little improvement in the child. The child also reported better adjustment with the school environment.

Individual Counselling or case study approach is extremely helpful in understanding the child, the environment around, the problem and developing the insight in the child to deal with the problem.

8

Group Guidance Programme

What is a Group?

When we talk about group guidance programme, it is imperative to know what a 'group' is? According to Webster's dictionary a group is "two or more figures forming a design or a unit in a design; an assemblage of persons or things forming a separate unit, a cluster, an aggregation, an assemblage of objects having some relationship, resemblance or common characteristic." Various other scholars defined the term 'group' in a number of ways according to purpose, or the way some interaction takes place among people, or dependence upon each other etc. According to Delamator, "A comprehensive definition of 'group' can be formulated in terms of the following properties: interaction between individuals, perceptions of other members and the development of shared perceptions, the development of affective ties, and the development of interdependence of roles." This definition emphasises the existence of interaction, sharing of perceptions, ties and interdependence on each other's roles as group characteristics. From the point of view of guidance, a group would consist of persons with similar problems and similar goals.

Some examples of groups in a school system that could be formed in guidance programmes can be.:

A group of persons who need to be motivated to take up self- employment	A group of students of class X who want to make a choice of subjects	A group of parents with problems of aggressive children
A group of job seekers who want to know about the job opportunities available after middle schooling or High Schooling	A group of slow learners	Group of students with Tech- addiction like Mobiles

Figure 8.1: *Examples of Groups in a School*

Type of Groups

There can be various types of groups. Some commonly used terms of types of groups are:

1. *T-Groups*: Training groups are referred to as T-Groups. Here group members learn through interaction among themselves. They also feel

how people behave and function in groups. One's own behaviour in-group learning is also explored. The basis of T-Groups lies in the fact that people learn automatically by making relationships with each other in a group.

2. *Sensitivity Group*: It is also a kind of T-Group. But here the individual remains in the focus and not the group. With group interaction, one develops self-insight. The basic objective is the personal development of the individual.
3. *Encounter Groups*: Encounter groups are those in which one member tries to express his inner feelings to others. He tries to open up. The intention is to free himself from some of the internal stresses and in the process change his mind set and behaviour.
4. *Mini Groups*: When the group consists of 4-5 members it is called a Mini group. Here, the possibilities of interaction with each other are more being a small group.
5. *Primary Groups and Secondary Groups*: A Primary group is that group with which the individual is associated involuntarily. The individual has no choice in being with or outside that group. An example of such primary group is 'family'. Secondary groups are those where an individual may choose to be a member such as school, society, community. These secondary groups may be formal/informal, organised/unorganised groups, social groups, small or big groups.

Formation of a Group for Guidance

Group could be of any type, but for guidance purposes a group of students should have a common goal. Just a collection of students may not be called a group for organising guidance activities. Selection of group members will have to depend on:

- Sharing a common problem
- Volunteering to be members
- Willingness to group activities
- Homogeneity

What is Group Guidance?

The services rendered to people in groups are termed as Group Guidance.

While the individual guidance is one to one interaction the group guidance is multi-channel interaction and communication which can happen in several ways

- One person talking
- Two way communication or Multi-channel communication

See figure no. 8.2.

Crow and Crow define group guidance as "Guidance in group situations usually is thought of as referring to those guidance services that are made

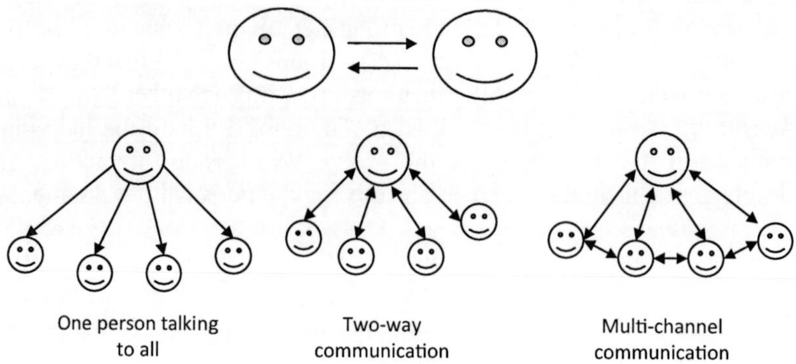

Figure 8.2: *Type of Communication Channels in Group Guidance*

available by school personnel to large or small group of pupils". According to Jones, "Group guidance is any group enterprise or activity in which the primary purpose is to assist each individual in the group to solve his problems and to make his adjustments." Froehlich observed that this phrase "encompasses the activities of the guidance programme in providing organised group services to help students acquire needed experiences for intelligent personal planning ... The important point is that they are essential services which, if the guidance programme is to be successful, must be available to all the students".

In other words, if guidance is to be made available to all, it is possible only if certain activities are planned in groups. Moreover, certain activities under guidance programme do not require individualised interaction. For example, to orientate students or the teachers or the parents about the guidance programme activities can be organised under group guidance. Similarly, to provide information about educational courses or vocational fields, the same may be organised forming homogenous groups. Group guidance, in fact, also prepares foundation for individual guidance as the guidance worker may identify the individuals participating in group guidance programme that require individual attention and guidance later.

Objectives of Group Guidance

The aim of group guidance is not only curative but also preventive because a developmental process takes place, which makes individuals self-sufficient in developing coping strategies for future problems. Please see specific objectives of group guidance in figure no. 8.3.

Advantages of Group Guidance

1. *Therapeutic Effect*: The individual with a certain problem does not feel that he alone is sailing in troubled waters. When he is in a group, he knows that others also have similar or other kinds of problems, which consoles him automatically.

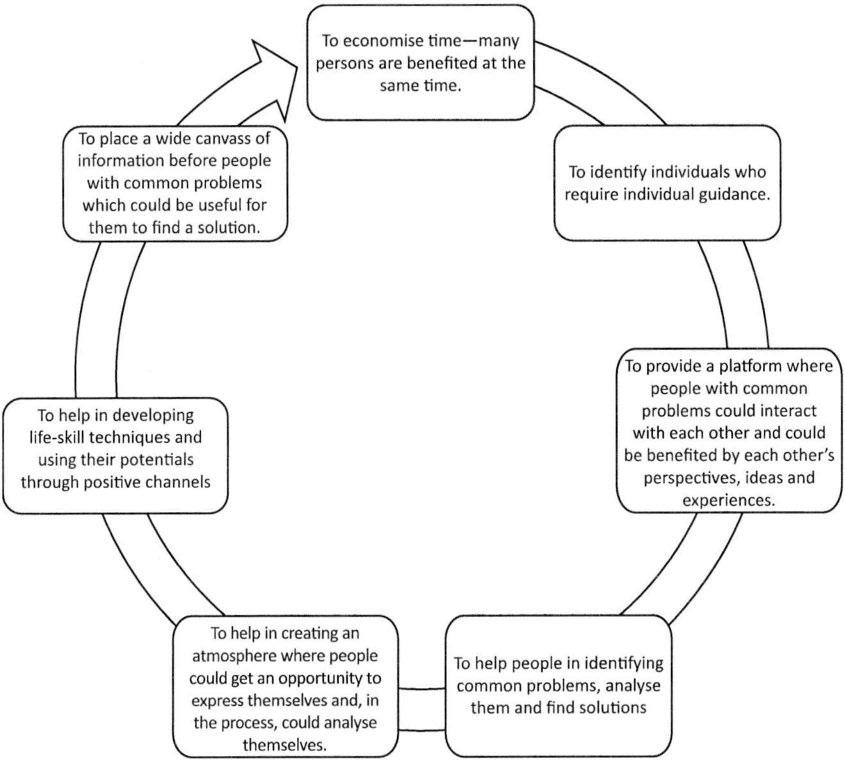

Figure 8.3: *Objectives of Group Guidance*

2. *Interaction with Others*: Each person can be benefited with the experiences and ideas of others. It also improves communication with others. One may find a solution to his problems during such communications.
3. *Develop Social Skills*: With group participation one develops team spirit, learns about group dynamics and analyses his own self. Interactions with people with varying attitudes, habits, backgrounds help in development of self-confidence.

   One example would explain how group guidance helps in developing social skills.

   > Sunita was a brilliant student. She excelled not only in school and college examinations but also cleared a number of competitive written tests. But at the time of interview, she always failed. She was unable to communicate and felt extremely nervous. She developed phobia for interviews. During group guidance programme 'mock sessions' for interviews were arranged, where a number of students with the same problems participated. With a group of ten such participants, 5

persons were made interviewers and the other 5 interviewees. After one session, the roles were reversed. During this process Sunita learnt to communicate. When she was interviewer, she became very confident. The confidence once developed could be seen when she was playing the part of interviewee. After such programme, she was finally able to compete in real life interview session also.

4. *Insight into the Problem*: During discussions among the group, one analyses the problems in his own perspective as well as in others' perspective and the probability is quite high that he gets insight into how to solve his problems. Due to communication of the problems with others, personal tensions also get released and one is able to think with a proper and positive frame of mind.

   Example:
   A group of four young boys failed in the Board examination of class XII. All were extremely frustrated. They participated in a Group Guidance programme of the school. Here is the communication of 4 boys (a, b, c, d) and how the process of change occurred.
   (a) I belong to a very poor family. After passing XII examination I wanted to take up a job. Now I have nowhere to go. I was so tense that I even thought of committing suicide.
   (b) I am also a poor person. But I don't think about committing suicide, although I don't know what to do.
   (c) I belong to a rich family. My father wanted me to help him in his business but I wanted to study. All my aspirations are now over.
   (d) I was not a good student from the very beginning. I told my family that I didn't want to study. But they insisted on me to take science subjects and study. When I failed, they have scolded me. I don't know how to go back home. I don't want to go home.
   At this point, guidance worker discussed with them about several options which were available with them. He also discussed the life skill techniques to cope up with their frustration.
   The group of four interacted among themselves. The guidance worker also talked with the parents of four boys. During such interaction 'a' asked 'c' if he could get a job with his father, 'b' got the idea of doing a technical course, 'c' thought he would re- appear in the examination and 'd' decided to change his subjects, his parents also agreed. The tension of all the four abated and they could think in a positive manner. They also helped each other in solving their problems with the help of the counsellor.

5. *Study the Behaviour of Students in Groups*: Group guidance is provided through various techniques, which pose various situations before the students. The counsellor may observe their behaviour and reactions during such group situation, which may not be possible otherwise.

6. *Collective Decisions*: Many problems are common among the students. Group guidance provides an outlet where students can discuss the problems freely. They may not come out with their problems in individual interactions. With various suggestions coming from various corners, they are able to take collective decisions. They also learn to work in teams and take decisions in-group situations.

Planning a Group Guidance Programme

Planning is extremely essential for the conduct of a Group Guidance Programme. It makes the programme focused and effective. A example will indicate the importance of planning a group guidance activity. A senior manager from a Bank visited an Employment Exchange, and stated that he had been invited to tell the participants about the loan facilities available for them to start self-employment ventures. It was understood that he was invited by the Employment Officer in charge of the Employment Exchange, who suddenly proceeded on leave without informing anybody in the office about the visit of the Manager. The next person in command collected some students who actually came for getting their names registered and told them that they would be registered only if they will listen to the lecture. Most of them were not interested but they had to attend the lecture. Most of them were only waiting for the lecture to end. It is evident that any unplanned programme would lead to disaster.

How to Plan

(a) Objectives of the Programme should be clear.
(b) Target group should be defined: In the above example target group could be those people who are in the process of starting their own ventures and want to know the details of obtaining loans.
(c) Time management: The programme should be of proper duration, neither too long nor too short. If a lecture has to be organised, time limit can be 40 minutes +15 minutes for discussion. If it is group discussion, it should be between 20 minutes to 30 minutes and 10 minutes to wrap up discussion. Too long a programme can create monotony and too short a programme may not provide desired information.
(d) Identification of Support Services: A group programme may require support of many other agencies and organisations. For example, for organising a Career Conference, help is required from the experts in the field, a place, printing of material etc.
(e) Homogeneous Group: Groups should be formed according to the objectives of a group guidance programme, which are homogeneous in character. In a class talk of 'What after XII', the students of XI and XII

should be called or if the talk is on 'options for XII for students with Science' only students from science stream should be invited.

Scope of Group Guidance Programme

As group guidance is rendered through organising group activities, it is assumed that there are certain issues that can be addressed in groups even when guidance is to help an 'individual'. The scope of group guidance is limited to only common issues. Some such issues can be as follows:

- Discussion of a single occupation in details. For example 'Details of competitive examination or entrance exam for engineering or job profile of an architect, etc.
- Discussions on occupational field visits.
- Motivational programmes, such as promoting self-employment.
- General information like interview technique, how to improve handwriting, how to develop good reading habits, etc.
- General problems of work environment and work adjustment.
- Educational planning – the options available.

It may be observed from the above that most of the activities in group guidance relate to information sharing and therapeutic healing together.

9

Identifying Problems and Role of Guidance Personnel

Types of Problems of Students

Before a guidance worker tries to help a student, he should be aware of the entire gamut of the students' problems, and know how to identify the specific problem of the students. A child may face more than one problem at a time and with varying frequency. The counsellor has to tackle the problems in their entirety. He cannot focus on one problem at a time leaving the others. Various experts have tried to classify the problems keeping in mind, the various areas and fields a person belongs to.

Many times, personal problems of a child are the basic cause of all of his educational and vocational problems. The student may not be able to get good grades due to his health problems, which he may or may not be aware of. The counsellor should identify if he has frequent fever, cold and cough, fatigue, visual difficulties, etc. In such cases a child should be referred to the physician. The counsellor should also identify the physically challenged students and appropriate guidance should be given to the teachers dealing with disabilities.

Jones has classified the problems according to 8 such areas:

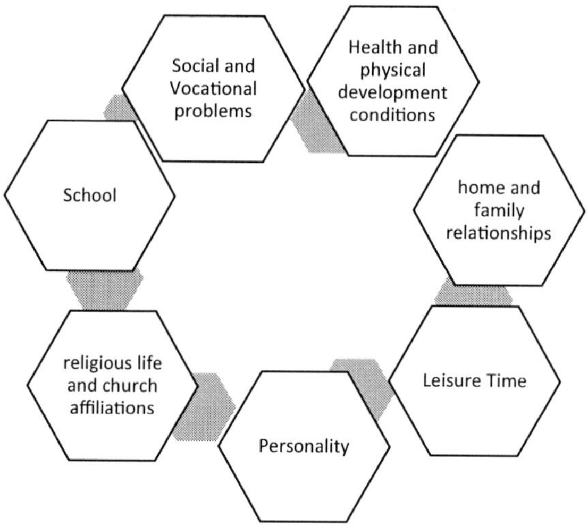

Figure 9.1: *Major Areas of Problems*

Under these 8 major areas, Myers has analysed specific conditions, a child may face.

1. Health and physical development conditions:
   (a) Physical defects—sight, hearing speech, deformity
   (b) Inability to excel in athletics
   (c) Lack of physical coordination
   (d) Lack of physical vigour
   (e) Malnutrition
   (f) Physical unattractiveness
   (g) Sickness
   (h) Undersize or oversize
2. Home and family relationships conditions:
   (a) Dominance of parents
   (b) Lack of control by parents
   (c) Lack of home fellowship
   (d) Broken homes—death, divorce, separation
   (e) Home duties—too few or too many
   (f) Jealousy or friction among children
   (g) Non-wholesome home conditions—physical, social, moral
   (h) Disapproving family
   (i) Lack of cooperation with school
3. Leisure time conditions:
   (a) Lack of interest in sports and games
   (b) Inability because of poor health or physical handicaps to engage in sports
   (c) Limited resources for enjoyment
   (d) Lack of interest in reading
   (e) Lack of skill in handicraft
4. Personality conditions:
   (a) Extreme sensitiveness
   (b) Shyness
   (c) Lack of aggressiveness
   (d) Strong aversions
   (e) Self-confidence or its lack
   (f) Excessive conceit, egotism
   (g) Carelessness
   (h) Inability to get along with people
   (i) Delusions
   (j) Lack of sportsmanship
   (k) Inferiority complex
   (l) Superiority complex
   (m) Lack of social-mindedness
   (n) Emotional instability

5. Religious life and church affiliations conditions:
   (a) Religious doubts and conflicts
   (b) Extreme religious attitude of parents
   (c) Conversion
   (d) Excessive religious activity
   (e) Apparent conflict between science and religion
6. School conditions:
   (a) Budgeting time
   (b) Ineffective study habits
   (c) Lack of application
   (d) Lack of independence
   (e) Too much help given by teacher
   (f) Lack of interest in schoolwork
   (g) Feeling of boredom
   (h) Inability to see value in certain subjects
   (i) Fear of failure
   (j) Unwillingness to put forth effort
   (k) Dislike for teacher or for school
   (l) Too long assignments
   (m) Impatience with slower pupils
   (n) Poor study conditions in school or at home
   (o) Lack of adjustment of work to mental ability of pupil
   (p) Poor preparation
   (q) Too much attention to athletics or other student activities
   (r) Feeling of injustice
   (s) Poor orientation in general
   (t) Feeling that no one takes an interest in him
   (u) Poor choice of school or of subject
   (v) Choice of school or college
   (w) Planning work in preparation for college
   (x) Truancy
7. Social (including moral and civic) conditions:
   (a) Cheating, lying, stealing
   (b) Lack of moral standards
   (c) Manners
   (d) Antisocial tendencies
   (e) Racial handicaps and antipathies
   (f) Insufficient social life
   (g) Excessive social life
   (h) Unwise use of leisure
   (i) Smoking and drinking
   (j) Discourtesy
   (k) Rebellion against authority

(l) Intolerance of others' beliefs and opinions
(m) Choice of friends of opposite sex
(n) "Petting" and "necking"
(o) Flirting
(p) Disappointment in love
(q) Being in love
(r) Unreasonable restriction on friendship with opposite sex
(s) Double standards of morality
(t) Low ideals of civic responsibility
(u) Unwillingness to assume citizenship duties
(v) Inability to choose leaders wisely
(w) Unwillingness to follow chosen leaders
(x) Unwillingness to accept responsibility as a leader

8. Vocational conditions:
(a) Insistence by parents on a certain vocation
(b) Inability to choose among several vocations
(c) Unwise choice of vocation
(d) Determining fitness for a given vocation
(e) Choosing the best preparation for the vocation
(f) Lack of time or money to secure the preparation necessary for the vocation chosen.
(g) Lack of opportunities in the vocation chosen Difficulty in finding a job
(h) Difficulty in adjustment to the conditions of the job.

Another way of identifying the problems of the people is the technique of problem checklists developed by Mooney. These problem checklists have been developed in five forms – for junior high school students, senior high school students, college students, nurses and for rural youth. In every form there are various areas and items have been listed in each area. For example, in junior high school form, there are seven areas with 210 items in each area. In college and senior high school forms, there are 11 areas with 30 problems in each. This checklist may be given to the individuals to point out their problems, which can be helpful for the counsellors to identify the problem. Froehlich and Hoyt listed six areas of the problems, which included vocational, educational, social and personal, financial, family adjustment and health. They have also tried to identify the specific problems that could be common to students in each area. Bordin did not agree with this classification given by these two experts. He was of the view that the problems should be classified in terms of adjustment to environment. Therefore, the emphasis is on environment and not on the individual. He classifies the problems of individuals as dependence, lack of information, self-conflict, choice and anxiety. There may also be students who think that they cannot classify their problems.

To sum up, following may be some common problems of the students:

Table 9.1: *Summary of Problems*

Common Issues	*Personal*	*Finance Related*	*Family Relationship*	*Health*
Discrepancy between educational ambitions and abilities	Feelings of inferiority or lack of self-confidence	Restrictions on educational-vocational planning because of inadequate financial resources	Conflicts over educational and vocational plans	Frequent absence from school because of illness
Underachievement	Lack of the basic social skills necessary to make good social adjustments	Too much outside work to hamper achievement up to capacity	Over dependence of girls on their families	Educational or vocational limitations imposed by physical disabilities
Overachievement	Unpleasant or irritating personality traits	Educational-vocational plans dependent upon receiving financial aid	Difficulties in establishing independence from their families	Worry about health, due to real or imagined physical or mental ailments
Inefficiency in basic skills, such as reading or arithmetic or spelling				

Role of Guidance Personnel

How to Identify Problems

The guidance worker may adopt any checklist of the problem areas, but it should be kept in mind that the problems stated by the students should be verified, because a child may give wrong information or may not be able to classify his exact problem. The causes of the problem also need to be looked into; some of the problems may be identified by the guidance worker himself.

Educational Field

1. For identifying education-related problems, the guidance worker should compare the educational grades in the school with intelligence levels and capacities. Through this process, he can identify the slow achievers and over achievers. A special programme for each group is desired.
2. Guidance worker can help the students to deal with their time management. Some students do not get time to study all the subjects or their time table

does not include any leisure time or time for extra-curricular activities. Sometimes they do not have any time even to take their meals. Guidance worker can identify these problems.

3. There are students who lack motivation for studies and are always busy in extra-curricular activities. The reasons for lack of motivation are to be observed and motivational programme may be organised by the guidance worker.
4. Constant interaction may be had with teachers to identify the problems of the students in educational area.

Vocational Field

By administering aptitudes and interests test, the counsellor can see whether the choice of vocation made by the student corresponds to the aptitudes or not. May be that student has no choice at all. The counsellor has to provide occupational profiles that could be suitable for him. There is a possibility that a student has more than one choice and is not able to decide which line he should choose. His aspirations may also be unrealistic. All these problems may be taken care of by the counsellor by providing factual information about the individual as well as the occupation.

Within the vocational area, three types of people are there to be identified:

1. Students with discrepancy between ambitions and abilities
2. Students with inaccurate or inadequate information about job requirements or opportunities
3. Students with complete indecision (This may be due to the student's consideration of several possible and equally attractive choices, his responses to outside pressures from family members or others, or a complete lack of occupational information).

Personal Problems

Personal problems may be of various kinds. The student may not be able to get good grades due to his health problems, which he may or may not be aware of. The counsellor should identify if he has frequent fever, cold and cough, fatigue, visual difficulties, etc. In such cases a child should be referred to the physician. The counsellor should also identify the physically challenged students and appropriate guidance should be given to the teachers dealing with disabilities.

Finances may be another area of problems, which generally students have. The counsellor should be able to provide information about the financial assistance available to them. Other personal problems may be relating to socio-psychological adjustment in the school, with the peer group, with the seniors, with the teachers, etc. This may affect the scholastic achievement of the student. The child may also be emotionally disturbed, irritating and frustrated. Sometimes the family problems, such as preference for a particular child in the family and over-or-under domination, affect the child's overall development adversely.

Discrimination against girl children in some societies is very common. The counsellor's role is to help the child in his overall development and, therefore, he cannot ignore any of the problems a child might be experiencing. Personal problems may be identified with the help of classmates, friends, parents, teachers and other members of the community. The best source for providing information about his personal problem is the child himself.

Role and Functions of a Guidance Worker

Here it may be noted that words guidance worker and counsellor are used interchangeably. The role and functions of a guidance worker may vary according to the purpose, setting and target group. For example, in a community setting where a couple has approached the counsellor, regarding a problem in their marriage. The counsellor's efforts would be to help the couple to resolve their problems in marriage. On the other hand, the role of the guidance in a school setting would focus more about helping the individuals in choosing a right kind of career according to their capabilities, aptitudes, interests etc. The discussion in the following paragraphs would be restricted to the role of the guidance worker keeping in view the school setting.

In general, the intervention by a guidance person would be remedial, preventive or developmental depending upon the need and problems of the people. It can aim at individual, some individuals, associated groups or the settings and systems that are affecting the individual behaviour. Arthur, J.J. (1941) has defined the term school counsellor in the following manner:

> "The term "School Counsellor" is used to indicate the personnel or worker whose chief responsibility is to stimulate, initiate, develop and coordinate the guidance work of the entire school. He will, in many schools, also perform some or more forms of specialised guidance service; what this is will be determined by the type of organisation of the guidance activities in the school and the type of other personnel available. He must act as guidance leader and as a resource person in the school and should have superior qualifications and training for the task. In many schools he will be the only personnel worker and be directly responsible for the entire guidance programme".

Many other experts have analysed the role of a counsellor based on research studies. Bailey stated that personal advice, planning and supervision, making community contacts; interpretation and application of tests, planning and supervision of extracurricular activities are the duties of a counsellor. Cox, on other hand, analysed the functions of 100 selected counsellors and classified the same as:

(a) work with parents
(b) educational- vocational-emotional guidance of pupils
(c) supervision of tests – giving and interpreting test results
(d) Cooperation with law-enforcing agencies

(e) consultation with employers,
(f) discipline
(g) placement
(h) coordinating the guidance programme of the school
(i) home-room supervision
(j) cooperation with community guidance agencies
(k) teaching
(l) chaperoning parties
(m) follow-up of pupils who left school.

Functions of a counsellor according to Tooker (1957) are detailed below:

1. First of all, he is an educator.
2. He has direct responsibility for individual counselling of students assigned to him.
3. He often has responsibility for group methods in guidance.
4. He is expected to establish relationships with great numbers of individuals, so that students will come to identify him as a person to whom they can turn for advice and help within the school setting.
5. He is expected to be familiar enough with standardised tests of intelligence, achievement, aptitude, interest and personality so that he can utilise test results in the process of counselling
6. He is often given considerable responsibility in arranging transfers of students for both academic and personal reasons.
7. He is called upon to help in such important projects as building and maintaining cumulative record systems.
8. He is often expected to conduct follow-up studies of graduates and dropouts.
9. It is not unusual for him to be asked to function as a resource person in such educational projects as the setting up of systems of reporting to parents.
10. He is usually expected to know current college admission procedures and to serve as adviser to both parents and students in this area.
11. He is expected to participate in school activities and to assume his share of extracurricular activities.
12. He is expected to maintain a knowledge of and working relationships with local business and industry so that he may be in a better position to counsel students in the area of local vocational offerings.
13. He is often expected to help in the sponsoring of guidance-related activities such as college nights, career days, and guidance committees.
14. He is frequently called upon to provide leadership in broad areas where guidance aspects may seem remote.

In practice, one counsellor may do all the activities by himself or may do some activities depending upon the objectives and needs of students.

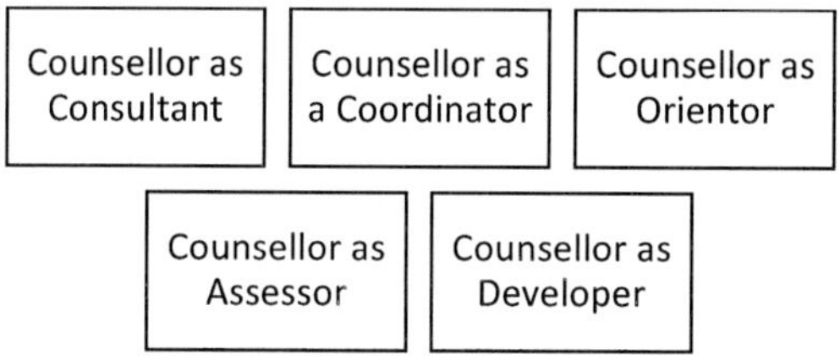

Figure 9.2: *Roles of a Counsellor or Guidance Worker*

To summarise, the role of a counsellor may be as described on the following lines.

1. *Counsellor as a Consultant*: In a role of a consultant, a counsellor has to interact with teachers, parents, support groups of the individual and other systems, which are influencing the individual.
2. *Counsellor as a Coordinator*: A counsellor has to coordinate from time to time with the other agencies which the students may need to approach from time to time, such as the employers, the hospitals, the employment exchanges, etc.
3. *Counsellor as an Orientor*: As an Orientor, the role of a counsellor is to gradually inform the pupil about the world of work, to help them in developing adjustment skills and creating an environment where the pupils could have positive experience of education and learning. Orientation of guidance services is of utmost importance.
4. *Counsellor as Assessor*: The counsellor has to assess the individual as well as his environment. Assessment of individual includes his academic achievements, aptitudes, interests, abilities, personality traits etc. while environment includes his family background, cultural and social roots and other factors that influence child's behaviour.
5. *Counsellor as a Developer*: A counsellor has to lay a strong foundation on which every pupil, specially at elementary school level, could develop himself in the desirable direction. At elementary stage, children have very little exposure to the world of work. If they have seen a teacher, milkman, or a postman at home, their choice would be to become the same in future. It is the responsibility of the counsellor to provide children a greater exposure to various avenues of work. At later stages also, his role as a developer is significant in terms of providing placement services, counselling for problems, helping the students in developing an insight to solve their problems. Career guidance becomes more important at secondary school level. The counsellor may also have to deal with adolescence problems of the students, inter-personal adjustments, etc.

Specific Functions of Guidance Counsellor in Personal Guidance

(a) Functions of a guidance worker in personal and social guidance, *inter alia,* include development of life skills. Life skill guidance relates to creating a 'drug free' atmosphere in the school, spread awareness about sex education in general and AIDS in particular, and develop the skills among the students to fight temptations. The guidance worker should help the students in controlling and managing the aggression and preventing violent tendencies. Inter-personal skills, communication skills techniques and team spirit have to be developed among the students.

Another life skill is to learn grief management. Everyone faces situations of grief one time or other. It could be failure, not achieving as per the aspirations or according to the expectations of parents or society, loss of some dear one, loss of a possession. Grief is of maximum intensity at the time something unwanted occurs but declines with passage of time. The time of occurrence of the event which is the cause of sadness is of crucial importance. One has to develop the skill to deal with such grief specially during the crucial periods. Counsellor has to help the student in developing coping strategies for such situations. Suicides by students at the time examination results are announced are becoming a common phenomenon. It indicates that such students feel a lot of mental pressure and succumb to it in the absence of necessary skill to deal with them.

Crisis management is another area where life skills are required. Crisis may occur in the school, in the community or at place of work and children should be ready to deal with crisis situations with a problem- solving approach. Crisis may be in terms of natural calamities or man- made calamity. Children should be made aware of such situations and should be mentally prepared to deal with them. These skills can be developed through 'role-playing' or 'simulation techniques.

Time management is another aspect of life skills. There are children who are glued to T.V. or computers for long hours. This affects their physical and mental health negatively. They gradually become conditioned to electronic equipments. They get no time for outdoor activities like games, physical activity, studies, and socialisation which is a must for normal growth. The busy parents also ask their toddlers to sit before T.V. so that they may not disturb them. Such situations should be avoided. Children should learn how to divide their time in varying types of activities and counsellors help the students in learning that.

How to be a good social being is a very important aspect of one's life. Being a good citizen in the society includes development of socially acceptable behaviours, be of use to the society, develop social skills that could help the individual to communicate among the people in a desirable manner, maintain harmony, develop helping attitudes etc. These are developed from the very beginning. It may be observed that initially a child in infancy is very possessive of his things like toys and clothes. As he grows, he develops the skills of sharing and caring. In the single child families, where parents do not allow the child to be social with the children of the community, the child may find it difficult to develop the skill of sharing. Such children, when admitted to school, face problems of adjustments, and if not helped in time, may develop as 'self-centred' adults when they grow up.

Considering the importance of life skills, they are being introduced in the new syllabus of the schools finalised by the government recently. No doubt regular teaching of life skills in the school from the very beginning will have its desired impact on young minds.

(b) Another important function of guidance counsellor in personal and social guidance is to assess the needs of the students and help them to meet their needs. For example, the students with some physical disability may require information about facilities available for them in or outside the school. The guidance worker should have such information and refer these students to the desired destination. He can also help the school administration to make the school environment and infrastructure user friendly.

(c) The counsellor has also to organise parental guidance services to help children deal their personal and emotional problems. The role of the counsellor in parental guidance would be discussion about the child – his capacities and shortcomings and make the parents accept 'what the child is'. Parents should have realistic aspirations. In other words, counsellors have to help the parents to understand and accept their child in a better way.

Characteristics of a Guidance Counsellor

Efforts have been made to list the characteristics of the counsellors that could make them effective in carrying out the functions of guidance. Bailey listed these characteristics as:

1. A sympathetic understanding of youth
2. Emotional Stability
3. Approachability
4. Broad scope of knowledge and interests
5. Good judgement and common sense

Committee of National Vocational Guidance Committee (1941) listed 12 characteristics:

1. A stable and well- adjusted personality
2. A high degree of intellectual capacity
3. A fundamental liking for persons
4. A sympathetic and objective understanding of people
5 Facility in establishing wholesome, effective, personal and social relations, including ability to work cooperatively with other people
6. Ability to stimulate students and colleagues and to challenge their best efforts in working for ends that they come to accept as desirable

7. Perspective – ability to see and understand the total situation and the separate parts in relation to the whole
8. An understanding and appreciation of one's own limitations in dealing with certain areas of problems and with certain individuals
9. Broad general knowledge and wide interests
10. An understanding of classroom conditions, teaching responsibilities and pupil-teacher relationships
11. An understanding of working conditions and employee-employer relationships in jobs outside of educational work or in non- professional vocational life
12. Understanding of social and economic conditions and influences– general and local

Rogers, in 1942, listed five characteristics of a counsellor. They included

(1) sensitivity to human relationships,
(2) objective attitude and an emotionally detached attitude,
(3) respect for the individual,
(4) understanding of himself, and
(5) knowledge of human behaviour.

Parsons stated that vocational counsellor should have

1. A practical working knowledge of the fundamental principles and methods of modern technology.
2. An experience involving sufficient human contact to give him an intimate acquaintance with human nature in a considerable number of its different phases; he must understand the dominant motives, interests, and ambitions that control the lives of men, and be able to recognise the symptoms that indicate the presence or absence of important elements of character.
3. Ability to deal with young people in a sympathetic, earnest, searching, candid, helpful and attractive way.
4. A knowledge of requirements and conditions of success, compensation, prospects, advantages, and disadvantages, etc., in the different lines of industry.
5. Information relating to courses of study and means of preparing for various callings and developing efficiency therein.
6. Scientific method – analysis and principles of investigation by which laws and causes are ascertained and facts are classified.

To sum up, a counsellor should be able to establish harmonious and trustworthy relationship with the students so that they could trust the counsellor and confide their problems. He should be accepting, listening, understanding and helping. He should be emotionally stable and mature to be able to deal the problems. He should also be intelligent enough to coordinate with various people, persons and agencies. He should also have good communication skills and knowledge of group dynamics.

Role of Career Master

Generally, the career master is a school teacher who gets some training in guidance and works for a few hours a week along with the counsellor. The career master helps the counsellor in collecting, collating and disseminating career information, gives class talks and helps in other day to day activities of the guidance programme. In the schools where there is no guidance counsellor, career master is in-charge of the guidance programme in the school along with his normal teaching assignments. A career master's role is more in providing orientation and information services in school. He can also play role in organizing group guidance activities and placement services. His role is less in Aptitude Testing Programme and Individual guidance. He should be fully trained in organizing these activities.

Role of Psychologist

A psychologist is fully trained personnel in the field of psychology and guidance and counselling. Generally, a guidance counsellor is a psychologist and therefore there is either a position of guidance counsellor or a psychologist in the school. When there is no guidance counsellor, the services of a psychologist are taken. The role of psychologist is more in organizing aptitude testing programme and organise individual counselling wherever both counsellor and psychologist are posted. If there is no counsellor, the psychologist has to carry out the whole programme in the school. If there is a counsellor in the school, services of a psychologist are taken to assess the capacities of the students, identify disabled children, counsel the problem children, convey the psychological test results etc.

Role of Other Guidance Programme Personnel

The guidance counsellor alone cannot implement a guidance programme. The cooperation from various people in the school and the agencies outside is imperative. Even otherwise there are stakeholders who will have their impact in the guidance services directly or indirectly. For example, when a child is being counselled his parents may have to be taken in confidence for a number of purposes. A guidance programme in a school cannot be successful if the principal is not in favour of these services. There are many instances where the guidance worker could not enlist the cooperation from the principal and was asked to teach the normal subjects in the school than prepare and execute the guidance activities. Similarly, there are various services in a guidance programme which require contacts with other agencies. These could be referral services where a child has to be referred to some hospital or the doctor. For placement of the students a guidance worker needs the cooperation from employers. Again, there are mass media like newspapers, T.V, radio, etc., all of which contribute in guidance activities. These are termed as information resources. The third category of resources may be of energy resources. These may include groups, organisations or individuals who may like to spare money time or other resources available with them for the guidance activities. All these play an important role in the implementation and effectiveness of a guidance programme.

There can be two types of resources, one relating to the school and other outside—the school resources and community resources.

School Resources

Role of the Principal: The principal is the main administrator and is "the key person in the whole situation, and how he works will determine the success of his efforts" (Schwartz – 1953), The principal of the school needs orientation about the guidance services. The methodology of the orientation would differ according to the level and the geographical area. For example, in an urban school the principal may be well versed with the guidance activity or the principal of a secondary school might be knowing the principles of a guidance services, while in case of the principal of a rural school or the principal of an elementary school the situation might be different. But in all cases their cooperation has to be sought for the proper functioning of a guidance programme. If the principal is cooperative, he can provide a place to the guidance counsellor to set up a Career Resources Centre. He may provide the time to the guidance worker for organising his activities within the school time table. The principal is also responsible to provide the budget for guidance activities. The principal can also convince the teachers and the parents about the importance of the guidance activities so that the counsellor may get cooperation from the staff and the parents. A principal, who is in the school for a long time, may also help the guidance worker to make contacts with the community resources. In case the principal is busy he can depute another person to help the guidance worker as and when required.

Role of the Teachers: The teachers directly interact with the students most of the time and therefore they can be a major source of information. The students also develop a special relationship with the teachers, specifically in the elementary school where most of the time one teacher remains in the class. The teacher is the key person who can also help the counsellor by providing the data for preparing Cumulative Record Cards. He may be mediator between the counsellor and the parents and provide information about the academic achievements of children. Teachers can be a resource for collecting information from various other sources. For example, the teachers in one school may refer the counsellor to their counterparts in other schools where guidance services are not available and the guidance worker is supposed to cater to the needs of the students in those schools also. The teachers can also assist in group guidance activities like preparation of the posters and charts. In this activity the help of art and drawing teacher may be had for hobby clubs or preparing the models. The assistance from music teacher and of the science teacher may also be taken. The teachers can also refer the students who need individual counselling for their undesirable behaviours or special problems in their school achievements. The teachers can interact with the counsellor on the issues of slow learners, first generation learners, the gifted children, the physically handicapped etc. Teachers can be helpful in evaluation of the guidance programme as well as the follow up services.

Role of the Doctor: Generally, all the schools have the services of a qualified doctor. Counsellor should maintain a good relationship with the doctor in order to refer the students who require health check-up or in need of some medical help. In such cases, the advice of the school doctor may be had and the child may be referred to a clinic or hospital outside in case of need. A regular health check-up programme of the students may be worked out in consultation with the doctor as many times neither the teachers nor the parents are able to identify the problems of the children relating to health. In other cases, the doctor may provide the information about the health status of the children to the counsellor for health-related guidance. The children with malnutrition may be identified and referred to the doctor for a diet advice. The health- related information about the children in the Cumulative Record Card might be filled up with the help of the doctor.

Role of the Librarian: A Librarian is a trained person who is well versed with the filing and dissemination of the information. His help may be taken by the counsellor for the career information services. The librarian may also help in collection of the information from various sources by writing letters to the concerned organisations, preparing the reference cards, displaying the material and preparation of career books. The school library may also be having lot of information that can be useful for the guidance worker. For example, the annual reports of the organisations which provide information about the employment trends, the apprenticeship training, the reports of the committees and other literature. If the counsellor has a harmonious relationship with the librarian, he can gather the information relevant for guidance activities from these documents easily. Sometimes, the space available in the library may also be utilised for guidance activities, if necessary.

Other School Personnel: The other non-teaching staff like a bus driver, canteen personnel may be helpful in providing information about the children's eating habits, the behaviour with the peer group, cooperation with others, etc.

There are a large number of resources available in the community, which can be helpful for guidance activities. A guidance worker should be able to explore these resources and should be able to ensure their cooperation.

Role of the Parents: The first communication of the child is with parents which continues even after the child leaves the school. Home is the place where behaviours of the child are formulated and his personality develops. The parents and the home have a lasting impact on the child's personality. Parents can be a good source about providing valuable information about the child. Parents know the various limitations of their children, their problems in the growth process and the limitations of the home. The parental involvement may be extremely helpful in identifying the problems of the children. The parent's help can also be taken to resolve these problems. There are cases where parents need counselling to deal with their children. These areas can be over authoritativeness of the parents, lack of control, imposing their own interest on the children and so on.

The parents can also provide health-related information about the child. Moreover, when the child is referred to any clinic or hospital, parents have to be taken with the child to the hospital.

Role of the Employers: The placement services in a guidance programme are based on the cooperation from the employers. A guidance worker should list out the employers in the vicinity, their activity, their needs for skills, the shortages, their expansion plans and future requirements of personnel. The employers can also be called to interact with the students. Field visits may be organised to the industries in case the counsellor has good rapports with the employers. During the Rozgar Melas and the career conferences, the employers may be requested to interact with the students.

Community Resources of Guidance

(a) *Hospitals*: Interaction with the hospitals in the area is necessary for referral services in the guidance programme. For health-related problems, the guidance worker may send the child to the appropriate place for health check-up and advice. These can be social welfare clinics, the general hospitals and the mental health clinics.

(b) *Clubs and Other Creative Organisations:* For development of the creativity in the children and for a better use of leisure time available with the children, the counsellor should keep a track of the youth organisations, hobby clubs and other community agencies that can be helpful for the development of the children. For example, SPIC – MACAY is one organisation that motivates youth to take to classical music. Similarly, the YMCA, the YWCA, the sports clubs, the health clubs, the GYMs are some of the organisations that can be a resource for the guidance services.

(c) *Banks and other Vocational Institutions:* Association with banks and other institutions that can provide financial assistance to the children is also an asset. The needy children may be referred to these organisations. There are several related organisations also that provide financial assistance to the needy children. Scholarship facilities are given to the good achievers and poor people. A guidance worker should maintain association with all such resources.

(d) *Educational Institutions and Libraries*: The information has to be collected for educational and vocational guidance from various educational institutions as they have the prospectuses on the dealing courses. Interaction should be had with all such institutions, departments, universities, and other agencies like Bureaus of Guidance, University Grants Commission and International Organisations that help for admissions outside like British Council, US Council. Community libraries and groups also organise career activities from time to time. Moreover, a substantial literature is also available with the libraries located outside the school. All such resources should also be taken into account by a guidance worker.

(e) *Computers*: The computer and the Internet is a modern resource providing a lot of information to the guidance programme. There are several web-sites dealing with careers, and educational and job-opportunities. The guidance worker may use the computer as tool. Some of the sites which can be useful for the guidance worker have been listed in the chapter on Guidance Services in India. Moreover, career information can be organised systematically on a computer system using 'menu-driven' approach, for easy access to the students.

Pupil Personnel Work

Meaning

Guidance programme is a team work where family, teachers, friends and peers, community all contribute in some or the other respect. All have specified roles to play to make guidance programme a success. The counsellor cannot work in isolation. For example, if a child in the school is not performing well in spite of his abilities and intelligence, the counsellor has to see the reasons behind it. To find out the reasons and help the child in overcoming his problems, the counsellor has to discuss with the teachers of his class or parents. Similarly, if a child has some health problems, the counsellor needs the health institutions of the community. Thus, guidance programme requires help from each and all at some or the other occasion.

George E. Myers has defined the pupil personnel work in terms of its nature and scope:

> "The only road to clearness in the matter seems to lie in restricting the term 'pupil-personnel work' to those activities which have for their purpose bringing the pupil into that part of the school environment *as it exists* which best suits his needs, in such condition that he will derive from it the maximum of individual development along lines that society considers wholesome for itself and for the individual".

Purpose

The goal of pupil personnel work is to enable every student to realize his full academic potential by maximizing strengths and addressing weaknesses coordinating between school, home and the community. It combines all activities which aim at bringing the pupils into that part of the school environment *as it exists* which best suits his needs so as to enable him/her, to derive the maximum healthy individual development.

Programmes

A pupil personnel worker is specialist trained to assess student needs, serve as a student advocate, and act as a motivating force in removing barriers to students' achievement. He is the link between the school, home and the community. He is an advocate for all students, a consultant to school staff and parents, a liaison for all departments of the school system and a source for referral to outside resources. His most common functions are:

- Counselling/guidance to individuals/groups
- Paying home visits to promote family involvement
- Tackling emergency student and family welfare situations
- Facilitating the adjustment of students in collaboration with class teachers
- Providing support to schools in times of crisis
- Explaining government and school policies and procedures to students and parents
- Monitoring and supervising home-schooling cases
- Providing case management for suspended/ore expelled students
- Arranging for special education for students with special needs

The pupil personnel worker develops and implements a school guidance and counselling programme that includes academic, career, personal and social development of the students. For this purpose, he acts as an advocate of for high academic achievement and social development of all students, provide prevention and intervention strategies and counselling services in the school, and provide advice to teachers and parents about the students' needs.

- He will assess all factors relating to home, personal, school and community at large, that may affect students' learning, develop and implement appropriate strategies for children and their families such as counselling, case management and intervention in times of crisis.
- He will consult with and advise other teachers and staff of the school on the emotional and social needs of the students.
- He will coordinate home, school and community resources on behalf of students.
- He will provide psychological counselling to individual and groups of students and parents, identify and assess special psycho-educational needs, provide services to address problems of adjustment and enhance academic achievement.
- He will coordinate intervention strategies in case of individual and school-wide crisis

- He will access appropriate services from both public and private providers of services such as law-enforcement, health and rehabilitation, and other social services
- He will enhance knowledge and awareness of the school staff about the government and school regulations regarding child welfare and school attendance
- He will develop and implement strategies to improve school attendance
- He will advise school authorities on policies and procedures which inhibit high academic achievement

As stated earlier, pupil personnel programmes are organised taking into account home, school and community. How these interactions take place and how the programmes programmed have been summarized in the following table:

Table 9.2: *Pupil Personnel Programme*

Home	*School*	*Community*
• Provide link between school policies and programmes to parents and other family members. • Services to children for their family related problems. • Helping the child in getting home teaching whenever need. • Pay home visits whenever needed to make liaison between child and family. • Identify and help deprived children and children with special needs to have better adjustments at home and find a place for homeless • Help in guardianship issues.	• Making liaison between school and home environment of the child. • Organise in-services for professionals. • Identify support system of the child and find out multi-disciplinary approach to solve the problems of the child. • Advocacy in crises situation or during disciplinary action against the child • Attend Parent-teacher meetings. •. Home visits to sort out school related matters. • Sort out attendance related issues. • Orient teachers and other staff about children's problem and role of guidance services.	• Orient the community about pupil personnel services. • Consult and interact with various community agencies as per need. • List and keep detailed information about community resources that could contribute to pupil personnel services like health facilities, financial aid available etc. • Refer and help cases of juvenile delinquency, alcoholism and drug-abuse to the concerned. • Represent at community organization

Here it is important to note that since a guidance worker has several responsibilities, a separate person can be involved for pupil personnel programme. But in case, such opportunity is not there, the guidance worker or a Counseller can do this liaison work on his/her own.

10

Techniques of Group Guidance

A number of techniques are used in organising group guidance. The important point is that the choice of technique should be according to the objective of the programme, the target group, the availability of time, the number of participants etc. To provide the information to a large number of students, lecture method can be used. But if there are ten or 15 participants and the purpose is to know their problem, their needs, etc. a group discussion can be organised. Some of the techniques that are used in group guidance are detailed below:

Group Discussions

Group discussions are organised in the groups of 10 to 15 students with some common problems. It is assumed that each individual of the group has something to contribute on the given topic. For example, if the topic is 'Importance of choosing a career', the group discussion may lead to economic, social, psychological aspects of career and how it affects the life style. People may discuss about positive and negative aspects of a career.

For organising a group discussion, considerations should be

- *Setting* – where the activity is to be organised, whether the room has adequate space, lightning, whether it is free from outside noises or not and whether the setting has proper seating arrangement so that group members would be able to see each other and listen properly. It is always better to have group discussions with a round table arrangement.
- *Size* – Size of the group is important. If it is too small, many ideas may not come up or, if it is too large, many persons may not get adequate time to put through their ideas.
- *Time* – How much time should be given to discuss the topic is an important aspect to be considered. Timing should be set according to the topic and number of participants. Ideally the time of group discussion should be between 20 minutes to 40 minutes.
- *Topic* – Topic for the group discussion should be chosen very carefully considering the socio-cultural background of the participants as well as their needs. The topic should not hurt the sentiments of anybody and it should be relevant to the problems of the target group.
- To-the-Point Discussions – It should be ensured that discussions are focused and take place in the right direction and in congenial atmosphere. Ideas straying from the main focus should not be encouraged.

Analysing Group Discussions

- *Participation* – It has to be observed how many members of the group participate and who generally remain, silent. There would be some people who are not participating or are getting interrupted by others or are shy to speak. Who is more frequently talking and with whom may also be observed. The left-outs may need special attention at later stages. The people with leadership qualities, communicative abilities, team spirits and innovative ideas may be identified.
- *Influence* – During the group discussion, leadership emerges. Who emerged as the leader in the group? Was he facilitating discussions or was he dominating? Was there more than one leader? Were there groups within the group with rivalry? Such observations should be noted.
- *Style of Influence* – Obviously some people will influence others. This style of influence may be positive or negative. Positive influence encourages others to give their ideas and communicate freely while negative influence sends others to their silent shells.
- *Decision-making Process* – It is to be observed whether any decision-making took place, and if so whether it was based on facts and ideas or was it imposed by some members of the group? Were suggestions coming to take decisions? How were ideas getting rejected? Were there good working relationships?
- *Expressions* – How was the communication in terms of tone, voice, pitch, gestures, etc.

Limitations of Group Discussions

Persons with communication problems and of introvert nature remain left out and do not come out with their ideas. They start feeling lower in self-esteem, thinking that they cannot participate in the group discussion.

If the topic is not told in advance, group members may not have much information to share

Rules and goal of organising the group discussion should be explained properly, as otherwise it may lead to needless arguments among the group members.

Career Guidance Exhibitions

It is said that one picture is worth ten thousand words. Organisation of exhibition is another technique where information can be disseminated to a large number of persons. For organising career exhibitions, display material posters and charts have to be prepared. While posters are generally intended to motivate, charts provide detailed information. Posters and charts can be prepared for all types of guidance, *i.e.,* educational, vocational and personal. For educational guidance, charts may be prepared giving details of various courses available at different stages, their admission criteria, etc. Under vocational guidance, information may be provided about various job options available after, middle or High schooling or Graduation levels, by various educational streams or details about one occupation such as entry qualifications, process of entry in the job, pay scale, nature of duties, working conditions, future prospects, etc. For personal guidance, posters may be prepared about coping strategies or motivating a person to develop good study habits, or to take up self-employment or to join defence forces.

Figure 10.1: *Example of Posters*

Courses in ITI				
Course	Duration	Eligibility	Number of Seats	Job Opportunities

Figure 10.2: *Example of Chart*

What to consider:

- Location (Where to organise)
- Budget (How much resources are available)
- Manpower (Who would prepare posters and charts?)
- Information (What are the sources of correct, accurate and updated information?)
- Quality
  - Posters and charts should be need-based.
  - They should be attractive and display should be eye-catching

- Series of posters containing details about one topic should be displayed together
- Visibility and clarity of writings on charts and language used should be easily understood.

Limitations:

- Posters and charts can give only limited information. If the client wants more details he may not get instantly. The posters/charts should indicate the sources of additional information.
- Motivating posters can be misleading. For example, everybody may not be able to get loans from the banks for starting self-employment.
- If proper publicity is not given about organisation of exhibition, many people may not visit.

Class Talks

The organisation of class talks may be extremely beneficial to provide information to a specific group of students. There can be various types of talks:

(a) *Educational Talks*: Educational talks may relate to some common education problems of a particular class. For example, educational talks may include problems like 'how to memorize', or'how to prepare for examination' or' options after class VIII.' The choice of the theme would depend upon the target group.

(b) *Vocational Talks*: Vocational talks may relate to the problems relating to vocational choice or giving information about a particular occupation or entry into the occupation etc.

(c) *Motivational Talks*: This type of talks are meant to inspire students to concentrate on their studies, setting up of their goals in life, motivating them to form positive attitudes towards life, work, etc.

(d) *General talks*: General talks may not be problem specific. These can be about informing the students about guidance services in schools or the role of employment exchanges or health facilities available near the school.

Purpose of Class Talk

To give exposure about various aspects of educational and vocational fields

- To provide motivation in certain areas
- To provide specific information
- To develop real self – concept

Choosing a Topic for the Talks

The nature of group – socio-economic and educational background. For example, a talk on what to do after passing Highschool would not be useful for students of mid-school students. Academic performance level should also be considered. The students with low academic achievements may not be interested in the topic like 'How to appear for Administrative Services'.

Employment availability is another important point to be considered. If there is already saturation in employment in a particular occupation, there is no point in providing information on that particular occupation.

Local needs of area should also be considered. If, in an area people are required for repairing household goods, a talk may be arranged on the openings and preparation for repairers.

Societal traditions and norms should be taken care of. In certain societies where girls are supposed to remain in 'Purdah' topic on how to enter in 'modeling' field would be a waste.

Topic may be chosen after discussions with the students.

Planning and Organisation of Class Talk

(a) *Where*: The place for the talk should be the classroom or a hall auditorium. It is to be decided whether the talk would be in the school or students are to be taken outside the school. The place chosen should have proper sitting arrangement and a place for displaying posters and charts. If using the audio-visual methods, appropriate equipment and proper place to use that equipment should be available.

(b) *When*: Timings of the talk are important. A talk on "Options available after high school may be useful for students passing out. Morning time may be better useful for the talk than the evening time.

(c) Who: Who would give the talk is to be decided – the guidance counsellor or some expert from outside.

(d) *Single Talk or Series of Talks*: It depends upon the topic. One talk may be sufficient, on memorisation process, but the topic of options available at various levels of education and details of these options may require more than one talk. In such cases, a series of talks may be planned. For example, 1. Competitive examinations after passing a certain level of education for further education. 2. Job options after passing out a level. 3. Jobs through competitive exams 4. Courses stream wise to a certain level of students, and so on.

(e) *Number of Participants*: The ideal number of participants for a talk is between 30 to 40 students.

(f) *Duration*: Duration should generally be between 30 to 40 minutes. After the talk, about 15 minutes time should be given for queries from the students.

(g) *Methodology*: How to deliver the talk should be decided in advance. Would it be in lecture form or question-answer form? Whether the talk would be followed by Power Point Presentations or some other audio-visual aids? It is always better to combine the talk with audio-visual material. With on-line education, one can organise such talks like using various computer based platforms like zoom etc.

(h) *Preparation*: For organising a class talk, the students should be informed well in advance about the topic, about the person who has been invited to speak, the time, the place, the duration etc. so that students may be mentally prepared to attend the talk. They may be asked to keep a notebook and a pen to note the desired information. They may also be asked to be ready with their queries. The class talk should be simple in language. Delivery should be slow and to the point.

Organisation of Contents

The contents of the talk would vary with the topic. For giving information about an occupation, the following contents may be incorporated:

1. Introduction – The Occupation
2. Importance of the Occupation
3. Nature of duties
4. Educational and Training requirements
5. Experience needed
6. Physical requirements if any
7. Personal traits needed
8. Entry into the occupation and preparation
9. Working conditions
10. Salaries and perks
11. Employers and organisations where the Occupation is found
12. Promotions and opportunities for development
13. Hazards, if any
14. Future trends of Occupation
15. Start-up facilities
16. Contacts for further details.

Precautions:

- Exaggerated statements should not be given. Real picture of an occupation should be provided
- So far as possible all the details must be given including negative aspects of pursuing a course or opting an occupation. The talk should include where to get additional information
- Information should include relevant statistics including projection for future
- Ornamental language should not be used
- Information should be relevant for the target group. For example, for the rural students of a village where there is no electricity, information about computers may not be relevant
- Choose the media, which is popular in the locality like puppets in Rajasthan.

Sample of Class Talk

Name of the school:
Class & Section:
No. of students:
Age Range:

Date:
Time:
Topic:
Medium of talk:

Objectives

1. General:
   A. To motivate students towards educational and vocational planning.
   B. To motivate the students to plan their future careers.
   C. To help them in assessing their own strengths and weaknesses.
   D. To make them aware of the world of work.
2. Specific:
   A. To help in realising the need for educational and vocational guidance.
   B. To make them aware of the need for educational and vocational planning.
   C. To make them aware of the factors which they should consider in career planning.
   D. To help them in realising the need for thinking about their own abilities, aptitudes and interests.

Topic -Need & importance of career planning (English)

Presentation

Introduction: If you want to climb on a ladder you have to go step by step. You can't reach the upper most level in one step. To reach there, you have to think how to get there. For example, if you have to arrange a party what would you do?

Expected answer: How to arrange? What to arrange? Where to arrange? Arrangement of crockery, tables, etc. Thus, before achieving some goal or before trying to get something, one has to think about how to reach it. He has to consider all the aspects of the matter, and this is known as planning. Without making a plan we cannot do anything. It will, otherwise, be just like wandering in the dark. No door of success can be opened without planning.

So, today we will discuss something about the need for and importance of educational and vocational planning.

Q. Narendra what do you think about yourself? What do you want to be when you grow up?

A. I want to be a doctor, or engineer or businessman.

Yes, I am happy to know that you want to do something in your life. Like you, everybody should make some plans for future. Most of you will be thinking as to what they will do when they grow up and what their friends will be when they grow up?

But attainment of goal is not a child's play. Choosing a vocation and preparing for it are such important tasks that one needs to think carefully before taking any steps in a particular direction. Your future depends upon your present planning, because what you have to study and where to study depends on what you want to be in your future. So your education depends on your vocational choice, just as your vocation generally depends on your educational preparation.

In this connection, it would be wise to put the following questions to yourself.

1. What do I know about myself? What are my interests and attainments in different school subjects?

2. Do I know what subjects I should study in college?
3. Up to what stage I should or can continue education?
4. Do I know that I am more suited for certain types of jobs than for others, if so what are they?
5. How to get a job and how to choose it?

For arriving at answers to all these questions you should know two things.

1. World of work
2. More and More knowledge about yourself.

Some important aspects of the world of work are: job opportunities in various fields, qualifications and skills needed for various jobs, training, experience required, age limits, physical conditions, hours of work shift, etc.

Q. Do you know how the jobs differ in their work requirements, attractions, etc?

Let us take the example of a pilot. There are some special physical requirements to become a pilot, such as the length of legs, eyesight, etc. To take another example, life of a businessman or a doctor is a very busy life. There are no vacations, no certainty of income in comparison with the job of a teacher.

One thing very important to mention here is that the choice of a vocation is the pivot around which the whole life moves. It affects the way of life as well as the life of the family. Choosing a vocation is also like tossing a dice. Once cast, the result is fixed.

Q. Ashok, can you tell me how a job determines the way of life?

A. One's status, income, circle of friendships, extra-curricular activities, prestige, etc. all depend upon the job which he is in. If you consider examples from the lives of people in different occupations, you will realise more clearly how people working in different occupations adopt different ways of life. As a businessman, one has no fixed holidays and no fixed salary. He is usually interested in keeping up to date information regarding market rates and the availability of goods. His circle of friendships will be within his own group, mostly comprising businessmen.

So, when you choose a vocation, you choose at the same time, a certain way of life also, and if you are careless in choosing the vocation, there will be no job satisfaction and you may face disappointment and difficulties in life. We people work for satisfaction of needs. Work is a medium for satisfying them because we get money and also mental satisfaction. So if there is any trouble or dissatisfaction in this medium, *i.e.,* work itself, life will become full of miseries.

Now we shall consider this aspect knowing more and more about yourself.

Q. Can everybody do the same type of work?

Expected Answer: No.

Yes, because there are individual differences. You ask yourself questions like: what things and activities do I like? In which subject do I do well? As you seek answers to these questions, you will gradually gain a better understanding of yourself.

First of all, physical health and strength have a close relationship with the vocational choice. You will do some jobs well and in some others you may be handicapped depending on your physical attributes.

Next, your interests and abilities play an important role in the choice of a vocation.

Q. Can you do every job with the same interest and enthusiasm?

Expected Answer: No.

Every body has his own hobbies and interests. According to such interests, people like to study science, commerce, fine arts, and some take up sports. Ideally, everybody should choose his vocation according to his own interests, as otherwise he wouldn't do the job honestly and enthusiastically.

However, interest alone is not enough. Every occupation, in order to be handled successfully, requires a certain level of general intelligence and also of specific ability. For example, for becoming a musician one should have an ear for music. Similarly, abilities to do something also differ from individual to individual. Some abilities are natural talents. Only to a certain extent abilities may be further developed, by hard work or extra attention.

I hope by now you have some idea as to how you should prepare yourself for choosing your career and also what things you should know in doing so. Though planning for a vocation is ultimately your own responsibility, you can benefit by the opinions and suggestions given by others.

If you closely observe your parents, your brothers, friends and their friends, you will realise how vast or varied the world of work is and how much planning goes into preparing for and getting a job. Haphazard choice may lead to continued frustration in life and you may feel you have missed the boat in life and be discouraged to think positively. So planning your future career by planning educationally and vocationally from the very beginning is very important.

I hope all of you will start thinking about your future from now

Finally, if you want to ask something about the subject we have discussed your questions are welcome.

Black Board Summary: Need and importance of career planning.

1. Introduction
2. Need for planning
3. Occupation affects the way of life
   Right choice, saves time, money, resources and protects from frustration.
4. Know your self
5. Know the world of work
   Support with success and stories of failures—film show

Career Conference

Career Conference is a technique through which information about a number of occupations and educational choices may be provided to a large number of students at one time. To organise career conference, pre-planning is extremely necessary.

How to Organise the Career Conference

- First of all the guidance worker should identify the needs of the students at various levels
- Career conference may be planned for two or three days
- The conference may be organised for the students of three or four schools located in the area
- Career conference may be followed by career exhibition.
- Topics may be chosen according to the needs of the students
- The place for organising the conference has to be decided. The experts for speaking on the chosen topics should be identified and contacted.

- The details of the topic to be covered in the talk may be provided to the experts
- Duration of each topic to be covered by the experts should be decided in advance.
- Career conference may include some career talks, motivational talks, group discussions as well as film shows to a smaller group.
- Activities like drama and group songs may be organised.
- To organise a career conference, help of the teachers, parents, community and experts has to be obtained
- The students should also be involved in preparation and organisation of the conference.
- The posters and charts may be obtained from various agencies for display. Some of these may be prepared with the help of the students.
- Topics should be chosen keeping the interest of the target groups
- Children of various classes may be invited according to the topic.
- Feedback from the students and other participants should be obtained.
- During the career conference, the employers, the bank personnel may also be invited so that they could interact with the students.
- Media people may also be invited to provide publicity to the activities.

There are several advantages of organising a career conference, which provides for orientation of the community at large about the guidance activity, direct contact with the community people, and students' interaction with the experts and employers.

Field Visits

Field trips provide a direct experience to the students. The visits may be organised to the employment exchanges so that the students may see the actual functioning of the exchange and may establish the rapport with the concerned officials. The field trips may also be organised to various educational institutions so that the students could observe the educational atmosphere of the institution. They could interact with the students studying there and get their opinion about the course. Visits to employers and industries provide a first-hand experience to the students about the nature of occupations and jobs, working atmosphere, and relative strengths and weaknesses of various organisations. The students may discuss with the employees of the organisation and gain knowledge about the hazards of a particular job.

To organise the field visits, the concerned institution, organisation or industries should be contacted in advance through writing a letter and contacting on phone. Later on, time, date and duration should be fixed. The groups should comprise about 30 to 40 students. The students should be briefed about the field visit in advance. The number of participants to be visiting the organisation should be conveyed the plan of the field visit in consultation with the organisation to be visited. The Manager of the organisation may be requested to deliver a lecture about the general activities of the organisation. Some experts may interact and address the queries of the students and after that the visits to the work site may be organised.

The field visits provide a very good learning experience for students to see and observe the kind of experience they may not have through talks or discussions outside.

After the visit the students may be asked to prepare a note on the field trip and their experience. A discussion session may be held after the visit to review the outcomes of the visit.

In case such visits are not possible, virtual visits can also be organised using technology which can be for large number of students.

Guidance through Co-Curricular Activities

It is a fact that direct advice may not have much impact as the indirect advice can have. It is also important who is telling whom and at which place? For example, the campaign for 'No Smoking' may not be effective if the parents advise the children that smoking is not good for health, but a good campaign in a television programme utilising some actor or actress whom the children like, providing this message will have impact. Children would like to listen. If the same is in their community setting through songs, drama and film shows, street plays, *nukkad natak*, puppetry, etc. they have a lasting impact. Guidance counsellor should encourage that kind of activities in the school. Hobby clubs may be established, students may be asked to choose a topic and prepare some activity related to that topic to be displayed. Sometimes, the counsellor himself may give the topic. Through these activities messages may be communicated. Such activities are more influential in case of tackling personal problems or motivating the students for studies or developing the desired behaviours.

These activities, on the one hand, transmit the message, and on the other, develop creativity in the children. Their communication skill also improves. Participation of a large number of students can be had in such activities. Flower shows, science fairs, building models may develop their hobbies, which they can learn to be creative and utilise their skills as well as leisure time in an appropriate manner.

Film Shows

It is not possible to take large number of students for the field visits. There is another method to provide direct experience of the work sites. This can be the organisation of film shows. When a class talk is given the education of the students gets diverted and they misuse all the information provided during the talk. If the same information is provided through film shows the interest of the students remains intact; the guidance counsellor should be able to choose the film which is most appropriate to the pupils' needs and is also attractive. The time of the film show and the target group should be identified in advance, proper sitting arrangement should be made and equipments may be kept ready to show the film. After the film show, students should be asked to give their opinion and prepare a note on the film show.

Use of Mass Media

Group guidance programmes may use another effective technique, which is mass media. It includes the use of press, magazines, radio, TV, computers. A career information magazine may be brought out in the schools itself or otherwise the already existing magazines may be used for the articles on educational, vocational information. The panel discussion, the phone-in programmes, the quiz programmes, vacancy information etc. may be given through radio and TV

Essential Planning

- Preparing Annual Plan
  - Consultation with AIR/TV, Newspapers
  - Subjects to be covered and the audience targeted
  - Availability of resources
- Collection of Information
  - Collection of information required
  - Labour market information
- Other information like facing interviews, facilities available according to topic chosen
- Selection of Medium
  - Radio or TV or Newspapers/Journals/Internet/Computer Data Base.
  - Talk or Panel Discussion/Play.
- Working out Details
  - Material to be covered/Time to be taken/Speaker or Panel Members/ Style of Presentation/ etc.
- Rehearsal
  - Presentation
  - Time taken
  - Impact Release of Programme Why Mass Media
- Communication through media has a greater impact due to glamour attached to it.
- Information may be given to a larger number of people in lesser time & lesser cost.
  - V.G. Programme may be publicised.
  - Information may reach to diverse groups simultaneously.

Limitations

- Immediate feedback is not available
- Due to paucity of space/time details of information may be left out

- Information may not reach to the needy as many people do not read newspaper or have a TV/PC.

Some Agencies Related to Mass Media Communications in India

- All India Radio
- Doordarshan
- Press Information Bureau
- Film Division
- Directorate of Advertising & Visual Publicity
- Publication Division
- Song & Drama Division
- Directorate of Field Publicity
- Photo Division
- Registrars of Newspapers of India
- Indian Institute of Mass Communications
- Film & Television Institute of India
- Children's Film Society
- National Film Development Corporation
- Directorate of Evaluation
- Research & Reference Division

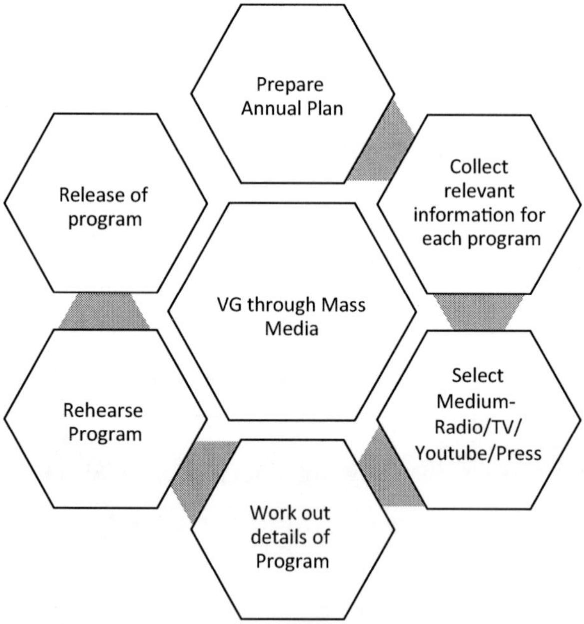

Figure 10.2: *Vocational Guidance Using Mass media*

Computers are becoming very popular among the students. A database on information may be developed and disseminated through computers.

Role Play

Moreno gave the concept of Role-playing. According to him, it involves the "staging of a situation in which selected members of the group are "the actors" and the other members are "the spectators". Participation in role playing technique permits the individual to express his inner needs and reactions to pressures. Through Catharsis (release of tension), better insight into his repressed self is achieved. It is assumed further that constructive forces come into play, and that, by permitting them to direct the individuals-believe acting, he realizes more complete and realistic understanding of himself." Super Role-playing is voluntary, unrehearsed and spontaneous. It can be of two types.

1. Socio-drama
2. Psycho-drama

Both types are almost similar so far as their procedure and basic concepts are concerned. The basic difference between the two is the subject matter. While socio-drama takes up the topics related to social issues, under psycho- drama themes are of personal nature.

The Procedure:

(a) *Selection of a Situation:* First of all, a theme has to be selected on which the role-play is going to take place. Theme should be such that it relates to most of the members and also easy to act.
(b) *Discussion with the Group*: Group should be appraised of the situation in details and the method of role-playing.
(c) *Role Taking:* Two groups may be constituted. One group that would enact and the other to observe the role-playing. Actors should be warmed up for taking the roles. Assigning of roles should be voluntary.
(d) *Actual Dramatization*: Actors act while observers would watch. Acting has to be based on spontaneity. Not much time should be given for preparation.
(e) *Discussions:* After the enactment, discussion should be held. Observers should give their views; actors should interact and the whole process should bring out the learning experience.
(f) *Re-play*: The same role-playing may be re-played with changed roles in two groups.

Role-playing is extremely helpful and is becoming popular. Enacting over a problem provides insight. Warmth, problem solving, problem analysis and exploration of resources take place in the process. Internal feelings are expressed freely and in many such situations, catharsis takes place. Once the tension is released, person starts thinking in positive direction. Shy persons are able to overcome their shyness and cultural barriers get removed.

For using this technique, communication skills are required. Problem should be understood properly.

Importance of Group Guidance in School

The importance of group guidance activities in a school needs to be understood. Such programme can be planned for large number of students facing similar issues which would save time money and energy. Group guidance can also be imparted when some information is to be provided to several students. It also paves way for catharsis when students discuss their problems in a group. Their mind set and behaviour can change in the desired direction when they hear others. Others perspective towards a particular problem provide wider horizon which leads to collective judgement. A guidance worker can use group guidance programme to observe students' behaviours and can identify unexplained needs. The guidance worker can plan a holistic programme for students in need.

11

Importance of Self-Concept in Education and Role of Guidance

It is extremely essential to understand the perception of self-concept an individual has. Sometimes a person or a child looks himself or herself as lacking self-worth and has a very negative self-concept. Some people have very vulnerable self- perception. With a little setback in the lives, their self-perception becomes negative from positive. A positive self-concept helps in development and achieving success in education. Of recent, there is a lot of focus on developing a positive self-concept in each individual. The NEP also refers to its importance.

Meaning and Purpose of Self-Concept

Self-concept is some total of self-perceptions which means how a person sees himself. A person experiences so many things during his growing but the perceptions about his own personal existence are most important. Keeping this in view, self-concept has been defined as a totality of a complex, organized, and dynamic system of learned beliefs, attitudes and opinions that each person holds to be true about his or her personal existence. Sometimes self-concept is treated as similar to self-esteem, self-image, self- regard, etc. But self-esteem is more towards the feeling of self-worth or the level of satisfaction one gets from the self. Carl Rogers had been a prominent psychologist who has worked on self-concept theory. According to his ideas 'self' is the central component of human personality.

In the words of Fitts 'The self-concept is seen as a means of understanding the individual from his own frame of reference and as a resource for better planning and assistance by those who would help him toward rehabilitation and or self-actualisation'. Thus, the self-concept is associated with the person's real self.

Thus, self-concept is image of oneself the individual has. These include the beliefs about themselves in terms of physical, psychological, social and emotional characteristics. The self-concept also includes the image of oneself in terms of the individual's aspirations, performance and achievements.

There are two dimensions of self-concept.

1. *Physical*: The physical dimension relates to the perceptions of persons about their appearance, adequacy and importance of body, their sex appropriation and how they see their physique.

2. *Psychological*: The psychological aspect includes the perception of individuals about their abilities, worth and their relationships with others. Behaviours take place on the basis of these two aspects of self-concept.

The physical self-image is generally formed first and psychological self-image is formed after the physical self-image. The psychological self-images also include emotions and feelings, courage, honesty, independence, self- confidence, etc. As the people grow the physical and psychological self- concepts merge in each other and they see themselves as unified individuals.

The origin of self-concept starts with those people who have a meaning in the child's life and who are around the child. These are parents, teachers, peers and other members of the community. If these people think about the child in a positive manner the child also thinks about himself favourably and if these people do not have favourable feelings about the child or if they comment on the child's abilities or behaviours negatively, the child also develops a negative self-concept. Components of Self-Concept:

(i) Self-concepts are learned
(ii) They are organized
(iii) They are dynamic

Self-concept Theories

While writing principles of philosophy Rene Descartes in 1944 talked about the non-physical inner self which was related to thinking and perceptions. A second milestone was established by Sigmund Freud in 1900 when he detailed the theory of self-concept in which he elaborated the importance of internal mental processes. Freud did not specifically mention about the self-concept but later in 1946 his daughter Anna gave emphasis upon the ego development and self- perceptions. In 1945 Prescolt Lecky stated the idea of self- consistency as a motivating force of human behaviours. Raimy in 1948 talked about the measures of self -concept and stated that psychotherapy is a process which helps in changing the individual's perceptions about themselves. Raimy said that measurement of self- concept is important for counselling.

In 1947 Carl Rogers elaborated the self- concept theory in detail. He said that all educational, vocational guidance and personal counselling is possible through understanding the importance of self.

A number of researches have been conducted since 1970s on the notion of self -concept. Recently new awareness has been generated about self-concepts due to the problems of drug abuse, alcoholism, behavioural problems, dysfunctional families, etc. It is believed that these problems could be tackled if a healthy self- concept is developed. Researches by Cognitive theorists like Mc Adam, 1986; Ryan, Short & Weed (1986) show that negative self- concepts lead to irrational thinking about oneself as well as about others.

Development of Self-concept

Concepts of self are hierarchical. The basic self-concept which is known as primary self-concept develops first with the interaction of the child with his interaction at home. It includes both physical and psychological self- images. The psychological images emerge with the interaction of the child with siblings. When the siblings are compared by the parents the concepts of self are formed. The roles and responsibilities among the child develop with parenting styles.

The secondary self-concepts develop when the child interacts with others. This includes how the other people think about the child. At this stage children also analyze their self-images developed at home in terms of the views of others. Whenever there are less discrepancies in primary and secondary self-concepts a child is likely to be well adjusted. Development of self-concept takes place with these interactions to understand sex differences, sex roles and other differences which occur due to the community and traditions.

By adolescence, self-concepts are generally established. Since these are not static, they keep on modifying as the children come into contact with new persons and experiences. For example, a child may excel in music at home and in school. He may form a belief that his is very good in music. But once he comes across with other musicians, he revises his opinion that he has learned everything in music or he is the best He may understand that although he is good in music but he is yet to learn a lot.

According to Rozers "Self is a social product. Therefore, it develops out of inter personal relationships. In his opinion, every human being wants to have positive perception about self He also wants that other people should also have positive regard for him. The process involves self-actualisation and development. Development of self-concept takes place with an enabling environment.

According to Super (1990) self-concept gets developed due to interface between a number of factors. These factors are shown in Figure 11.1.

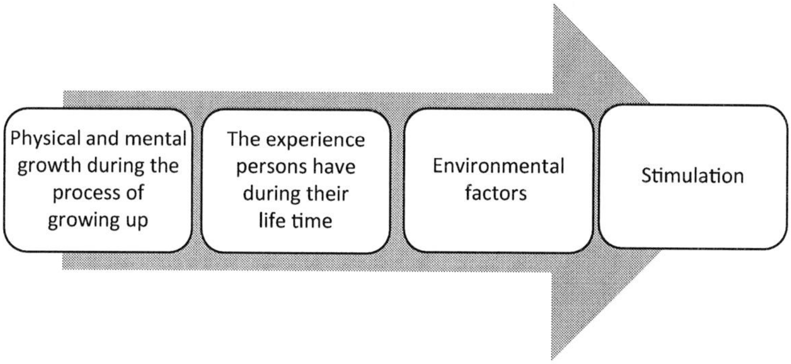

Figure 11.1: *Factors in Development of Self-Concept*

Super feels that self-concept continues to evolve as experiences of the person and interactions between a person and his environment continues.

Objectives

Self-concept is related to the academic achievement, attitudes and quality of life. It is extremely essential that children develop a positive self-concept so as to develop positive personalities and to excel in life. In this context, the purpose of self-concept is directly linked with performance and achievements in life. It has been seen through researches that children coming from deprived environment fail to achieve scholastic achievements. Self-concept is the core of the personality. The positive self-concept inculcates self-confidence, self-regard and higher levels of self-esteem. With a negative self-concept develop inferiority complex and a feeling of self-inadequacy. When they grow it leads to poor personal and social adjustments.

Measurement of Self-Concept

Self-concepts can be measured through testing and non-testing techniques of guidance. In testing techniques a number of self-concept scales and inventories can be administered. The non-testing techniques include the observation technique, anecdotal records, case histories and analysis of diaries prepared by the children. It is always better to collect information from more than one source. It is also advisable that a trained person measures the self-concept.

Role of Guidance in Developing Healthy Self-concept

Self-concept and vocational choice are interrelated. The guidance helps the individual in knowing self as well as the world of work. With the help of guidance, one gathers knowledge about occupations, their requirements, conditions of work, and career development. Similarly, one can know about his own interests, abilities, weaknesses, personality characteristics, etc. with the help of guidance. One can match his strengths or his own value systems with that of the demand of vocations and can excel in life. Choice of a right career enhances the continued development of a positive self-concept.

Everybody in life comes across with some or the other failures, stresses, anxieties and other negativities of life. A healthy self-concept can be developed when he knows how to cope with these problems. Guidance helps in developing coping strategies for dealing with negative aspects of life so that a positive self-concept could emerge and sustain. The planning for the life starts from the very beginning and a person has to play multiple roles in the society. These roles are played effectively and harmoniously to accept the self is possible through a guidance programme at the school stage.

12

Guidance for Encouraging Creativity among Students

Introduction

Creativity is the talent to produce new ideas, new products, new styles, new art forms, and, in short, the power to employ one's brain to create something out of the ordinary. If creativity is not there, life would be a burden and boring. Novelty contributes not only to happiness, enthusiasm and all-round satisfaction of the individual himself but that of the public at large. Creativity is needed in tackling effectively new types of problems, in planning strategies in various life and work situations and in attaining personal satisfaction.

In the words of Michael D. Higgins—

> "The roots of a creative society are in basic education. The sheer volume of facts to be digested by the students of today leaves little time for a deeper interrogation of their moral worth. The result has been a generation of technicians rather than visionaries, each one taking a career rather than an idea seriously. The answer must be reform in our educational methods so that students are encouraged to ask about "know-why" as well as "know-how". Once the arts are restored to a more central role in educational Institutions, there could be a tremendous unleashing of creative energy in other disciplines too."

Characteristics of Creativity

Advice or guidance on *what* creative thing is to be produced does not contribute to creativity. For example, small children love to draw and colour the drawings, if they draw as they please and colour the drawings as they please, amazing works of art are sometimes produced. If, however, they are told what colours are to be used where, the result would no longer be a creative piece of work but a standardized product without any novelty. Ramanujan, the mathematical genius, could not have been told what mathematical results he should produce. He was creative because he was allowed to sleep with the problems and wake up with solutions. However sometimes some small 'clues' through guidance can make students being creative.

The following major characteristics contribute to creativity:

1. Thinking on own.
2. Imagination and Imaginative behaviour.

3. The imaginative behaviour has some purpose which implies that it would lead to achieve specified objective.
4. The process of thinking and imagination are unique and produce something new and original.
5. The original product is valuable.

No doubt creativity contributes to discovery, innovation and dynamism to the society. It should be understood that creativity is a process and that is continuous. The New Education Policy lays particular emphasis on the development of the creative potential of each individual. It is based on the principle that education must develop not only cognitive capacities such as critical thinking and problem solving – but also social, ethical, and emotional capacities and dispositions. One of the principles of New policy is creativity and critical thinking to encourage logical decision-making and innovation. To meet this objective the Policy states that 'Curriculum content will be reduced in each subject to its core essentials, to make space for critical thinking and more holistic, inquiry-based, discovery-based, discussion-based, and analysis based learning. … and classroom sessions will regularly contain more fun, creative, collaborative, and exploratory activities for students for deeper and more experiential learning. In all stages, experiential learning will be adopted, including hands-on learning, arts-integrated and sports-integrated education, story-telling-based pedagogy, among others, as standard pedagogy within each subject, and with explorations of relations among different subjects.' All these promote creativity in students. 'Art-integration is a cross-curricular pedagogical approach that utilizes various aspects and forms of art and culture as the basis for learning of concepts across subjects. As a part of the thrust on experiential learning, art-integrated education will be embedded in classroom transactions not only for creating joyful classrooms, but also for imbibing the Indian ethos through integration of Indian art and culture in the teaching and learning process at every level. The need to integrate sports in education is well recognized as it serves to National Education Policy 2020. Foster holistic development by promoting physical and psychological well-being while also enhancing cognitive abilities is essential.

Developing Creativity among Children

Table 12.1: *Development of Creativity among Children*

Why	*How*	*Support*
Creative children have curiosity	They should be allowed to question and face challenges	Teachers and Guidance worker should provide support and facilitate them to find answers to their questions in innovative manner

(Table Continued)

(Table Continued)

Why	*How*	*Support*
Children connect things in their own manner and applying their own methods	Instead of applying the common rules to solve a problem, the creative children can apply new methods	A classroom teaching should be flexible.
Creative children think about alternatives. They explore, invent and create new options	Such children should be allowed to keep their minds open, learn through trial and error.	Do not insist learning through a designed pre-conceived manner
Creative children discuss their ideas, take feedback and use it, take criticism in positive manner, try to make link in ideas, behaviours and actions and its outcome with logic	They should be provided an environment where they could experiment	Encourage and motivate for their efforts
Students are prepared to take risks for their creativity	Risk taking should be encouraged among children to enhance their creativity	Counselling needed on shortcomings and setbacks
They need some Clues to experiment	Children should be provided various types of raw materials to experiment with their ideas.	Role models of creativity should be presented before children to motivate them to be creative. Children should be given sufficient time to explore, try and create

Dos and Donts

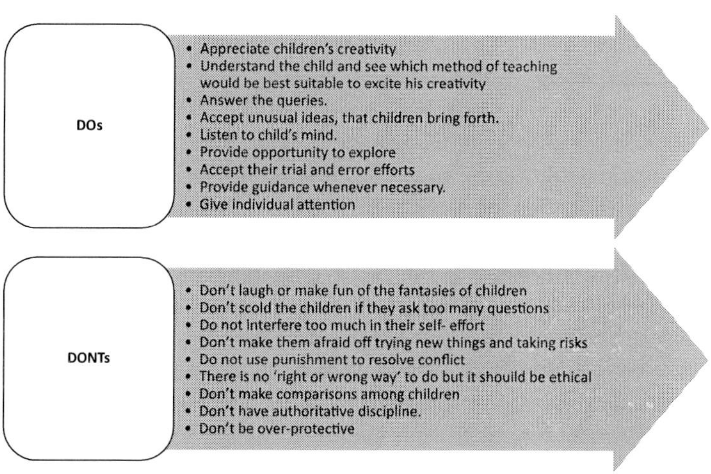

Figure 12.1: *Dos and Do Nots in Development of Creativity Among Students*

Role of Guidance in Developing Creativity

- With the help of guidance, creativity among children can be identified and nurtured.
- Guidance helps in creating an enabling environment in the school.
- Guidance can work as a bridge between the creativity of the child and aspirations of parents. Parents are to be counselled to understand their child's creativity.
- With the help of guidance worker, teachers can accept creative approaches to teach so as to make learning thought provoking, interesting and engaging.
- Guidance can help students to choose a career suitable to their creativity.
- Guidance can provide information on ways, manners and places that can help in nurturing the creativity.
- Guidance can organise various events to show case students creativity.
- Guidance can provide role models and examples of creativity.

Guidance and Adjustment for Well-Being

Life calls for adjustments at every stage. Adjusting to new and often unanticipated events is part of life. Every individual has to alter his way of thinking and behaviour suitably to be able to live in harmony with the emerging environment or situation that presents itself to him, be it at home, in the school or in the society at large. While people try to accommodate these changes without undergoing undue stress or hardship, often there may arise particularly unfamiliar and difficult situations which can severely strain their mental poise. For example, for a child entering a new and school with a sophisticated atmosphere unfamiliar to him or being forced to live with a step parent, for an adult losing a job or compelled to take up a job in which he has little or no interest, and for a couple losing faith in each other but still living together, the situation can be extremely challenging. Sometimes, several seemingly insignificant situations causing minor stresses could add up to create a feeling of helplessness and despair. Suitable adjustments in one's thinking and approach to the situation can help in maximising one's mental peace and consequently the potential for self-development in consonance with the external environment.

Defining adjustment Traxler says—"Occasionally in the use of the term adjustment' we imply that the more desirable state of adjustment is one in which the individual is perfectly happy and satisfied with all aspects of his life and one in which he has reached the level in all his contacts with his environment that he would be glad to see persist through his life".

The situation appears to be ideal but an effort to this direction and the extent to which one is able to reach is a continuous process of adjustment of individuals in their lives. The adjustment should come as an initiative not as a force. The adjustment is basically the degree of harmony between the individual and the environment.

Scope of Adjustment

1. First of all the person has to adjust with himself. He has to accept what he is i.e. his physical appearance, his strengths and weaknesses, his personality as a whole.
2. The person has to make adjustment in the home with his family and extended family.
3. The person has to adjust with his friends and colleagues.
4. The person has to adjust in a school atmosphere with his studies and daily routine.
5. The person has to adjust with his work place, recreational activities.
6. Adjustment in the community according to the social needs.
7. One also has to make adjustment in using his time that leads to learning time management.
8. The person also has to make adjustment with his finances, the future aspirations, the realities of life and other situations that come from time to time.

The proper adjustments in life situations lead to total wellbeing of a person. A well-adjusted person will be physically, emotionally and mentally healthy which is also connected with creativity.

Symptoms of Adjustment Problems

Difficulties in coping with the life-changing situation manifest themselves through various symptoms. Children who are unsuccessfully trying to adjust to new difficult situations may exhibit new behavioural problems like aggressive airs, or have trouble expressing feelings. Old behaviours also may re-emerge. Among adults, sometimes the normal ways of coping or finding solutions to life's problems just don't work and sometimes the situation is so complex that no possible solution presents itself. Adjustment problems may result in a feeling of stress, anxiety, agression or even hopelessness. Left unattended, this could lead to depression, mood disorders or alcoholism and in extreme cases to loss of mental balance and suicides.

Situations Calling for Adjustments

- *Family*: Difficult parent or parents, large families, poor academic environment, over discipline or total lack of it, own illness or illness in the family, lack of encouragement for fields of one's interest, un-cooperative attitude of sibs, discord with spouse and children, etc.
- *Economic*: Poverty, lack of satisfying facilities for studies, differences in levels of living with the neighbourhood, dependence on others.
- *School*: With school atmosphere and school discipline, with peers in the class, with teachers and teaching methods, with curriculum and participation in other school activities, with levels of achievement.

- *Work Place*: With nature of work, colleagues, subordinates and superiors, working conditions and advancement in career.
- *Others*: With friends, lack of opportunities for hobbies and pursuing one's interests

Need for Guidance

Individuals generally do not like to change their way of thinking or manner of behaviour. They do not always realize by themselves that a slight adjustment in their thinking and manner of acting can lead to substantial improvement in their relations to the external world and bring in immense personal happiness and success in life. It is in such a situation that professional guidance can help in identifying in what direction the adjustment should take place and by how much. A guidance worker can help the individual in the adjustment process in the following manner:

1. Identifying the specific adjustment problem.
2. Giving insight to the individual about his problems and reasons thereof.
3. Helping the individual to think about the probable solutions to his problems.
4. Helping the individual in making decisions and dealing with his problem.
5. Providing counselling about the mall-adjusted behaviour and change the person to the desired direction.
6. Working as a bridge between the child and teacher or child and parent or child and peers and solving the adjustment problems.
7. Create an enabling environment so that maximum harmony between the individual and his environment could be obtained.
8. Helping the individual in understanding and accepting himself.

Well-adjusted students in school and surroundings will use their talents in bringing out their creativity. It is very important that students are facilitated to develop a positive self- concept confidence and positive image about selves to encourage their creativity.

13

Mental Health and Guidance of Children with Special Needs

Almost every child in the school, who is old enough to understand the significance of being better than his/her peers, strives for academic excellence; and certainly, all the parents expect that their children excel in all fields of studies. This, however, does not always happen. Sometimes, the overall level of achievement of the class as a whole, or even that of the school as a whole, is well below expectations. It is more common to see that some children in the class, for various reasons, lag behind the others substantially in their academics, either in all or some subjects. The former situation of general or absolute academic deficiency is usually the result of unfair expectations of standards by the school administrations, inferior teaching and teaching methods and other factors beyond the control of individual student like school atmosphere not conducive to studies and has to be tackled at school level. The other situation of relative deficiency primarily arises out of family and individual differences of various types.

Reasons for Academic Deficiency

Academic deficiency can arise from a variety of reasons, some of the important of which are:

- *School-related*: Absence of proper school atmosphere required to promote learning, inappropriate and uninteresting curricula and teaching methods (lecturing without bothering to know whether all the students are following), ignoring of the backward students by the teachers
- *Family-related*: Lack of conducive atmosphere to stimulate academic achievement (as in the families of first- generation learners, large families, a parental attitude of indifference to achievement, etc), inability to afford costs of supplementary effort to improve achievement (like home tuitions, purchase of equipment to boost learning); unreasonable parental expectations and belief in the ability of their children
- *Individual Academic Differences*: Differences abilities (in one or more subjects), in level of motivation to do well in academics, in methods of learning and study habits
- *Individual Psychological Differences*: Aptitudes in the fields chosen (e.g. science instead of arts stream), communication (oral and written)

and listening skills, time management (answering the question paper in time allotted), self-confidence (e.g. to ask questions in the class and clear doubts), ability to mix with fellow students (and in the process learn from them), problems like fear and anxiety, inferiority complex, etc.

Role of Guidance

According to Braddock, the purposes of guidance and counselling services in school are toImprove academic achievement

- Foster positive attitudes toward school, learning, and work
- Increase acquisitions and application of conflict resolution skills.
- Decrease dropouts

Guidance services are necessary to assist students with problems like lack of relationship between ability and achievement, deficiency in one or several subjects, defective and inappropriate study habits, psychological problems of anxiety and fear, and inferior self-management skills in general. Guidance, thus, plays a vital role in removing the educational, personal, social, mental, emotional and other similar problems of the students and contributes to enhancing their cognitive, social, and self-management skills, and thereby their academic achievement.

Francis and others (1987) also examined the positive effects of counselling on students' communication patterns, study habits and academic achievement. The secondary school guidance programme should be a part of the total school programme and complement learning in the classroom. It should be child centered, preventive and developmental. The guidance programme should aim at maximizing the student's potential by encouraging their social, emotional and personal growth at each stage of their development.

A guidance worker must identify the problem of the child at an early stage so as to prepare an action plan to help him. This detection is possible through comparing the child's academic performance with that of his intelligence and abilities. The guidance worker can prepare Bi-variate graphs for comparing the academic achievements and intelligence. Reports from the teachers can also be taken into account. The guidance worker has to see the reason behind the low performance of the child. It could be that the child is learning disabled or coming from a backward area and is not able to adjust, the child could be a first-generation learner and may have no support system. The reasons of lagging behind in the academic performance could be many which are to be identified by the guidance worker. After ascertaining the reason child should be helped in improving his performance according to adopting various strategies. These strategies can be counselling of the child, arrangement of remedial classes, creation of enabling home/school environment, counselling of parents and teachers and so on.

Guidance and Mental Health

New discoveries and innovations have led to the new connotations relating to health. It has been established through researches that psycho-social problems and inadequate behaviour patterns are directly related to physical illness. The state of mind, the lifestyles, the interactions with others, relationships all are linked with physical and mental health. The concept of psychosomatic machines that emerged in early 1900s emphasised the role of interaction between mind and body in producing illness. Depressions, anxiety, migraines, asthma, ulcers etc. have been found to be linked with the state of mind. According to Miller, 1983—"The enormously important new area of medicine encompasses professionals from many disciplines, including psychology, psychiatry, sociology, anthropology, epidemiology, physiology, pharmacology, nutrition, neuroanatomy, endocrinology, immunology, nursing, social work, health education and public health." Due to the interdisciplinary approach, it has become easy to learn the effects of behaviours on physical and mental health. Health psychology has emerged as a new discipline.

Definition—Mental Health

Mental health is a term used to describe either a level of cognitive or emotional well-being or an absence of a mental disorder. The World Health Organization defines mental health as "a state of well-being in which the individual realizes his or her own abilities, can cope with the normal stresses of life, can work productively and fruitfully, and is able to make a contribution to his or her community."

Types of Mental Disorders

A study conducted in 1996 by the World Health Organization, the World Bank, and Harvard University found that the ten leading causes of disability (counting lost years of healthy life) were:

1. Major Depressive Disorder,
2. Alcohol Use,
3. Road Traffic Accidents,
4. Schizophrenia,
5. Self-inflicted Injuries,
6. Bipolar disorder,
7. Drug Use,
8. Obsessive-Compulsive Disorders,
9. Osteoarthritis,
10. Violence

Millions of people all over the world are affected by mental, behavioural, neurological and substance use disorders. For example, estimates made by WHO in 2017 showed that 792 millions persons had some or the other mental disorder globally which indicates that one in ten people is suffering with some mental issue. As per estimates about 264 millions had depression, 284 millions anxiety disorders, 46 millions Bipolar disorder, 16 millions eating disorder, 20 millions schizophrenia etc. and other about 970 millions substance abuse and so on. Situation is more alarming due to COVID-19 and is prevalent world wide. Indian situation is also a matter of concern. As per Public Health Foundation of India, 2019 estimates about 197 millions persons were suffering from mental disorders. Depression and anxiety are more common. Experts predicated rise in cases of anxiety and panic post Covid.

It is also experienced that cases of substance abuse even in small children as well suicides are increasing. In addition, many other disorders affect the nervous system or produce neurological sequelae. Projections based on a WHO study show that worldwide in 2005, 326 million people suffer from migraine; 61 million from cerebrovascular diseases; 18 million from neuro infections or neurological sequelae of infections. Number of people with neurological sequelae of nutritional disorders and neuropathies (352 million) and neurological sequelae secondary to injuries (170 million) also add substantially to the above burden.

Some of the behaviours that directly have negative effect on mental health are smoking, poor nutrition, obesity, lack of coping behaviour to face stresses, alcoholism, drug abuse, inadequate life style with lack of physical activity, lack of sleep etc. Researches show that not only stress affect our body and mind negatively, but also the thought process, the feeling and emotions in stress are directly associated with mental and physical health.

Principles of Maintaining Mental Health

Lack of good mental health is not a one- time affair or just a stage. It is the result of a complex interaction of individual's genetic, environmental, developmental and physiological factors.

The guiding principles for good mental health are:

Principles of Seeking Adjustment with Oneself

1. Principle of knowing the self
2. Principle of accepting one's self
3. Principle of balancing one's development
4. Principle of self -drive and shaping
5. Principle of self- control.

Principles of Seeking Adjustment with Environment and Developmental Factors

1. Principle of understanding others
2. Principle of accepting and understanding others
3. Principle of socialising oneself
4. Principle of satisfying needs adequately
5. Principle of training emotions
6. Principle of adjusting with the world of work

7. Principle of developing positive attitude towards life
8. Principle of bearing the stresses and strains of life
9. Principle of good physical health
10. Principle of faith in God
11. Principle of managing anger
12. Principle of learning coping strategies.

Taking Care of Children for Good Mental Health

It is essential to take care of the mental health of a child from the beginning as the effects of events and environment on the child's mind last for long. If these effects are negative then the child may suffer certain serious mental problems during the adulthood. There is a direct relation between the mental pattern developed during early childhood and the attitudes and way of life of the person during later stage of life. Many criminals were supposed to have a depressed childhood and frustrated school days.

- Mental exercises and mind games arc useful in dealing with feelings of depression. These exercises give you a brighter outlook towards life. Mind games like Suduko, crosswords and electronic games will improve brain's memory and speed.
- Meditation is one of the best exercises for your mind, body and soul. It gives your brain a complete workout along with complete relaxation of whole body.
- Healthy food like walnuts and fish oil. Nuts.
- Tell good stories to store memories of people and events.
- Spending time with nature and outdoor activities than sitting at home
- Watching TV together with children.
- Good physical exercise.
- Focus on learning new things.
- Use brain training techniques.

Role of Guidance for Sound Mental Health

The goal of education is to prepare children for their optimal intellectual, occupational and social functioning as adults. It has been observed through researches that when a comprehensive range of school and community- based services including quality mental health services are provided, students achieve excellence in educational performance and behavioural adjustments. Each and every child is in need of guidance at some or the other time to keep his good mental health. Mental health services which include coordination with teachers and parents help in mental health of the children.

Children in today's world have to face a lot of challenges. These include parent-child maladjustment, parent's and school's demands, changes in physical appearances, peer pressure, cultural adjustments, lack of support system, illness, disabilities, lack of emotional management, failures etc. These problems manifests in behavioural disorders. Illegal sex, assaults, suicides, drug abuse have become common phenomenon. These symptoms are of lack of good mental health.

A guidance worker helps to keep up the sound mental health of children in the following manner:

1. Use of various strategies to identify and address the child's needs and improve his mental health.
2. Organise programmes and activities for teachers and parents to develop effective teaching and learning strategies.
3. Keep liaison and discuss the problems of children with parents and other family members to develop effective techniques to manage behaviours of children at home.
4. Help the teachers and parents in identifying children with special needs and or creative children and meet their needs.
5. Develop life skill techniques to cope up with stresses, anxiety, anger and other daily routine problems.
6. Provide acceptance and encouragement to each and every child.
7. Link mental health to learning and behaviour to promote high academic achievement.
8. Prevent mental disorders by helping in creating harmonious environment at home and school.
9. Keep liaison with community to help children in getting needed help from community resources that could help in developing sound mental health in the child.
10. Develop a positive self-concept to have sound mental health.

Guidance For Children With Special Needs

Children in the school come from varying cultures, traditions and socio-economic background. Their educational, emotional and adjustment needs may differ. A uniform educational programme or a uniform system of dealing with the children may not meet the needs of all the children. A system has to be evolved in the school that may cater to the needs of children. Guidance plays an important role to deal with children with special needs. How can the children with special needs be defined? Children with special needs are those children who do things differently than the average normal children. If a child is not able to understand what is being taught in the class while all other children can, obviously that child has some special problem. Another child who sits in the back of the classroom but comes to the front whenever something is written on the blackboard needs to be taken care of. May be his eyesight is weak and he requires a seat in the front. There may be a number of other problem cases. On the other hand, there may be children with extra energy and are always hyperactive. They feel whatever is being taught is very boring. Such children require a special curriculum where provisions are there for extra activities. These hyperactive children are generally ignored otherwise. Similarly there are children who have some physical handicap or some mental disability called as 'Divyang' in India.

About one billion disabled persons live in the world which is about 15 per cent of the world's population. Nearly 240 millions of them are children. Out of these 100 million are Indians. About 12.60 million such children are school children. It is also to be mentioned here that this does not include those with a number of disabilities such as cerebral palsy, learning disabilities, epilepsy etc. as these are not covered under the definition of Disability Act.

14

Types of Children with Special Needs

Children with Learning Disabilities

Children with learning disabilities are known as 'slow-learners'. Generally, these children are considered as mentally retarded by the teachers. But that is not a correct assumption. These slow learners are not necessarily mentally retarded children but suffer from some other problem. These problems could be due to difficulty in memorising, writing, concentrating. Some children may have difficulty in reading or they may lack motor coordination. These children with learning difficulty are to be identified. Generally, these children have normal or sometimes even above average intelligence. Golick (1970) has classified learning disabilities in the following categories.

1. Poor body awareness: child cannot locate various body parts, difficulty in telling right or left
2. Poor ability to combine vision and movement: poor eye-hand coordination.
3. Visual inefficiency: Even after normal vision, child may not be able to give selective vision.
4. Poor listening ability: easily distracted towards notice.
5. Poor integration of information from sensory channels – child is not able to integrate the alphabets with their sounds.
6. Poor grasp of sequence: child is not able to remember the sequence of things like counting 1 to 10 he will not narrate in order.
7. Poor sense of rhythm: difficulty in narrating a poem.
8. Problems with concepts: child has difficulty in identifying the similarities and variations in various objects. Poor concepts of time or number.
9. Problems in learning: like difficulty in arithmetic, remembering numbers or names, difficulty specially in memorising
10. Poor general knowledge: child has difficulty in learning general information like home address, occupation of parents, names of friends, etc.

How to Deal with Learning Disabled Children

As a first step, it is important to identify children with learning disability and to identify their specific problem. Some might be facing problems in reading or understanding, others in writing. Some children may have problem with solving mathematical problems. Apart from learning difficulties, learning disabled children may face difficulty in having inter-personal relations or social interactions. There may be various categories of learning disability ranging from mild to extremely severe. Severely learning- disabled children require intensive intervention, may need special schools or constant supervision or continuous tutorials. In the regular classroom, special tutorials with direct instructions would be helpful. Social skill training, use of equipment to overcome learning problems, practice in speaking and writing, adapted curriculum should be provided. Behaviour management is another area which should be given due attention. Patience is required to deal with such students. They should be encouraged for appropriate behaviours. Simple assignments should be given and those students should not be punished because of their slow pace of learning. The special assistance should be reduced in a phased manner.

Mentally Retarded Children

Another category may be of the children whose intelligence level is lower than the desired. There are four categories of mentally retarded – profoundly retarded, severely retarded, trainable and educable retarded. Profoundly retarded children have very low levels of intelligence and may suffer from more than one handicap. Such children need support of special institutions. Severely retarded category children also have very low levels of intelligence and constantly require supervision or care in special homes. The trainable retarded children can be trained to take care of themselves in routine and repetitive jobs. However, they have difficulty in reading or doing mathematics. Some such children have some other special ability like that of singing. They are capable of performing some activities in sheltered workshops such as candle making, sorting jobs etc. Special training facilities are required for such children.

The educable mentally retarded children are those children who are borderline cases so far as intelligence levels are concerned. The physical appearance of these children is generally normal. These are termed as mildly retarded children. They require special programmes and extra classes to handle school curriculum. They are generally aggressive and need special and individual attention. They can learn to do simple routine jobs and study up to a certain level. Some of these children are very good in languages, physical activities, making craft items. Teachers need special training to deal with such students.

Table 14.1: *Categories of Mental Retardation and IQ Level*

Category	*IQ Level*
Profound mental retardation	Below 20
Severe mental retardation	20-34
Moderate mental retardation	35-49
Mild mental retardation	50-69
Borderline deficiency	70-79

The borderline retarded children can be taught to manage their daily routine activities and also to pursue academics up to a certain level. These children should be provided some vocational training along with the educational syllabus. This vocational training should involve repetitive work. Such children should be treated with care and concern. Sometimes a mentally retarded child acts in such a way that is not considered normal. He may make different poses or may be aggressive without any valid reason. Other students generally laugh at such activities of a mentally retarded child. The guidance worker has to organise community awareness programmes so that others may know about the status of the child and could deal with him with empathetic attitude.

Teaching for mentally retarded has to be extremely gentle as such children take a long time in learning an activity. Specific and continued training with patience may be helpful. The concept of gentle teaching has emerged from the Psychology of Interdependence. The Psychology of Interdependence is based on the assumption that each individual wishes to have a feeling of companionship which can modify the behaviours in the desired direction.

The parents and other family members have to play an important role in the development of a retarded child. Most of the times, parents scold the child for not learning or behaving in the desirable manner. Counsellor should help the parents in understanding the needs of the child. Parents may take professional or institutional help on a life- long basis for such children.

The syllabus has to be adapted according to the needs of the child in the school. For example, generally, the retarded child is unable to do mathematical problems. Extra tutorials may also be arranged in the school so that the needs of the children could be met.

Gifted Children

There are always some children in the class who are more capable than others. They have high IQ, can do more than one activity at a time do not take much interest in doing simple things. They feel happy undertaking extra and complex work. They can finish their tasks in a lesser time than others. They may have special innate abilities such as aptitude for music or other performing arts, aptitude for doing finer things, aptitude for doing mechanical things etc. These are the gifted children. Some special curriculum with extra and creative activities is required for such children. Special training opportunities are needed to nurture their special talents.

Various methods have been adopted to deal with the gifted children. Ability groups are made and they are kept in a separate section. Sometimes they are promoted a class higher. Having a separate section for the gifted sometimes makes them alien from the others. The other alternative is to organise enrichment programmes to enable the gifted develop their potentials and utilise the special talent they have. During the regular classes, special creative assignments are given to such students. Such children are restless in the class, cannot sit for a longer time with one activity or if they finish their task, they start disturbing others. It is, therefore, essential that they are kept busy where they can utilise their extra intelligence.

Parents are also to be guided about such children. Parents should be encouraged to provide such opportunities in the home environment where the gifted child may be able to nurture his talent.

The NEP 2020 takes into account the talents of gifted children and details as to how their talents will be encouraged in schools. NEP states 'Teachers will aim to encourage students with singular interests and/or talents in the classroom by giving them supplementary enrichment material and guidance and encouragement. Topic-centered and Project-based Clubs and Circles will be encouraged and supported at the levels of schools, school complexes, districts, and beyond. Examples include Science Circles, Math Circles, Music & Dance Performance Circles, Chess Circles, Poetry Circles, Language Circles, Drama Circles, Debate Circles, Sports Circles, Eco-Clubs, Health & Well-being Clubs/ Yoga Clubs and so on. Along these lines, high-quality national residential summer programmes for secondary school students in various subjects will also be encouraged, with a rigorous merit-based but equitable admission process to attract the very best students and teachers from across the country including from socio-economically disadvantaged groups'.

First-generation Learners

Another category of children, which is very common in schools especially in government run schools, is of first-generation learners. Due to the special schemes initiated by the government, emphasis is on the education for each child. Parents, in the changed scenario are also aware of the importance of education and are sending their children to schools. These children are the first in their families to attend the school. No body from the family is educated. These children have peculiar problems of making adjustments in the school, learning discipline, and understanding the importance of education. There is also nobody at home to help them in doing their homework. Teachers often scold them for not bringing the relevant textbooks or notebooks to the school or for not doing the homework. Their special needs are to be understood and taken care of.

Children with Different Physical Abilities

There may be children in a class who have some physical deformity like polio, lack of hand coordination, visual handicap, hearing disability. Or they might be suffering from severe allergies like allergy from dust, perfumes, smoke or some eating things. They might be having chronic disease like arthritis, diabetes, heart ailments, etc. Some children may suffer from epilepsy. A common problem in the students may be observed in speech. Children may not be good articulates, they may omit some words or may stammer. Sometimes speech problems occur due to emotional disturbances. Some such handicaps have been detailed below:

Hearing Impairment

The deaf child can be of various categories. There are children who are both deaf and dumb, others can speak but cannot hear and some others are hard of hearing. The hard-of- hearing children can use the hearing device. The children of the other two categories are to be taught through sight and touch and using the sign language. Researches show that such children can do extremely well in the activities involving manual dexterity, athletics, artistic abilities and creativity. A balanced and well-designed curriculum is needed for such children keeping in mind their specific abilities. All India Federation of Deaf, Deaf and Dumb Society, Delhi Association of Deaf, are some of the organisations that help deaf and dumb persons in getting employment. The most important aspect to rehabilitate the deaf child is early identification of the disability, arrangement for well-fitted hearing aids and early training in 'lip reading'.

A number of facilities and equipments are available these days which make the life of hearing-impaired children easy and smooth. Deaf persons can use Telecommunication devices for communicating through telephone. Mobile text-phone equipments have come in the market. In developed countries like U.K and USA telephone relay services are available. A deaf person can communicate through a human translator. Other equipments available are the flashing lights to signal events, for example, a fire alarm or doorbell.

Orthopaedically Handicapped

The orthopaedically children generally use artificial limbs. It is felt by the society that due to loss of hand, or leg, one is not capable of competing in normal society. There are people who are born disabled, while some others become handicapped due to some accident or injury. The latter category feels a drastic change in their lives. They feel more depressed and anxious than the persons who are born handicapped. One need of such persons is that the society understands them properly and helps them in coming out of their trauma.

Orthopaedically handicapped children require a suitable accommodation, a proper sitting arrangement and hindrance free architecture, especially the children who are using a wheel chair. Proper transportation to suit their disability is also necessary. Medical facilities should be available in the school or nearby school. Library facilities should be accessible to these children.

Visually Impaired Children

Visually impaired children may be of various types. They can be totally blind, partially sighted or colour blind. In the category of totally blind are those children who are not able to see anything, while partially sighted children require special arrangements for vision. Colour-blind children are those who cannot differentiate various colours.

Blindness may occur in some children by birth while in others it may be caused due to some accident. In some children it may develop as they grow.

Blindness in legal terms has been defined as the vision of the child in the better eye, after correction is 20/200 or worse than this. A person does not come under the category of blind if the one eye has 20/200 or worse and the other eye has better than 20/200. A person is not visually impaired if he can do his normal work after using glasses. This means that a legally blind individual would have to stand 20 feet from an object to see it with the same degree of clarity as a normally sighted person could from 200 feet. In many areas, people with average acuity who nonetheless have a visual field of less than 20 degrees (the norm being 180 degrees) are also classified as being legally blind.

In educational terms, a child is designated as visually impaired if he cannot read through sight and is required to use Braille system or any other system to read. Partially sighted children, can read the normal books, but have sight problems up to the extent that requires special arrangements for instructions e.g. writing in big print etc.

Specific needs and programmes for the visually impaired children:

- Orientation of these children for school, facilities available and how to be mobile.
- Provide them technical support and orient them towards the technology like tape recorders, computers.
- Provide information about Braill books and help in reading them.
- Develop confidence in themselves and learn inter personal skills.
- Orient the other students of the class to have a positive attitude towards the children with special needs.
- Support of a person during examinations to write the answers.
- Special curriculum and alternative questions where one is required to draw a graph etc.
- Use of actual objects for learning.
- All the written material on the black-board should be orally explained.
- Information about safety, use of electrical equipment etc.

Some Major Problems of Differently-abled

1. *Architectural Hindrance*: Architecture of the school building or the working place is one of the major barriers for the disabled. For example, if the building is multi-storied and one is supposed to use lift, there should be a provision of announcement about the floors, numbers should be written in Braille, the children confined to a wheel chair should have the accessibility of lift. Children affected with polio or using a wheel chair should have proper facilities of toilets.
2. *The Attitudes*: Generally, the disabled are neglected by the society or if some people do not neglect them, they pity them. Such attitudes give negative signals to the disabled. They develop a sense of self-pity and feel as if they do not have a place in the society. They are not able to

develop a sense of belonging. Sometimes even parents do not want to accompany disabled children as they feel embarrassed, especially in case of children with mental retardation. Some measures have been initiated for mainstreaming of disabled children by keeping them in the normal school along with other normal children. There is a need to make the fellow students aware. Acceptance in the society is extremely necessary.

3. *Jobs and Disabled*: Although there is 3% reservation for the physically handicapped in the jobs, employers are apathetic towards employing them. Even if they employ the disabled due to compulsion, they do not have a positive attitude towards them. The capabilities of disabled are not given due respect; jobs are not assigned to them. The disabled are treated as a liability and not as an asset, while it has been seen that certain jobs can be done better by the disabled. Physically handicapped are not occupationally handicapped. There is a need to identify suitable jobs for various categories of handicapped. Success stories may be helpful in changing the mis-conceptions on the part of employers. In the activities where lot of noise is involved, the deaf and dumb can do excellent job.
4. *Education System*: The education system in the country is yet to be made disabled friendly. It has to be employment-oriented. More academic education would not help them in their future quest for livelihood. Jobs should be identified for them and proper training, including the mental readiness for a particular job, should be given from the very beginning. For example, the work of call centres is flourishing. Visually impaired can be prepared for such jobs.
5. *The Inferiority Complex*: Another major problem which most of the disabled suffer from the feeling of inferiority and low levels of self-esteem. Due to the handicap, they feel that they are not like other normal children. It affects their performance. There is a need to develop their personalities in the areas where they can excel. School has to provide such opportunities to the disabled students.

Identifying Children with Special Needs

The first step to meet the needs of different categories of children is to identify them and their special needs in the class. They can be helped as early as they are identified. Teachers should be able to spot the special-needs-children for example, children suffering with physical handicap; mental retardation may be discovered through administering IQ tests. Doctors may help in identifying physical ailments. Psychologists also administer diagnostic tests for identifying learning disabilities. Parents can help in talking about the child's difficulties, for example, late development of speech of the child, any emotional problem the child has suffered from, etc. The detailed information about the child's health and dreams and other background may be had from Cumulative Record Card, if the child has come from some other school. Psychological tests can also identify the children with special talents. Sometimes other classmates and friends talk about the child's problems and exceptional abilities.

Role of Guidance Worker

A guidance counsellor has a very important role in providing services to the children with special needs. He has to perform the following functions:

- Identify the children with special needs.
- Assess their capabilities and weakness.
- Identify what these children can do and what they cannot do.
- Ascertain what specific facilities these children require in the school and outside.
- Discuss and make the teachers, parents, principal, peer group aware about the special needs of these children.
- Map the resources available inside and outside the school to help these children.
- Collect, collate and disseminate the information that may be required for the children with special needs.
- Provide counselling to such children wherever required.
- Prepare a plan for various activities in consultation with teachers which various categories of special-needs-children may require.
- Help the teachers and school in implementation of the plan.
- Provide referral services. For example, the child who has problem in speech should be referred to speech correctionist or a physically handicapped child may be referred to occupational therapist. Referral services may also be had to assess the residual capacities of children with special needs.
- Preventive measures can be taken to curtail incidence of disability. Guidance worker should make the students and community aware of the importance of immunisation against various diseases, adopt a safe life style, follow traffic rules while on road, use safety measures while working in school laboratories.
- One of the most important functions of the counsellor is mainstreaming of disabled children in the school and community with providing awareness about various disabilities.
- The National Educational Policy calls for equitable and inclusive education and learning for all. Various provisions have been made to make these implementable.

15

Appraisal of Students for Guidance: Psychological Tests

Psychological Tests

Sometimes psychologists or counsellors are considered as predictors or astrologers or magicians by common man. A gentleman 'X' was travelling by train and chatting with co-passengers. During the conversation they could get to know that 'X' was a psychologist. All of a sudden many people crowded around 'X' and started asking questions like 'Tell me about my personality'; 'See my face and tell my strengths'; 'What can I do in future', etc. It took some time for 'X' to convince the people around him that no simple answers can be given to these questions. Counsellors are neither astrologers nor magicians. They only make a study of the individual, his environment and his situation and help him to reach a conclusion or decision. In this process, they may conduct appropriate scientific investigations.

Psychological tests are instruments in the hands of the counsellor that are helpful in the assessment of an individual's skills – abilities, aptitudes, personality traits, attitudes, interests and achievements. They constitute a scientific method of individual's appraisal. A psychological test has been defined as "an objective and standardised measure of a sample of behaviour" (Anastasy, 1968). Cronback (1970) has defined a test as "a test is a systematic procedure for observing a person's behaviour and describing it with the aid of a numerical scale or category system". The definitions show that while it may be extremely difficult to tell about a person's skills or behaviours using only non-testing techniques psychological tests make it possible to arrive at quantitative indicators of his strengths, weakness, behaviour patterns, etc. Moreover, the results of these tests enable comparisons between individuals and the same individual in different situations.

Objectives of Using Psychological Tests in a Guidance Programme

While non-testing techniques of guidance like case study or observation method are subjective, the testing techniques are objective and unbiased. The objectives of using psychological tests as tools for guidance are given in Figure 15.1.

Classification of Tests

Classification of tests has been done using various criteria. For example, *on the criterion of the process of administrability*—these have been classified

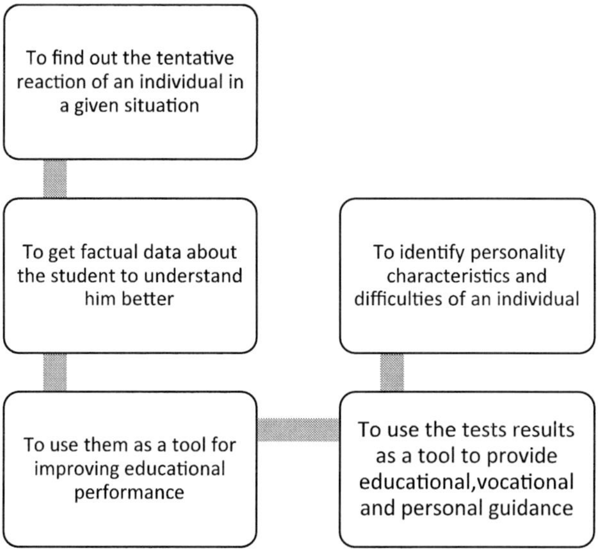

Figure 15.1: *Objectives of Using Psychological Tests in Guidance*

as individual tests and group tests. Individual tests are those which are administered to the individual. Group tests are administered to a group of people at a time. *On technical basis*—these have been classified as paper-pencil tests or performance tests. Performance tests are language free and free from cultural bias while paper-pencil tests require reading and language ability. *According to the purpose*—these tests can be classified as survey tests where the purpose is to collect the information about the individual on various variables or diagnostic tests meant for diagnosing the specific problem of the individual.

Characteristics of a Good Test

A scientifically prepared test should have the following characteristics:

1. *Objectivity*: Objectivity of a test denotes unbiasedness in administration, scoring and interpretation of the test. The test should be such that the Guidance workers' attitudes or ideals do not get reflected in the administration, interpretation and scoring of the test. The scores on the tests should be the same even when examined by more than one examiner. Higher this objectivity, higher is the probability of the test being good. Objectivity of a test is also measured in terms of item difficulty. Item difficulty in a test should be based on empirical findings. For example, if a large number of individuals are able to solve a particular item in a test, it implies that the item is easy, and the items which are solved by only a few people are termed as difficult. This shows that construction of a test should be based on experimental measurement of difficulty level.

2. *Reliability*: The reliability of a test denotes consistency of the results. In other words, if a test is administered repeatedly to an individual the test results should be more or less similar. For example, if on an intelligence test an individual's score is above average and the test is repeated, the scores should not be below average or average.

   Anastasi has defined reliability as: "Test reliability is the consistency of scores obtained by the same persons, when retested with the identical test or with an equivalent form of test."

   For use of any test for guidance purposes only those tests should be used whose reliability has been tested and is high. The formulation of the test should also explain the method by which reliability of the test has been checked.

   The reliability of a test can be measured through various techniques:

   (a) *Test-retest reliability*: Test-retest reliability is the technique where the test is repeated on the same individual or individuals a second time. The extent to which the scores are equal indicates the extent of reliability. It should be kept in mind that the conditions during the administration of the test during the second administration should remain the same as during the first administration and the time gap between the two administrations should not be too large. This interval may vary from one month to six months. Tests, which have a probability of improved performance due to familiarity, should not be tested through this method.

   (b) *Alternate form reliability*: It is also known as parallel form reliability. In this technique, two parallel tests are constructed and administered one-by-one on the same set of individuals. The correlation in the scores obtained on these two parallel forms refers to the reliability coefficient. This overcomes the problems in the technique of test-retest method to a certain extent. But in using the parallel form, it should be ensured that the two tests are truly parallel. The level of difficulty, the content, the procedure of administration, the time limit, the format, the illustrations all should have equivalence, which is very difficult in practice. Thus, many tests available do not have an equivalent form.

   (c) *Split half reliability*: In this technique, one test is divided into two equivalent halves. This can be divided choosing the odd even number, or first half and second half. The division of a test depends on how the items in the test have been arranged. In this procedure the test is administered only once and two scores are obtained by splitting the test in two forms. The reliability coefficient is then measured by the correlation coefficient between the scores of the two half tests.

3. *Validity*: Anastasy has defined 'validity' as "what the test measures and how well it does so. It tells us what can be inferred from test scores."

For example, if people are to be recruited for defence services, the validity of the test depends on whether the test can predict who is suitable for this particular occupation. Validity of a test is measured on the basis of some criteria. If the correlation of the constructed test is high with the criteria, the test is known to have high validity. An aptitude test for pilots can be validated choosing criteria of achievement in flight training. Validity is based on the relationship between the performance and other variables such as behaviour characteristics. Validity of a test has several aspects to it.

(a) *Content validity*: Content validation refers to the extent to which a person has learnt a specific skill. For example, to repair a car, it is necessary to ascertain whether a person knows the details of repairing the car. The content of the test for this purpose should be such that it can measure the ability of a person in repairing the car. The content to measure specific skill or skills should be properly defined and should include the objectives, factual knowledge, application of this knowledge in practical situations, interpretation of data etc..

(b) *Face validity*: 'Content validity' is sometimes misinterpreted as 'face validity' while the two terms are different. 'Face validity' is the relevance of the test to a particular target group or the situation. In other words, the test should be acceptable to the target group. They should feel that the test is not superficial or childish. Test items should be relevant to the cultural ethos of the type of group it is meant for, e.g., the test, which has to be used for recruitment of science teachers, should ask questions relating to science and those eliciting the scientific mind of the examinees. If questions relating to literature are included in this test they would not have any relevance and the test would lose its 'face validity'. It is commonly advised that a test constructed for a particular culture should be adapted before it is chosen for use in another cultural setting.

(c) *Concurrent validity*: Concurrent validity of a test requires that the test scores should be consistent with other test of assessment. For example, if a test of intelligence is correlated with the other available test of intelligence of similar nature, it is known as measuring the concurrent validity.

(d) *Predictive validity*: Predictive validity of a test is measured when the test has to predict the performance for future.

Standardisation of a Test

Whenever the term psychological testing is used, the question of 'standardisation' arises. It is said that while choosing a test to be administered, it should be ensured that it is a standardised test. What is the meaning of standardisation? It is "uniformity of procedure in administering and scoring the test".

For ensuring the uniformity of procedure of administration, detailed instructions for administration of the test should be made available. It includes time duration, sample items, verbal instructions, the material required, conditions, if any. Standardisation implies that all the individuals being tested should receive exactly the same information, directions, examples, time limit.

Norms

For maintaining the uniformity of scoring, the second aspect of standardisation, proper 'norms' should be established. A 'norm' is the average performance with which the individual's performance could be compared. For example, if, on an average, children of 12 years are able to complete 30 items out of 50 on an abstract reasoning test, then the norm for a 12 year's old child would be 30 and the scores obtained by an individual are compared with this norm. The actual scores obtained by individuals are known as raw scores. For establishing such norms of test scores, a test is administered to a large number of persons of a specified age group, educational level, according to the fixed time limit and controlling other variables. The scores are averaged to prepare norms.

Evaluation of a Test Score

Once the norms for a test are available, and a person is administered the test and scored, the question arises as to how the score is to be evaluated. The obvious way to measure the individual's score against a norm is to take the deviation of the score from the norm. For example, if the norm is 'm' and the individual score is X, the deviation is X – m. How to evaluate the magnitude of this deviation? Usually, in distributions based on large number of individuals, the statistical measure called the 'standard deviation' (denoted by 's') can be used to divide the population into sections containing fixed percentage of scores. For example, about 68 per cent of the scores would lie within one standard deviation's distance from the mean (34 per cent on each side). About 96 per cent of the scores would lie within two standard deviation' distance from the mean (48 per cent on each side) and over 99 per cent with three standard deviations' distance.

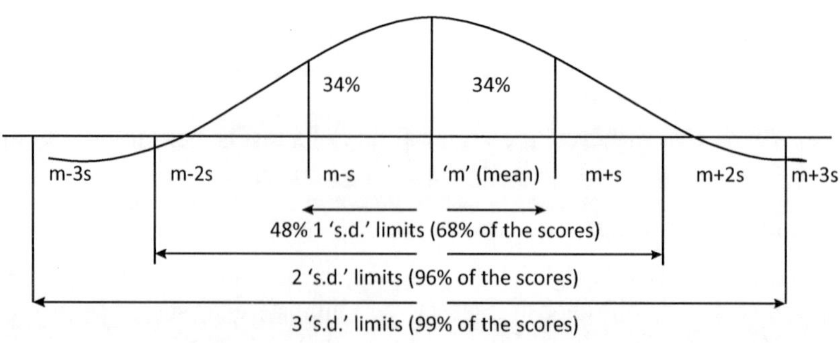

Figure 15.2: *Distribution of Scores*

In view of this, an individual score is evaluated not merely as its deviation from the norm, but as the ratio of the deviation to the standard deviation, as this ratio enables us to evaluate how the deviation observed in the case of the individual compares with the standard deviation and whether the observed deviation can be expected with a high level of probability. This ratio, called the

'Z' score, is $Z = \dfrac{X - m}{s}$.

Thus, from the raw scores obtained by the individuals 'Z' scores are derived. 'Z' scores are amenable to further statistical analysis and interpretation. Statistical tables are available, with the help of which it may be inferred if, for example, an observed 'Z' score can lead to the conclusion that there is no 'significant' deviation from the norm, or whether it is 'significantly' different from the norm.

Statistical Concepts

In evaluating psychological tests, one has to deal with the scores of several (at times thousands) of individuals. These raw scores by themselves do not lead us to any worthwhile conclusion. Questions like "Is there any value around which the scores center, and which can be taken as a representative value of the population's score?" or "Are the individual scores closely packed or are dispersed over a wide range?" arise. The first question is answered by computing what are called 'measures of central tendency'. These measures are:

1. *Mean*: The arithmetic average of all scores. For example, if there are 6 individuals with scores of 60, 30, 70, 80, 40 & 80, the average is (60+30+70+80+40+80)/6 = 60.
2. *Median*: The value of the score, which divides all individuals into two equal groups. Sometimes, there may be more than one such value In the above example, any value between 60 and 70 divides the population into two equal groups, the first group consisting of individuals with scores of 30, 40 and 60 and the second group consisting of individuals with scores 70,80 and 80. In this case, the average of 60 and 70, i.e., 65, is taken as median.
3. *Mode*: The value of the score which is attained by maximum number of individuals. In the present example, the mode is obviously 80.

The example given also serves as an illustration of the problems in using the three measures. The 'mean' is the simplest to understand and amenable to mathematical manipulations, but is influenced by a few extreme values. Median is not affected by extreme cases, but need not be unique. There can be similarly more than one mode. Both median and mode are relatively difficult to handle statistically.

The second question raised above is answered by what are called 'measures of dispersion'. Some measures of dispersion used in the context of testing are standard deviation, range and percentiles.

1. Standard deviation is computed by the formula-

$$s = \sqrt{\frac{1}{n}\sum_{1}^{n}(x_i - m)^2}$$

   where X_i is the individual score of the 'i'th individual, m is the average score of all individuals and 'n' is the total number of individuals. The formula derives standard deviation as the square root of the average of the squares of deviations of the individual scores from the mean.
2. Range of a distribution of scores is the difference between the maximum and minimum of the scores. In the example given above, the minimum score is 30 and the maximum is 80. The range is therefore 50. It may be noted that the Range is dependent only on the minimum and maximum scores and does not take account of the other scores.
3. Percentiles are the levels of scores, which divide the population into fixed, equal percentage groups. For example, 'quartiles' divide the population into four equal groups and 'deciles' divide into ten equal groups. There will be four quartiles Q1,Q2,Q3,Q4 and one- fourth of the scores would be less than Q1, one-fourth between Q2 and Q3, one-fourth between Q3 and Q4 and the remaining one- fourth above Q4. Similarly, in the case of deciles, D1,D2,....D10, one tenth of the individuals have scores less than D1, one-tenth between D1 and D2, and so on, and one tenth above D10.

Uses of Psychological Tests

1. Tests are useful in measuring the individual differences.
2. They can indicate the behaviours of an individual in various circumstances, enabling identification of problems in adjustments.
3. They can identify children with special talents and also the slow learners.
4. On the basis of the psychological tests students may be provided education and vocational guidance, after assessing their suitability to various technical and professional courses.
5. The tests are helpful to the employers to hire employees according to the needs of specific jobs. For example, these tests are used in recruitment in the Defence Services.
6. Similarly tests are helpful to professional educational institutions in their admissions, *e.g.,* in Management courses.
7. The result of the tests may be helpful for the parents in understanding their children better and making a future plan along with their children.

8. The tests results are useful for teachers in understanding the children and preparing remedial plans wherever required. With such an understanding teachers may be able to deal with the child in a better way.
9. Tests provide a foundation for self-understanding, which helps an individual in taking decisions. The emotionally disturbed persons may also be identified through tests for individual counselling.
10. Tests provide data for conducting researches on a number of issues such as developmental process and problems therein, group variations, cultural variations, etc.

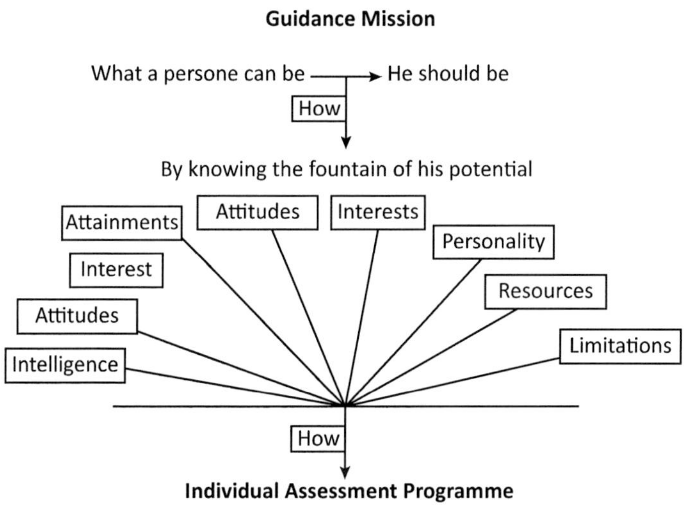

Figure 15.3: *Guidance Mission*

Various types of tests that can be used for assessment are detailed in chapters 16, 17.

16

Intelligence, Aptitude and Achievement Assessment

Intelligence and aptitudes are sometimes used interchangeably, but there are differences in these two terms. While intelligence is the general ability related to one's potential for learning, aptitudes measure specific ability, such as for clerical, mechanical or artistic work. Intelligence was considered to be an innate characteristic that could not be changed while aptitude could be developed and nurtured.

Intelligence Tests

It is common to hear people say 'she is brilliant', or 'he is very intelligent' or 'he is so dull that he cannot understand anything'. What does it mean? What is intelligence?

Various psychologists on the basis of their researches have defined the term. Terman (1921) defined it as the 'ability to think abstractly'. Wechsler (1944), who also developed tests to measure intelligence said that "intelligence is the ability to act purposefully, to think rationally, and to deal effectively with the environment". There are different points of view from which the term may be defined. One view emphasises the role of heredity (organic view) in the individual's attempts to adapt himself to environment. Another view focuses its attention on environment (social view) that influences person's adaptation to environment, and the third view (behaviouristic view), which stresses the importance of the capacities of the individual to adapt himself to the situation. According to this view both heredity and environment play a vital role in determining intelligence. With this concept, intelligence is the 'ability to adapt oneself'. Garrett (1946) defined 'intelligence' keeping its operational part in view and said it is "... the abilities demanded in the solution of problems which require the comprehension and the use of symbols". This definition provides a criterion for intelligent action. More recently Sternberg and Salter (1982) defined it as "a person's capacity for goal-directed adaptive behaviour".

Theories of Intelligence

There are a few theoretical models on which the concept of intelligence has developed.

1. *Sternberg's Information – Processing Model*: Sternberg (1979, 1981, 1982) observed the manners in which people process information to deal with various situations. He listed six steps in the process – Encoding, Inferring, Mapping, Application, Justification and Response. During his research, he found that intelligent people analyse a problem more thoroughly at the initial stage (encoding). He saw that intelligence and speed were not necessarily inter-correlated.

   In this model people can be motivated to devise their own problem solving technique. In this approach, information about facts is important.
2. *Spearman's Two factor Model*: This model is based on the structure of intelligence. On the basis of his experiments, Spearman stated that intelligence is made up of two factors. One is 'g' factor, *i.e.*, general factor and another 's' factor – a collection of specific abilities. He was of the view that every body is endowed with some general intelligence, which is reflected in all his behaviours. Specific factors help in doing some specific activities.
3. *Thurston's Primary Mental Abilities Model*: Contrary to Spearman, Thurston's research and factor analysis didn't find any general factor. He argued that intelligence consists of seven primary abilities. These are verbal comprehension, numerical ability, spatial ability, perceptual speed, word fluency, memory and inductive reasoning. According to him each ability is independent and can be measured independently. To see the overall intelligence of a person, there is a need to measure all seven primary abilities.
4. *Guilford's Structure of Intellect Model*: Guilford conducted researches during the period 1967 to 1982 and based his model of intelligence on factor analysis. According to him, there is no general mental ability but intelligence consists of 150 separate abilities. He believed that each task involves three major intellectual functions.
   (a) Operations – how we think
   (b) Content – what we think about
   (c) Products – applying particular operation to a particular content

Each of the above major functions has numerous sub-functions. Guilford identified 150 such sub-functions

Measurement of Intelligence

(a) In 1905, Simon and Binet devised an intelligence test, which was revised in 1908 and again in 1911. Terman further revised this later in 1916. This revision is known as Stanford-Binet test. The test has been devised to be used at various age levels with varying levels of difficulty. In this revised form, the concept of IQ (Intelligence Quotient) was introduced for the first time. The basic idea behind the scale is that intelligence can be measured through behaviours. The Stanford-Binet test assumes that intellectual ability improves with age. Thus, a child's composite score on the test was his mental level. A 5-year-old child who scores the same on this test as an 8 year-old child scores, is said to have a mental age of 8 years.

Intelligence Quotient: On the basis of the Binet's work, Stanford gave a formula to calculate mental age corresponding to chronological age (actual age of a person). Stanford used the ratio of a person's mental age (MA) to his chronological age (CA) to measure the intelligence level and designated it as Intelligence Quotient (IQ). To avoid the problems of fractions, the ratio is multiplied by 100. Thus, IQ = MA/CA x 100. In the above example, the I.Q. of the child is 8/5 x 100 = 160

To Recapitualte: *Mental age* can be defined as a measure of mental ability defined in terms of the average capabilities of individual at each age. It means his mental ability as distinct from age in years

Chronological Age – Actual age: IQ – Index of intelligence defined as a person's mental age divided by his chronological age multiplied by 100.

(b) *The Wechsler Intelligence Scale*: Wechsler Scale is in three forms, one designed for adults, one for school-age children and one for pre-school children. Wechsler scale has verbal and non-verbal sub-tests. It is possible in this test to have separate scores for the verbal test and non-verbal test and also a composite score.

Both the Binet scale and Wechsler Scale are individual tests and can be administered to one person at a time. There are other tests that can be administered to groups also. Group tests are economical as well as less time consuming. Initially, two tests called Army Alpha test and Army Beta test were developed as group tests. These tests were developed, as their names suggest, to be used for soldiers.

As said earlier, administration of individual test is very time consuming. Verbal tests have cultural bias. Tests have, therefore, been designed, which can be administered to groups and are also free from cultural bias. Some such tests are:

(i) *Raven's Progressive Matrices (RPM)*: This test was designed to measure the 'general' factor of intelligence propounded by Spearman. The test contains abstract design items in the form of matrices. From each of these matrices, a part is missing. Alternatives for this missing part have been provided and the client is asked to choose the correct missing part from the given alternatives. The administration and scoring of the test is simple.

The test is available in three forms. Coloured Progressive Matrices (CPM) is for young children, Standard Progressive Matrices (SPM) is for school children and Advanced Progressive Matrices (APM) is for above average adolescents and adults.

Example of the Test-

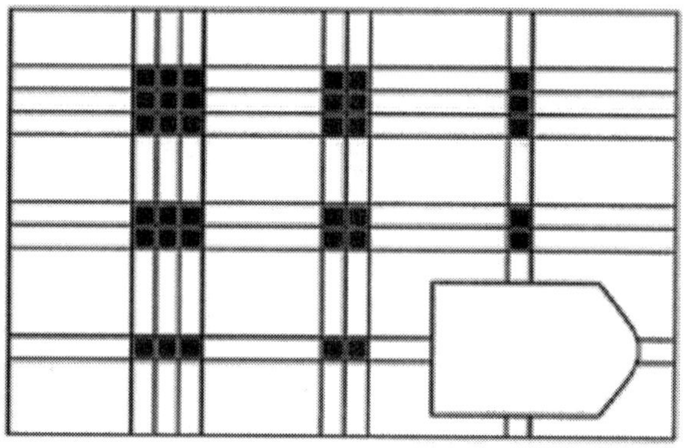

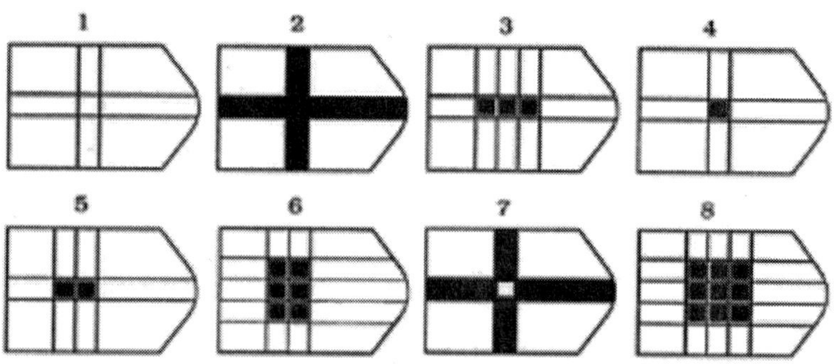

This test is being used widely in Indian schools. Indian norms have also been developed.

(ii) *Bhatia Battery*: Shri C.M. Bhatia developed a performance test of intelligence to be used with the vast illiterate population of India applicable for both rural and urban children. The test contains 5 sub-tests. These are:

1. Koh's Block Design test
2. Pass Along test
3. Pattern Drawing test
4. Immediate Memory test
5. Picture Construction test

The reliability and validity of this test battery has been checked. It is an individual test. The test has been standardised both on rural and urban children and norms have been developed for comparison. The Battery is used in selection of children at primary level.

The MMY series provides evaluative information about various tests for test selection. These volumes are brought out every three years.

To choose a test in the guidance programme, a well-designed test, with high reliability and validity should be taken. Local norms to compare the results should also be available.

How do the intelligence/knowledge level of a student help a counsellor in implementing the guidance programme? Researches have shown that there is high correlation between scores on intelligence test and academic achievements. High scores on intelligence are related to high academic achievements, and *vice-versa.* In case a child is high on intelligence score but not getting good grades in school, he may be identified for counselling. The counsellor should prepare bi-variate charts for each individual to compare the results of intelligence and school grades and monitor the performance after counselling. Through counselling his problem may be identified – it could be family disturbances, lack of concentration, personal problems, etc. A guidance worker may help him to come out of his problem and improve the academic grades. Intelligence tests are also used to predict occupational success but here they should be used in combination with other information and observations. On the basis of the intelligence scores occupational choices can be indicated.

Emotional Intelligence

Wikipedia defines Emotional intelligence (EI) as the ability to perceive, use, understand, manage, and handle emotions. People with high emotional intelligence can identify and accept their emotions as well as those of others. They have ability to manage their thinking and day to day behaviour according to the emotions of self and others. They are also capable to deal with their emotions so as to adjust with the environment around. One can understand the specific behaviours that are affected by emotions. The term emotional intelligence was first used in 1964, but it became popular in 1995 with a book on *Emotional Intelligence*, written by Daniel Goleman. (https://en.wikipedia.org/wiki/Emotional_intelligence - cite_note-2)

Emotional intelligence in schools is important in achieving academic excellence and being a useful partner in a team. High emotional intelligence keeps a person balanced during failures, submitting assignments on time, dealing with various types of students and develop healthy relationships. It can control impulsive behaviours acts of unsocial behaviours.

Emotional intelligence can be measured through tests which include self-reporting tests. Alternatively, a guidance counsellor can administer these tests on the students and can identify problems related to emotions.

Elements of Emotional Intelligence

Daniel Goleman defines the five key elements of EI (see Table 16.1).

Table 16.1: *Elements of Emotional Intelligence*

Elements	*How it helps*
1. Self Awareness	Self-awareness leads to identify what triggers the emotions and how other people re affected by these emotions
2. Self Regulation	This ability can make adjustments in emotions to have positive effect
3. Motivation	Positive emotions create motivation to do something
4. Empathy	With empathy one can understand feeling of others. In a school if a student is feeling stressed due to some or the other reason, the person with empathy can help him easing the stress.
5. Social skills	These help in good communication with others. Good social skills lead to listening and resolving conflicts effectively.

How to Develop Emotional Intelligence

Sometimes emotional intelligence is innate but some other scholars opine that it can be developed also. One can practice the following to develop emotional intelligence:

1. Observe Others: see and observe how others behave in a particular situation and how you react. Compare the two and analyse. Take a decision if you can change your own behaviour. For example, getting low marks in a subject one student can think that he should put more efforts, but the other one may start crying.
2. Introspect: Think and see how your actions are governed by emotions. Sometimes a joke on you can increase the anger within. You analyse if you are impulsive and reactive in your behaviour.
3. Displaying the emotions: Some people are very vulnerable and easily share all their feelings to many people while others may like to manage their emotions on your own.
4. Learnings: Every one has failures in life. Some people always blame others for their failures which minimises the chances to improve themselves. One should learn from their experience and modify.
5. Listening: People react without listening which make them reactive and impulsive over a period of time. Developing habit of listening is important.
6. Others' Perspective: It is always to see how others are feeling. Just describing your own feelings without noticing how other are reacting to it will not help. Understanding body language is also important in seeing others' perspective.
7. Positivity: Create positivity around with positive thinking. Students with positive thinking can solve problem situations very easily.
8. Taking Criticism:

9. Practice being Calm: There are various stressed situations that comes in life for everyone. One needs to practice these situations with a calm mind. Daily exercise, walking, meditation, spending time in hobbies, playing, being with family and friends help in being calm.

Aptitude Tests

Aptitudes are generally known as latent and undeveloped abilities which can be developed through their proper identification and training. In Warren's dictionary aptitude has been defined as "a condition or set of characteristics regarded as symptomatic of an individual's ability to acquire with training some (usually specific) knowledge, skill, or set of responses such as the ability to speak a language, to produce music etc." The definition shows that aptitude is a present indication of skill that is capable of future development.

Taking this definition into account Bingham (1937) defined 'aptitude' as "a condition symptomatic of a person's relative fitness, of which one essential aspect is his readiness to acquire proficiency – his potential ability – and another is his readiness to develop an interest in that ability". Super in 1949 stated that "an aptitude is not necessarily an entity, but rather a constellation of entities; the set of characteristics which enables one person to learn something may even be different from that which enables another person to learn the same thing". Thus Super indicates the unitary character of aptitudes. Hann and MacLeanc (1955) gave a more comprehensive definition of 'aptitude' as "latent potentialities, undeveloped capacities to acquire abilities and skills and to demonstrate achievements".

Thus, aptitudes are latent potentials, which can be developed. With the development of such potential one can acquire and excel in related activity. For example, if a child has potential for music, with training in music he can be a singer, a composer or a music teacher. A child may be found dancing on listening to various musical tunes, or a small child may be able to solve mathematical sums very fast and comfortably. It can be said in the former case that the child has musical aptitude and in the latter case an aptitude for mathematics. If given an opportunity and training both these children may excel in their respective fields.

Basic Characteristics of Aptitudes

(a) Aptitudes are relatively stable for a long time. If a child has aptitude for music, it is relatively consistent throughout his adulthood.
(b) Relative differences in traits can be identified, and measured with accuracy.
(c) Individuals can excel and develop their aptitudes if provided training and an environment to develop themselves. It may be observed that some children who have good aptitudes for art, painting or music, if not encouraged by teachers or parents, loose their aptitudes in the long run.

Objectives of Using Aptitude Tests

(a) To identify individual's potential, of which he is not aware. Thus, these tests help in self-discovery
(b) To develop the special identified potentials.
(c) To help in educational and vocational choice on the basis of specific potentials identified.
(d) To predict academic and vocational success.
(e) To enable grouping of individuals for educational purposes according to their aptitudes.

How to measure aptitudes: A number of tests are available to measure relative strength of aptitudes in an individual that are used by counsellors. The aptitude areas identified are:

1. Verbal Aptitude: whether an individual is able to understand the meaning of words and their related ideas, ability to present ideas through language, comprehend and understand the information or not.
2. Numerical Aptitude: Numerical aptitude relates to the ability to understand and calculate the arithmetic problems with speed and accuracy.
3. Verbal Reasoning: It is the ability to identify the concepts in a text and their inter linkages. It is not the language proficiency but ability to reason, think, read and take out the substance of a written or verbal communication.
4. Clerical Aptitude: Clerical aptitude is the ability to understand details of tabulated material and to observe accuracy in handling words and numbers.
5. Spatial Aptitude: It is the ability to observe two or three dimensional objects.
6. Form Perception: This aptitude relates to the ability to perceive details in graphic or pictorial material and observe similarities and differences in shapes.
7. Motor Coordination: The ability to coordinate eyes and hands.
8. Finger Dexterity: The ability to move fingers to place small objects in right positions with accuracy and speed.
9. Manual Dexterity: It is the coordination of hands to move skillfully so that the work could be performed in a desirable way.

Some examples of classification of aptitudes may be seen in the Tables 16.2a and 16.2b.

A number of Tests and Test Batteries are available to measure various aptitudes. While Test is a single test, measuring a single aptitude, a test battery consists of number of tests, which can measure a number of aptitudes simultaneously. Scores of a test battery provide information about relative strengths of various aptitudes, while a single test can tell whether a person has

Table 16.2a: *Classification of Human Aptitudes and Abilities (By Kelly and Williamson)*

Aptitude or ability and description (By Kelly)*	*Aptitude or ability and description† (By Williamson)*	*Occupational outiets†*
Verbal – Ability to define, understand, and use words as symbols or meaning and experiences.	Verbal and linguistic – Fluency in use of one's own language and facility in learning other languages. Perception of verbal relations	Author, lawyer, professor, minister, editor, advertising copywriter, etc.
Numerical – Ability to manipulate (menially) numbers as symbols of experience or meaning; to solve problems which Involve numbers. Spatial -Ability to think or solve problems (mentally) invoivīng objects and the geometrical forms wnich represent actual objects in space.	Mathematical – Facility with abstract symbols (and relations of cause and effect). Perception of complex number relations. Constructive and mechanical -Perception of spatial relations, facility in designing, calculating, working with machinery, etc.	Mathematics teacher, accountant, statistician, engineer, comptroller etc. Engineer, architect, inventor, toolmaker. printer, etc.
Memory for detail Drill – Routine memorising or learning.	Manual skills – Dextenty in using tools. Skill with hands and fingers, precision in coordinating movements.	Surgeon, dentist, sculptor, artist, skilled mechanic, special skilled trades, etc.
Physical ability – Ability to coordinate large and small muscles; to manipulate objects with speed and precision.	Artistic (inc. musical) – Appreciation of form and color, facility in crafts and in imaginative interpretations	Artist, sculptor, architect, designer, composer, actor, dancer, etc.
Musical – Ability to understand musical forms and to perform on a musical instrument Artistic – Ability to understand form, balance, color harmony, and interpretation.	Social – Sociability, cooperativeness. tact, personal plea sing ness, helpfulness. Scientific – Facility in defining, classifying, grasping principles, inductive relation of rule to example.	Politician, teacher, personnel or social welfare worker, salesman, etc. Research worker, physician, physicist, chemist, geologist, psychologist, etc.
Social – Ability to work with people without friction; leadership	Clerical and commercial – Accuracy and speed in handling numbers, names, systems, and details. Executive – Initiative, self-reliance, ambition, leadership, etc. Practical – Efficiency in practical affairs, calmness under pressure, persistence, courage.	Bookkeeper, credit man, purchasing agent, cashier, clerk. Director, manager, foreman, Inspector, etc. Airplane pilot, sea captain, army officer, surgeon, etc.

* Kelly, T.L., 1929. *Interpretation of educational measurements.*Yonkers, N.Y.: World Book, pp.124-125

† Williamson, *E.G.* 1937. *Students and occupations.* New York: Holt. pp. 31-33.

Table 16.2b: *Classifications of Human Aptitudes and Abilities (By Paterson, Gerken and Hahn)*

*Aptitude or ability and description**	*Levels**	*Occupational outlets**
Academic – The ability to understand and manage ideas and symbols.	Professional, semiprofessional, and executive occupations Technical, clerical, supervisory Skilled tradesmen, low-grade clerical	Lawyers, college presidents, president of a large manufacturing concern, teachers at all levels. Minor executive, or highly technical work, railroad clerks, shop foreman, stenographers. Auto mechanic, stationary engineer, typist
Mechanical – Includes both the ability to manipulate concrete objects – to work with tools and machinery and the materials of the physical world – and the ability to deal menially with mechanical movements.	Professional and higher technological Skilled tradesman, high level Skilled tradesman, low level Semi-and unskilled tradesmen Professional Commerical	Inventive mechanical genius, mechanical engineer, toolmaker. Draftsman, engraver, general automobile mechanic, bricklayer. Boiler maker, tire repairer, cobbler. Wrapper, bench assembly worker
Artistic – Refers both to the capacity to create forms of artistic rnerit and the capacity to recognize the comparative merits of forms already created.	Crafts and mechanical Persuasive – direct or indirect Administrative	Sculptor, artist, teacher, university art teacher. Magazine illustrator, interior decorator, landscape gardener. Potter, draftsman, weaver.
Social – The ability to understand and manage people; to act wisely in human relations.	Business contact and service	Politician, life insurance salesman, minister, social service worker Executives, foreman, lawyer, physician. Sales clerk, information clerk, hotel clerk, telephone salesman.
Clerical – The ability to do rapidly and accurately detail work such as checking, measuring, classifying, computing, recording, proofreading. and similar activities.	Professional and higher technical Technical Routine	Accountant, actuary, statistician, secretary, bank teller Bookkeeper, stenographer, calculating machine operator, railway mail clerk. File clerk, mimeograph operator, retail sales clerk, messenger
Musical – The capacity to sense sounds, to image these sounds in reproductive and creative imagination, to be aroused by them emotionally, to be capable of sustained thinking, to give some form of musical expression	Creative, interpretive, higher professional Technical, lower professional General and mechanical	Composer, concert artist, symphony soloist, teacher in university. Arranger of music, critic, player in dance orchestra. Instrument repairman, music store clerk, factory instrument tester.

* Paterson, Donald G., Gerken, Clayton d'A., and Hahn, Milton E. 1953. The Minnesota Occupational Rating Scales (revised). Minneapolis: University of Minnesota Press.

aptitude for a particular skill or not. Some commonly used tests for measuring aptitudes are:

(a) *Differential Aptitude Test (DAT)*: DAT is a test battery, which can be administered to a group of people at a time. This is a commonly used battery, which is useful for educational and vocational guidance purposes. This battery has 8 sub-tests – Verbal Reasoning, Numerical Reasoning, Abstract Reasoning, Perceptual Speed and Accuracy, Mechanical Reasoning, Space Relations and Spelling and Language Usage. Instructions are available in the tests on how to administer them. Sample items in each sub-test are available to understand the test and practice. This test battery has been updated for computerised testing and is known as CAT.

Shri J.M. Ojha has adapted this Aptitude Test Battery for Indian Conditions also. Norms are available for Indian children.

Sample items from the Indian Adaptation of DAT are given below.

1. Abstract Reasoning

Problem

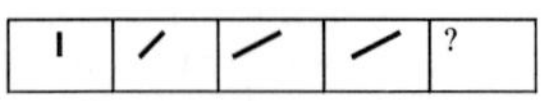

Answer alternatives

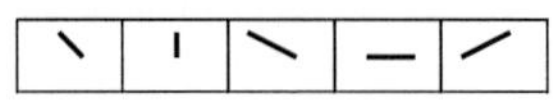

The correct answer is 'd'. a b c d e

2. Clerical Speed & Accuracy:

Underline the same alphabet or number pairs in the answer sheet, which are underlined in question sheet.

Question sheet

AC	AE	AF	AB	AD
BA	Ba	Bb	aA	aB
7B	B7	AB	7A	A7
Aa	bA	bB	Ba	BA
BB	3B	B3	1A	33

Answer sheet

AB	AC	AD	AE	AF
aA	aB	Ba	Ba	Bb
A7	7A	B7	7B	AB
Aa	Ba	bA	BA	bB
3A	3B	33	BB	BB

Some other popular test batteries are General Aptitude Test Battery, which has 12 sub-tests. The Flanigan Aptitude Classification Tests has 19 subjects. Administration of these Tests takes 8 hours.

A number of aptitude tests suitable for Indian population covering various aptitudes are available with norms for comparability.

Scientific Aptitude Test Battery has 4 divisions relating to logic testing, arithmetic ability, scientific information and science vocabulary. Teaching Aptitude Test designed by Dr. S.D. Kapoor measures the aptitude for teaching in 10 areas – cooperative attitude, kindliness, patience, wide interest, fairness, moral character, discipline, optimism, scholarly taste and enthusiasm. Norms have been developed for the test.

Thus, a number of Test Batteries are available, which measure a number of aptitudes and tell their relative strengths. Each of these batteries consists of a series of sub-tests. It is convenient to administer and less time consuming. Comparable set of scores on various aptitudes may be considered to make a judgment. The Differential Aptitude Test Battery, commonly used to measure the aptitudes, in India includes the tests on verbal reasoning, numerical ability, abstract reasoning, space relations, mechanical reasoning, clerical speed and accuracy and language usage. The norms on Indian population are available for this test battery.

Interests Tests

People lose concentration and attention towards an activity as, according to them 'they don't have interest in it'. It is common to hear people say 'I would like to pursue my studies in literature as I am interested in that' or 'I have interest in flying, so I want to be a pilot'. What is interest? These examples show that interests are the motivating factors towards some activities or preferences for doing certain activities.

Super (1949) has defined interests as "the product of interaction between inherited aptitudes and endocrine factors on the one hand, and opportunity and social evaluation on the other". This shows that social approval is required for interest. It would vary from culture to culture.

Strong (1953) was of the view that "since interest involves reaction to specific things, they must all be learned. Accordingly, they may be modified later on by re-education".

Cronback (1949) states that "An interest may be defined a tendency to seek out an activity or object, or a tendency to choose it rather than some alternative".

Interests are thus, determined both by heredity and environment and lead to personal satisfaction. Here it may also be mentioned that the interests may not always be related to individuals' capabilities or aptitudes. One may be interested in music but may not have ability to be a musician.

Characteristics of Interests

1. Interests relate to personality shaping
2. New interests can be created through exposure
3. Preferences may be expressed towards certain occupational activities through a wide range of stimuli
4. Interest may not necessarily be associated with academic or occupational achievement
5. Peer groups, friends and family influence interests.
6. Interests need social confirmation also. Interest in smoking may not develop if the culture disapproves it.
7. Interest patterns are visible at the age of 15and become crystallised at a later age. Some persons are not able to identify their interests, which lead them to change jobs frequently.
8. The interests that are measured through inventories show the needs and motivations of a person. These are not necessarily be reflective of success

in a specific occupation. However, they can predict certain kind of job satisfaction.

9. A number of jobs are available to persons having a particular interest.
10. Interest test results should be seen in combination with the results on personality assessment and aptitudes.

How to Measure Interests

Several methods can be used to measure the interests, such as putting direct questions to the individual, observing the behaviour of the individual and by using interests tests or inventories. Using interests tests or inventories is a more scientific method and is as such more objective.

There are two most popular Interest Inventories known as Kuder Preference Records and Strong Vocational Interest Blanks. Kuder developed a number of interest inventories of which Kuder Preference Record is most commonly used. The interest items in this record are arranged in triads' alternatives from which the most preferred and the least preferred have to be chosen. The results can be used in the occupational choices relating to outdoor activities, mechanical, computational, scientific, persuasive, artistic, literacy, music, social service and clerical. Kuder Inventory is interpreted as 'relative degree of interests' in the given areas.

Strong Vocational Interest Blank was revised as Strong – Campbell Interest Inventory. This has 325 items grouped according to occupations, school subjects, activities, amusements, types of people, preference between activities and personal characteristics. Results can be obtained on a variety of scales through computers.

How a Guidance Worker can use the Interest Test Results

1. Tests may bring out hidden interest, of which a person may not be aware.
2. An individual expresses some interests during conversation. Inventories may confirm these interests, and the results can be utilised to help the student in choosing an educational/vocational stream.
3. When all the results on the psychological tests are analysed, discrepancies among aptitudes, interests, claimed interests and personality may be identified to guide the student in right direction.
4. If the interests are not on desired patterns, counselling can be done.

Achievement Tests

Achievement tests are used to measure the outcome of specific education. These are related to course curriculum. Examinations held in the school system are a kind of achievement test. Achievement can be measured using two types of tests, one the objective type and another the subjective type. The objective type achievement tests have only one correct answer. These can be either in the form of 'True', 'False' answer type, or of multiple choice answer type. Subjective kinds of achievement tests are where a student has to write 'Essay' type answers. Essay type method of measuring achievement is very subjective and scoring depends not only upon the person's understanding, but also the expectations of the person correcting the papers. Such teacher made achievement tests are not standardised.

Attempts have been made to make standardised tests also. Thorndike developed a handwriting scale. After World War II Iowa Tests of Educational Development and the Sequential Tests of Educational Progress were developed. The Iowa test contains 9 objective tests which measure the understanding of social concepts, natural sciences, correctness and appropriateness of expression, qualitative thinking, interpretation of reading materials in social studies, interpretation of reading materials in natural sciences, interpretation of literary materials, general vocabulary, and use of sources of information. This test can be given to IX to XII grade students.

The Sequential Tests of Educational Progress measures critical skills in the areas of essay writing, listening comprehension, reading comprehension, writing, science, mathematics and social studies. The tests are available for various students of various grades.

There are other tests such as Stanford Achievement Tests available in J, K, L, M and N Forms applicable for students of various grades.

A number of Achievements Tests have been developed for Indian students also. Some of these are Mathematics Attainment Test Series, Progress in English, Biology Achievement Test, Statistics achievement etc.

The achievement tests measure the present level of educational status of the student, and are helpful in guidance programme to get the achievement level of the student in different areas. The standardised test scores can supplement the judgements received from the teachers and comparison among the students can be made. On the basis of these test results students may be guided to plan their future course of action or to improve the areas where they are lacking. Tests results may also be used to make prediction for future success in various educational streams.

17

Personality Assessment

Personality is a term, which is used in various ways. Sometimes it is referred to how a person looks, *i.e.,* the outer looks of a person; sometimes it is referred to the manner in which a person behaves. From another point of view, it is the combination of both. Various words are used to type a person such as 'he is lazy', 'he is shy and introvert', 'he is quick tempered', 'he is arrogant', etc. So, let us first define personality. Coleman (1960) defined personality as "the individual's unique pattern of traits, the pattern that distinguishes him as an individual and accounts for his unique and relatively consistent way of interacting with his environment'.

More recently, Mischel (1986) defined 'personality' as what "usually refers to the distinctive patterns of behaviour (including thoughts and emotions) that characterise each individual's adaptation to the situations of his or her life". This is the common theme of various definitions of personality and the emphasis is on individual. The function of personality test is "the measurement of emotional, motivational, interpersonal and attitudinal characteristics, as distinguished from abilities", Aiken (1993), Surger (1993) and Maddi (1989).

Theories of Personality

(a) Trait Theories

Trait theorists believe that personality is the sum of certain traits that each individual has in clusters. Allport said that the pattern of these traits is unique in each individual and it determines his behaviours. He said "bona fide mental structures in each personality that account for the consistency of its behaviour (1937)". This consistency in behaviours is because of the endurance of traits. If the personalities of two persons, one being outgoing and another being introvert, are compared it can be observed that the out-going person would be social, happy go lucky and would make friends easily while the introvert's behaviour would be of shyness. He would not be happy in meeting people. He would be withdrawn and would not socialise. Thus, the traits in one's personality determine his reactions to various situations.

Allport described three major traits – cardinal trait, central trait and secondary traits in personality. The special trait in the personality that makes a person totally different from others and provides uniqueness is known as cardinal trait. Allport is of the view that some extraordinary people have this trait. The cardinal trait can be seen in almost all the behaviours throughout one's life. A child who becomes the monitor of the class since beginning tries to lead in sports and games, instructs people at work place, can be said to have 'leading' as cardinal trait. Central trait refers to major characteristics such as honesty, dependability, cooperativeness etc. These are the general traits of a person. Finally, secondary trait relate to the behaviours in special situations. These traits are less enduring. A person is invited for an interview. He may wear a suit for this purpose but in general he may like to wear casuals. Allport's approach to study the individual is known as 'idiographic' approach. This approach emphasises the study of individuals in depth on some distinctive qualities of their personalities. Another approach, termed as 'nomothetic' approach, propagated by Cattell emphasises the study of personality as studies of groups of people and not as individual. Cattell argued that personality is made of two types of traits – the surface traits and the source traits. He identified some general traits and named them as surface traits. He researched on these surface traits and applied factor analysis and found 16 source traits that he called the care factors of personality. He listed each of these traits as pairs of polar opposites as Reserved/Outgoing, Submissive/Dominant, etc.

Trait theories have been criticised on the ground that they are silent on the issue how the personality develops.

(b) Psycho-analytic Theory

Freud propounded the psychoanalytic theory, which states that personalities of people develop through on-going conflict between their primary drives (sex and aggression) and social pressures, and that early childhood experience are extremely important in the development of the personality.

(i) *Structure of personality*: The structure of personality consists of Id, Ego and Supere go as detailed below :

Structure	*Consciousness level*	*Function*
1. Id	Unconscious	Need immediate gratification of
2. Ego	Predominantly conscious	desires Rational and logical
3. Super ego	Both conscious and unconscious	Idealistic and perfectionist

(ii) *Dynamics of personality*:

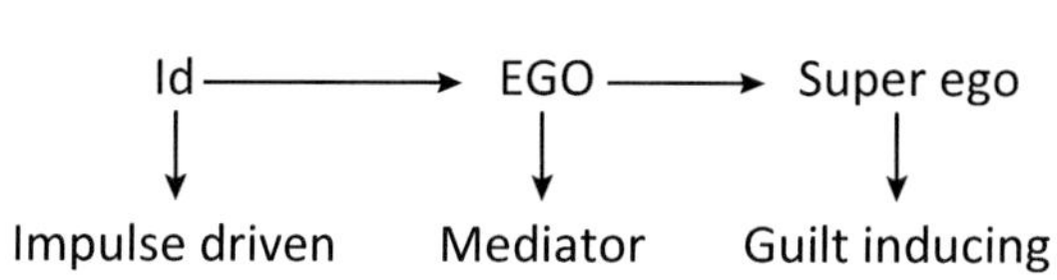

Acting as mediator, ego is pressurised with anxiety by Id and super ego. To release this anxiety, ego uses a number of defence mechanisms to save the personality from disintegration. These mechanisms are repression, rationalisation, projection, displacement, sublimation, regression and reaction formation.

(iii) *Personality development*: Freud was of the view that personality is formed during the first few years of life. He emphasised on psycho-sexual development, which has three stages – the oral stage – (first 12 to 18 months), the anal stage (12-18 months to 3 years) and the phallic stage (3 to 5 or 6 years). He said that during these three phases, a child goes through psychosexual development. If this psychosexual development is not proper, it may influence the adult behaviours. For example, frustration at oral stage may result in verbal hostility. Excessive gratification at this stage where a child is always given milk or a substitute may develop as dependent adult. This situation is termed as 'fixation'.

This theory has been criticised due to its overemphasis on childhood experiences. It is also not clear in stating as to how specific experiences would affect the personality in specific manner. This theory also does not take into account the importance of healthy personalities.

(c) Behaviour Theories

Contrary to the view that internal system shapes the personality, behavioural and social learning theories are based on the concept that environmental events build personality. Skinner, the pioneer of this approach, said that two persons may react to the same situation differently not because of their varying traits or their super egos but because they have different experiences of events in their lives. The reinforcements to certain behaviour or lack of them shape a person's personality. Social learning theorists also believe that events have a cognitive analysis dimension. The role of thoughts, feelings, perceptions in shaping the personalities cannot be ignored. Bandura gave the concept of learning through observing others.

Behaviourist theorists were interested in modifications of behaviours and they concentrated on how the interaction between cognitive factors and environmental factors can result in modifications of behaviours.

These theories have been criticised for overemphasising the role of external factors and ignoring the human dimensions of personalities like spontaneity or creativity.

(d) Humanistic Theories

Humanistic theories believe that each individual is motivated to develop and tries to develop his full potential and capabilities Rogers was the pioneer of this school of thought. He said that congruence between the self-concept and experiences determining the happiness. Maslow's theory of need hierarchy says that people try to achieve highest order need, which is self-actualisation.

Humanistic theories have been criticised as being based on abstract and non-verifiable concepts.

How to Measure Personality

Personality tests are available but one drawback with such tests is that a person may manipulate the answer if he does not want to be honest. In such a situation, the real picture of the personality would not emerge.

Some commonly used tests are:

1. *Mooney problem checklist*: It consists of a series of problems and the person has to identify the problem as most important for him and the least important. This checklist is useful to identify individuals from groups for counselling.
2. *Minnesota multiphasic personality inventory (MMPI)*: In this Inventory, there are 556 statements about behaviour, thoughts, or emotional reactions, which a person rates as 'true', 'false' or 'cannot say'. Hathaway & McKinley prepared the Inventory in 1942. The statements are like 'I am a happy person'. Trained persons should use this Inventory. Generally, this is not used in school settings.
3. *Cattel's 16 personality Factors (16PF)*: As discussed earlier, Cattel's researches on personalities of people show that there are certain surface traits, which occur in clusters. His analysis led a list of 16 primary traits, which he says is the core of personality. He listed these traits in bi-polar method as Reserved/Out-going or Submissive/Dominant etc. On the basis of 16 P F Questionnaire, individual profiles may be developed. This is designed for persons of the age 16 years and above. It provides 16 scores on the trait clusters of social, boldness, dominance, vigilance, emotional stability and rule conscious.
4. *California psychological inventory (CPI)*: This Inventory was developed by Gough. Its format is similar to that of MMPI. There are 15 traits that can be identified in each individual. The Questionnaire has good predictive validity.

The Inventory has been developed to be used with normal adult population.

There are numerous scale Inventories and Tests that measure one or more traits of personality. There are adjustment scales, locus of control scales, anxiety tests, self-esteem inventories, emotional problem measurement scales, leadership traits measurement questionnaire, etc. A number of these scales are available in India, many tests for personality measurement have been adapted and developed for Indian population also, which are available with Indian dealers dealing with psychological assessment tools. Udai Pareek has compiled a number of personality measurement tools in the form of books, which may be consulted for detailed information.

Projective Techniques to Measure Personality

Projective techniques to measure personality have been developed to delve into the unconscious thoughts and feelings of a person. As explained by *Anastasy*,

"It is expected that the test materials will serve as a sort of screen on which respondents 'project' their characteristic thought processes, needs, anxieties, and conflicts." The purpose of the projective technique is to measure the whole personality and not any specific trait.

Strong defined projective technique as a "method of understanding the inner world of the individual." Murray said that "The purpose of this procedure is to stimulate literacy creativity and thereby evoke fantasies that reveal covert and unconscious complexes. The test is based on the well- recognised fact that when a person interprets an ambiguous social situation, he is apt to expose his own personality as much as the phenomenon to which he is attending."

Several methods are in use to know the personality through projective methods. Two most popular tests are Rorschach Inkblot Test and Thematic Apperception Test (TAT). The Inkblot Test was developed by Rorschach (1921). There are 10 cards in this test with inkblots in them. During the administration of this test the client is shown the cards, one by one, and is asked to tell what he sees in the card. The psychologist also records duration of response, remarks, emotional expressions and other non-verbal clues. A system to analyse the responses received from the client has been given in the Manual Sample of design. A sample of this test may be seen as follows:

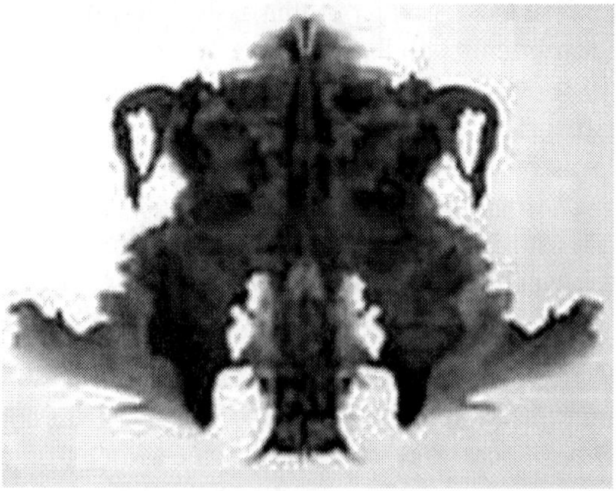

Figure 17.1: *Samples from Rorschach Test*

(a) *TAT*: TAT was developed by Henry Murray in 1938. The test has 20 cards having pictures of various situations. Out of these 20 cards, one card is blank. The client is asked to interpret pictures in the cards in a story form. Here the pictures are more structured in comparison to Rorschach test. After the administration of the test, a procedure to analyse the results has been given which is based on content analysis.

This test is popularly used in clinical settings. Many adaptations of TAT have been made.

A sample from the test:

Figure 17.2: *Samples from TAT*

(b) *Children's apperception test (CAT)* developed by Bellak is used on children. The methodology is similar to that of TAT, the difference being that TAT is used for adult population. Indian adaptation has been done by Dr. Uma Chowdhary.

(c) *The Rosenzweig picture – Frustration study*: This technique is different from TAT and Inkblot tests. Here free play of fantacies is not allowed. It requires simpler response from the clients. It is available in two forms – the first for children aging 4-13 and the other for adults of age 14 and above. This test provides a series of cartoons in which one person poses a frustrating situation to another. The client has to tell what the other person would say in reply to the frustrating situation. This test is relatively more structured and the scoring procedure has been explained.

Besides these popular tests, several other techniques are used. Galton (1879) introduced "Free Association Test" which is also known as 'Word-Association Test'. Under this technique some words are told to the client one by one and he is asked to respond to it by giving any other word, which comes to his mind after listening to this word. This technique is being used to study the thought processes. It is also used for clinical purposes. Sometimes clients are asked to use the word in sentences and the way they use the words may be analysed to assess their personality characteristics. This technique is a verbal projective technique, which requires language skills. For example, if the word said is 'snake', the client can answer by saying 'poison', 'pretty', 'scares', etc., or for sentence completion, if the word is 'accident', the client may use it as – 'I saw an accident, victim died', 'Accidents on road are very common', 'I met with him accidentally'. When given a series of words either for making the sentences or for responding by another word, the full picture of the personality emerges – the complexes, the positive-negative thinking, the anxiety, etc.

Another verbal technique is 'sentence completion test'. In this test, half a sentence is already there and client is supposed to complete the sentence. There can be several possible answers to complete the sentence. For example, the sentence may be "My brother...". To complete the sentence, one may say 'is lively', 'is cruel', 'is not good', 'beats me', 'loves my sister more than me'. The type of sentence the client uses is expected to reveal his internal feelings and thoughts.

Both word Association Tests and Sentence Completion tests have been standardised.

Drawing and Painting

Drawing and painting technique is known as performance technique of projective method. This activity provides a platform for self-expression. This technique is generally used with children. Machover (1949) test of Draw-a-Person Test is very popular. In this test the child is asked to make a picture of a person on a paper. After completion of the picture if the picture is of a female, the child is asked to draw a picture of a male. After he completes the drawings, the child may be asked certain questions about the pictures he has made. The procedure for analysis has been detailed in the test, which is qualitative.

The other tests of this kind are House-Tree-Person technique where the child has to draw pictures of a house, a tree and a person, and Kinetic Family Drawing, where the child has to draw the picture of the family along with himself doing something. Emotional problems, internal conflicts, family adjustment indicators may be worked out through these tests.

Play Techniques

The toy tests where dolls, puppets, and other playing material used are also a kind of projective technique. The play material should be such that with it the person can associate himself. Psychologists have standarised such play material. Playing with toys tells about the child's feelings about his fears, attitudes towards siblings, family, and the problems he is facing. Which toy the child opts for and what he does with it is to be observed in this test. His non-verbal clues are also observed while he plays with the objects.

All the projective techniques provide generally qualitative data. Only a person with psychology background and well trained in using these techniques and interpreting the results should use it. Personal bias may affect the scoring and interpretation.

These techniques are useful as it is easy to form a rapport with the client. Information about the children can be derived easily with these techniques, which may be difficult with paper-pencil tests. Moreover, the clients would not be able to manipulate the responses under this technique as they can in self-reporting methods.

How to Use Personality Tests in Guidance

1. The tests can help in identifying the students who have adjustment problems.
2. They can help the students in assessing their suitability to various occupations. For example, a student with shy and introvert personality would not be suitable for jobs that require dealing with the public.
3. Personality tests may help the individuals in knowing their weaknesses. They can overcome some of these through special efforts.
4. Students may know their strengths and utilise them in proper channels.
5. Tests can help the students in identifying the reasons for their poor academic performance, as this may be related to their emotional handicaps.
6. Choice of educational stream may be made according to the personality characteristics.
7. Leisure time activities may be chosen suiting to the personality.
8. Ultimately, personality tests help a person in self-understanding, self-acceptance and self-realisation.

Administration of Tests

(a) *Who should administer*: A properly trained person with psychology background only, should administer the tests.

(b) *How the tests should be administered*: The counsellor should make the necessary preparations before the administration of tests. He should orient the students about the testing programme. He should decide which tests are to be given and at what level of difficulty, and whether it would be an individual testing programme or a group testing. The purpose of the assessment should properly be explained to the clients. The material such as booklets, answer sheets, pencils etc. should be kept ready and counted. The counsellor should be well versed with the instructions and examples to be explained that are given in the test.

(c) *General conditions to administer the test*: The counsellor should ensure a congenial environment where students could feel easy in taking the test programme. The place should be free from noise. It should have proper arrangement for ventilation, lighting, etc. Seating arrangement should be adequate for each student. To stop interruptions during the testing programme, a board 'Don't disturb', may be placed outside the room where the testing is on.

The students should be in proper mental and physical frame. If they have any pressures, *e.g.,* if they have to appear for some subject test soon after the psychological testing, it would affect their performance on these tests. Similarly, they will not do well in the test if they are sick.

To reduce the anxiety among students, the counsellor should form good rapport with them before administering the test.

(d) *Considerations for selection of test:*
- Purpose and target group
- What information is required
- Duration of test
- Test's reliability, validity and availability of norms
- Cost of test
- Scoring is easy or difficult
- Availability of information for interpretation. Objectivity in interpretation.

(e) *How to Communicate the test results*: Communication of test results is important as well as a delicate issue. Results can be useful for students, teachers as well as for parents in decision-making. Before communication of the results the counsellor should fully understand the purpose of the psychological assessment programme and limitations of various tests. The students, teachers and parents should be made familiar with the vocabulary used to interpret the test results. When to communicate the test results should be kept in mind. Results, specially when the results are not encouraging, should not be communicated at the time when students are preparing for some annual examinations. In case students or parents do not show much interest in the results, counsellor should not insist upon communicating the results.

Tests results should be communicated in such a manner that they do not lead to the development of negative self-concept or an individual gets demotivated. While communicating the test results it should be made clear that the test results show the present status of the child and the prediction of immediate future, and that as the child grows, many aspects may change in the long run. Some sensitive children may get emotional after knowing many things about themselves after the communication of test results. Counsellor should be able to handle such emotional reactions.

The test results should be authenticated with the information received from other sources also.

The results of the child should be communicated to parents in such a manner that it facilitates understanding of the child. The results should not disappoint the parents and should not lead to their exerting undue pressure on the child to act in a directed manner.

Similarly, the results should be told to teachers to facilitate proper handling of the student or planning remedial programmes in the weak areas of achievements.

18

Assessing Students without Using Tests

All the information about the total life of individual cannot be obtained only through psychological tests. Therefore, the guidance workers have to adopt a number of other techniques as well to gather information about the individual. Such non-testing techniques have, however, limitations as they are of qualitative nature, the results cannot be quantified. Therefore, they have an element of subjectivity in interpretation of data. Moreover, the guidance workers' mindset may also get reflected in the information collected through non-testing techniques. It is always better to use more than one technique and source to collect the information and organise the same in its totality. Information collected through various techniques may be verified from each other.

Non-testing techniques may be of the following types:

(a) Self-reporting
(b) Observational
(c) Socio-metric

Self-Reporting Methods

(i) Autobiography

Autobiography is a personal account of individual, in which he records about himself, his frustrations, tensions, goals, aspirations, etc. It helps the counsellor because, due to the paucity of time, it may not be possible for the counsellor to give time to each and every student to collect his life history. This autobiographical record may be had through obtaining his personal diary or through structured questionnaire that the students may fill. This can be given as a class assignment or as homework. When it is given as a class assignment, there may be obstruction to spontaneity. It is always better that students write it comfortably outside the school premises. The students may be asked to write their biographies in two ways. One way is to provide basic outlines of what is to be written and the second option is to ask them to write freely whatever relevant information they can think of. For dealing with the emotional problems of the students, the second option is always better, while in educational, vocational services, the structured autobiography may be obtained.

Autobiographies may be helpful in understanding the past experiences of the individuals, their environment, their friends circle, etc. In this process, the students should be assured that their writings would be used only for professional purposes. The autobiographical information may be verified with the students through further interviews or other sources to check the reliability and validity of the information.

Sample of Guidelines for an Autobiography

Write about yourself

1. Your schooling and academic achievements
2. Your strengths and weaknesses
3. Your likes and dislikes
4. Your family and friends
5. Your interests and hobbies
6. Your goals
7. Your problems and frustrations
8. How you deal with your problems
9. Who helps you in need – support system?

The above format may be modified according to the purpose and need of the student.

How to Analyse Autobiographies – A Sample Format

1. Identify important and relevant incidents
2. Support system available with the child or lack of it
3. Expression – whether there are certain omissions. If yes deliberate or inadvertent, the depth of expression, the tone.
4. Organisation of thoughts
5. Indicative problem
6. Verifiable information
7. Observations and comments

The limitation of this technique is the difficulty of expression through writing. Moreover, if a child does not want to disclose some information, he may mislead. To seek attention and sympathies from the counsellor, the student may record events that have never happened. It may also be difficult for the student to remember all the facts.

(ii) Self-Assessment

In this technique, the student is asked to indicate his strengths and weaknesses. He can also indicate the problems he is facing at home or in school.

It is generally observed that many people record only their plus points and do not mention their weaknesses. Some children with low self-esteem always mention about their inability in doing things.

The counsellor may look into the real problem of the child and verify the reported information from other sources.

(iii) Essays

Essay writing is a kind of self-reporting method, which resembles autobiographies. But while autobiographies are direct and the child has to write about his own background, essays can be on various topics. In essays, the client may reflect some of his feelings, which he otherwise does not want to disclose. The topics of the essay may be 'If I become a teacher', 'Importance of friends in life', etc. Such topics motivate a child to think also. He can imagine instead of giving only factual information as in the case of autobiography.

Observational Method

Assessment of people through observing their behaviours comes very naturally to all. All of us observe others and draw conclusions about them. This is a popular technique in guidance also. Teachers and the counsellor observe the behaviour of students in natural atmosphere and reach certain conclusions. These observations may be structured, where the students may be asked to do certain activity, or unstructured where observations are made about the students in their normal daily routines.

It is important to note here that drawing conclusion through observing a person during one incident is not appropriate. It is necessary to make observations over a long time in varying situations and circumstances with varying groups. Observations thus made should be verified with information from other sources. The totality of the situation should also be kept in mind. For example, if a person is showing aggressive behaviour, the situations where he is aggressive should be analysed properly before aiming at any definite conclusion. To reach any conclusion his behaviour should be observed in more than one situation. For structured observations, a number of techniques have been developed.

(i) Anecdotal Record

Randall has defined Anecdotal record as "A record of some significant item of conduct, a record of an episode in the life of the student, a word picture of the student in action... a word snapshot at the moment of the incident: any narration of events in which the student takes such a part as to reveal something which may be significant about his personality".

Anecdotal record is a useful instrument where the behaviour of a student is observed during some specific incident in which the student was also a party. It is also called a word picture because the person who observes the behaviour of the student describes the incident to show the real picture of his behaviour. The teacher may provide such records to the counsellor to understand the student better. The reporting person should be very clear and free from prejudices. He should not confuse between the facts and his own feelings. The purpose of anecdotal record is to narrate the behaviour of the student during the incident. Anecdotal records are used in combination of various other techniques.

Moreover, there should be a series of anecdotes at different timings. Only one incident cannot describe the behaviour of a person.

Anecdotal reports may be prepared in a given format.

A Sample Format of Anecdotal Report

1. Name of the Student
2. Class
3. Observation made by with date
4. Place where observation was made
5. Narration of the Incident
6. Situational details and setting
7. Any triggers identified
8. Observations of the observer
9. Comments from the observer
10. Recommendations

Such records about the individual should be maintained and collated for integration and guidance. This kind of behaviour observation may provide clues about the individual's relationship with peer group, with teachers, his aspirations and motivations, aggression, fears etc.

It is not possible to record anecdotes for each and every student. It has to be considered carefully as to who should be chosen and why. At primary level a teacher can identify a child who does not speak or at secondary level child can be identified who is a slow achiever. Anecdotes may be written about those children, who are difficult to understand during normal interactions.

Example

Name :	Miss Anita Singh
Class :	X
Observation made by	Mrs. Sushma Acharya, Games teacher
With date	on 10.9.04
Place where observation made	– Hockey ground
Narration of the incident –	While playing with the group, and situational details she was looking withdrawn. When she was unable to listen to the call of another girl Nina to pass the ball, the Nina commented What's wrong with you'?

On this Anita hit the other girl with her hockey stick.

Triggers identified:

(a) Anita was upset due to some reason.

(b) Comment of Nina hurt her and triggered her mental state.

Observations and Comments from the teacher:

Anita is good in sports. She is always cooperative and helping. She remains smiling while playing.

Recommendations: Guidance worker should find out the reason of such behaviour from Anita and provide help.

(ii) The (Problem) Checklist

Checklist method in observation is used when the purpose of the counsellor is to identify certain specific personality characteristics in a student. The list of traits is provided to the observer and he has to tick the trait, which he observes the individual to have. For example the traits may be hardworking, calm, decision maker, irritable, etc.

Example

Problems: A girl has mental ability. She is studying in IX standard. Her academic achievement is not upto mark.

Checklist:

- Concentrates in the class
- Takes notes
- Brings the books and note books to the class
- Irritable or calm
- Aggressive
- Talks with classmates during the class
- Writes something in the class
- She is hardworking
- Attentive to the lectures
- Takes interest in the subjects.

The above checklist would provide information about the listening and learning methods of the girl in the class, her characteristics whether she is hardworking and laborious. Analysis of what the real problem is can be made in the light of the fact.

(iii) Rating Scales

Rating scales may also be used as instruments for observation, Rating scales provide comparability of observations. These scales may be designed according to the purpose. Observations on a particular characteristic can be rated on 5 or 7 point scale.

Example

Purpose: To observe maladjustment with the peer group.

Items:	*Never*	*Rarely*	*Sometimes*	*Often*	*Always*
• Talks with the classmate sitting next to him					
• Talks with other classmates					
• Shares his things with others					
• During lunch time eats food all alone					
• During recess plays with others					

While Anecdotal records are 'observer descriptions', the Rating Scales are 'observer evaluations'. The Rating scales also provide information about the degree of the characteristics.

How to prepare Rating Scales: For preparing a Rating Scale, one should list out the characteristics that are to be rated. These could be self-confidence in the student, self-dependence, industriousness, cheerfulness, helping attitude. Each characteristic should be well defined and be understood by the Rater. Moreover, only such characteristics should be chosen that are relevant and observable in the given situation. In a school situation where teachers are supposed to rate a student's 'love for siblings' would not be an observable characteristic.

A few things should be kept in mind before making a Rating Scale.

(a) It should be free from prejudices and subjectivity. This difficulty may be overcome by choosing more than one Rater.

(b) Some observers have a tendency to rate a person at one point on all the characteristics. This is known as 'halo effect'. For example, the Rater may rate a student as excellent on all the characteristics. This does not give the real picture about the person. In such cases, more than one student may be rated on one characteristic, then on another, and so on.

The problems of rating scales may be lessened if the Rater is also asked to support his Ratings with justifications.

Follow up: Follow up was done after 15 days. Teacher reported a little improvement in the child. The child also reported better adjustment with the school environment.

Sociometric

The socio metric technique is used when information is required on how a person perceives himself and others in the group *That means* which members in the group are near to him and who are at a distance. This tells about the relationship of the person among peers; the leader in the group and the atmosphere. Whether the person is a rejected lot or he is accepted in the group.

In this technique, children are asked to name two or three of their peers, with whom they would like to work. Sometimes they are also asked to name those with whom they may not like to sit or work. This kind of technique is used where adequate group activities and interaction among people is there. Information, thus, collected provides clues on the patterns of interactions among individuals.

Moreno J.L., has defined sociometry as "the mathematical study of psychological properties of populations; the experimental technique of, and the results obtained by, application of quantitative and qualitative methods". Sociometry is a study of feelings, which come out spontaneously through this technique.

Example: Suppose there are 7 students (A, B, C, D, E, F and G). Each of them is asked to name three others in the group with whom they prefer to work, in the order of preferences – as first preference, second preference and third preference.

The following table shows how each of them indicated their preferences.

Table 18.1: *Relationship Preferences*

	About their relationship with others						
Selector/selected	*A*	*B*	*C*	*D*	*E*	*F*	*G*
A	–	1	2	–	–	3	–
B	–	–	2	1	–	–	3
C	2	–	–	1	3	–	–
D	3	2	–	–	–	1	–
E	1	–	–	2	–	–	3
F	–	1	–	–	3	–	2
G	1	–	3	–	2	–	–

For example, A indicated B as his first preference, C as second preference and F as third preference. Similarly, G's first preference is A, second preference is E and the third preference is C.

The following chart indicates the first choices of each of the seven students through arrows. For example, A's first choice is B, B's first choice is D, D's first choice is F. F's first choice is B, and so on. The number of times each student is picked up by his peers as their first choice is indicative of the student's popularity. In this example, there are 3 students A, B and D who are the first choices of two others (maximum number) and so may be considered as more popular than the other four.

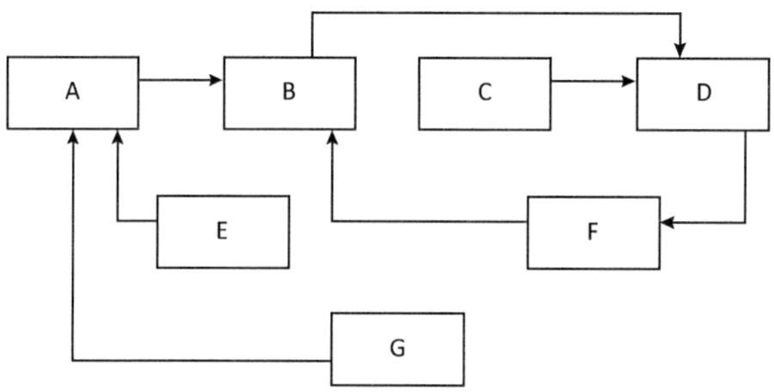

Figure 18.1: *Relationship Preferences*

The study may be made more comprehensive by including not only the first choices but the second and the third choices as well. The following diagram depicts the complete situation — simple → arrow indicating first preference, curved arrow indicating second choice and scribble line arrow suggesting the third choice. For combining all the preferences of each individual, it would be necessary to assign some sort of weights to each preference. For example, first choice may be assigned 5, second choice may be assigned 3 and the third choice 1. To obtain a combined score for an individual, the number of times he has chosen as first, second or third preference is multiplied by the respective weight and added.

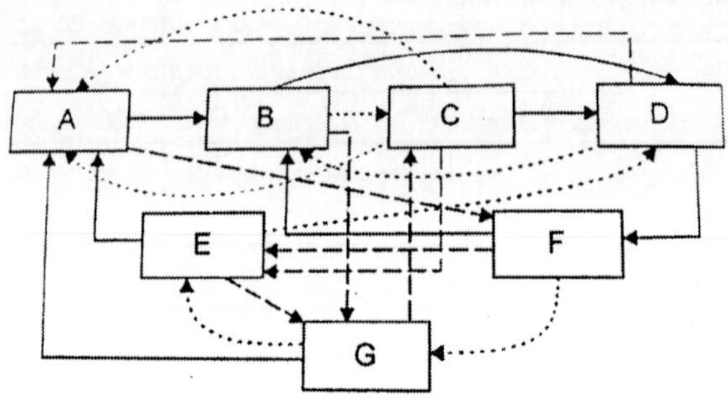

Figure 18.2: *Sociometric Presentation*

For example, A is chosen twice as first choice, and once each as second and third choice. The combined weighted sum of choices would be $2\times5 + 1\times3 + 1\times1 = 14$. In this manner, the following table may be generated:

Table 18.2: *Choices in Sociometry*

Student	*No. of others choosing him as*				*Sum of weighted choices*	*Rank based on*	
	First Choice	*Second Choice*	*Third Choice*	*Total*		*No. of times chosen*	*Sum of weighted choices*
(1)	(2)	(3)	(4)	(5)	(6)	(7)	(8)
A	2	1	1	4	14	1	1
B	2	1	–	3	13	2	2
C	–	2	1	3	7	2	4
D	2	1	–	3	13	2	2
E	–	1	2	3	5	2	6
F	1	–	1	2	6	3	5
G	–	2	2	4	8	1	3

For interpretation of the results, one could go either by the ranks on the basis of the number of times a person is chosen irrespective of the order of choice (Col. 7 of the table) or on the basis of the sum of weighted choices (Col.8 of the table). Each has its own limitation. While the rank based on simple number of times chosen ignores the orders of choice, the combined weighted sum depends on the subjectively chosen weights. However, if there is sufficient justification for the weights chosen, the latter is a more comprehensive indicator on one's popularity. In the present example, it may be observed that, whatever may be the method followed 'A' ranks above all the other six.

Non testing techniques are very useful in understanding child's behaviours and causes reflecting specific behaviour.

19

Information Needs and Maintenance of Guidance Records

Guidance is not a one-time affair. As has been discussed earlier, it is a continuous process. It is, therefore, extremely necessary to maintain records properly and adequately so that whenever needed, the necessary records could be referred to. Records are to be kept about the child, the resources available in and outside the school, the referral services, the information about educational and vocational facilities.

Records Needed

Registers

The counsellor should keep one register each for each of the services provided by him/her. For example, registers for class talk, psychological assessment, educational guidance, vocational guidance, personal or social guidance, group activities, career conference etc. should be maintained separately. For recording the data various columns may be prepared in the register. For example, in class-talk register following data should be recorded:

(a) Class & Section—e.g., V, VII or VIII
(b) No. of students attended
(c) Topic of the talk
(d) Date and time of delivery
(e) Follow up, if any
(f) Remarks & signatures of the counsellor.

An Action Plan

The counsellor should prepare an Action Plan for the academic year which should be displayed in advance. It should be class-wise and activity wise, indicating the resources required, the schedule of sessions etc.

Record of Resources Available Outside the School

The counsellor after mapping the resources should maintain a detailed record of resources available outside the school. These resources can be hospitals, clinics, therapy centres, gyms, places of equipment and appliances needed for children with disability, vocational training centres, places of historical and cultural importance in the vicinity, libraries, the recreation centres and so on. Records of these should indicate the name of the organisation, address, the contact person and his contact telephone number, e-mail, timings the distance of places from the school and other rules and regulations if any.

Cumulative Record Card (CRC)

The maintenance of Cumulative Record Card has been discussed in detail in the Chapter 'Guidance Services in School', which may be referred to. All the information relating to each child can be maintained through CRCs and updated as and when needed. These provide an important base for guiding the child and monitoring the progress. Data collected from various sources can be maintained in CRCs. The information about the child's environment, his home, his behaviours, his weaknesses and strengths are available at one place. On the basis of the information available in CRCs, the gifted, the slow-learners, the first- generation learners, the problem child etc. can be identified and helped. It can also be used as a tool while interacting with teachers, parents and peers whenever needed. CRCs can be transferred from one school to other if the child leaves one school and joins another. Maintenance of CRC should start from the very beginning i.e. at the time when child takes admission in the school. It should be upgraded with each class or with each set of new data coming up about the child. In cases of certain students, updation has to be done on a regular basis. For example, in case of under-achievers, progress has to be monitored on weekly or monthly basis and this should be recorded.

CRCs are maintained by the guidance worker or by teachers or Class Teacher. Who-so-ever is maintaining CRC, should be provided a proper training in filling and maintaining CRC. If a guidance worker has to maintain the CRC in the school, he has to take help from teachers and other authorities. An orientation of all concerned is necessary in this regard. Some precautions should be taken while maintaining CRCs and in using them. The information should be collected using more than one source to make it unbiased. Information collected from testing and non- testing techniques should be collated at one place, screened and necessary information only should be entered in CRC. It should be complete so that it could be used for guidance purposes. Doubtful information should not be entered till it is verified.

If the school has a computer, CRC should be maintained using a computer as updating the information is easy through computers.

Pupil Information Blank

As it has been said elsewhere, child is a good source of providing information. This information can be collected asking the child to write essays, or his autobiography. Another method can be a direct method, which involves preparation of a Pupil Information Blank, which can be distributed among students for filling. Pupil Information Blank can be culled out from CRC. Guidance worker should see what information in the CRC can be given by the child. The points on which child can provide information should be kept in Information Blank.

While analysing the information, it should be kept in mind that the child would be providing only his own opinion, which may not be factually correct.

Record of Psychological Assessment

Counsellors are supposed to maintain the record of psychological assessment programme. This information may not be entered in CRC in great details. Therefore, it is necessary to keep the details of the psychological assessment separately indicating which tests were used and when. Observations of the counsellor should also be recorded while interpreting the results.

Record of Educational and Vocational Information

Since the guidance worker has to make the student familiar with the world of work from the very beginning, he should collect information about various openings available for various streams, the training opportunities available, information regarding preparation for entrance examinations, apprenticeship training etc. and record them properly. Recording of such information is possible though preparation of posters, charts, small booklets, brochures which can be utilised by children. In case the information is voluminous, it should be arranged properly. For arranging such information, several methods can be used such as arranging these alphabetically, by level of education, by interest, by industry etc.

Besides the above, counsellor should also keep a record of meetings convened by him with teachers or parents or other experts; stock register, expenditure register and other day to day work record.

Wherever computers are available, they would be a good means for storage and quick retrieval of educational and vocational information.

Principles in Developing a Guidance Record System

A good record system should have the following:

Maintenance of guidance record is extremely important. Guidance is a continuous process. Various records are to be maintained including Cumulative Record Card resources available in and outside school, various registers for guidance service organized, pupil information, etc. Principles in developing a guidance record system includes usability, objectivity, continuity, purposefulness, etc.

Kinds of Information Needed for Guidance

Because of the vast changes in and expansion of the world of education and world of work, the decision-making process has become difficult and complex. Wrong decision in the choice of the educational stream and/or career may cost anyone a lot of money, time, energy and happiness. To make right decisions at the right time is the need of the day, which can be made only if supported by a proper information management system. Career information is the foundation

Table 19.1: *Developing Guidance Records*

Principles	*Details*
Usability	Record should be simple, neat and clean and to the point so as to increase their usability
Objectivity and Accuracy	Information recorded should be unbiased and accurate. It should be updated from time to time.
Continuity	Record must reflect the inter-connectivity of the information. They should show causes, trends, results and outcomes of an activity
Availability and Systemization	Records should be easily available when needed. Data should be recorded systematically
Efficiency	An efficient record system not only updates the data without delay but also increases its utility. Wherever possible computer should be used to record data.
Purposefulness	Record maintenance should be purposeful and to the point. Unnecessary information may increase the workload of the recorder as well as the user
Verifiability	Records are to be verified from time to time specially records of equipment, guidance tools, finances etc. Thus, these should be maintained in a manner which are easy to be verified.

of the career guidance programme. Hoppock has rightly pointed out that "choice always involves knowledge, one cannot choose what one does not know... the wise choice of an occupation requires accurate information about what occupations are available, what they require and what they offer." If a question is put to a small boy or girl of 3rd or 4th standard as to what he/she would like to be, his/her answer probably would be—a milkman, or a teacher or a gardener and so on. The reason is that they know only about these simple occupations they come across in everyday life. As they grow up, their choices change not because of growing but because they receive more and more information about the world of work. There is today an enormous variety of educational streams, skill development avenues and occupations, each requiring its own preparation and each having its own opportunities. The scene is getting increasingly complex day by day with innumerable number of specialisations in each field. Thus, it would almost be impossible to organise a guidance programme unless there is a strong information system.

Specific Need for the Information

(a) There are gaps in the information available and information required. Moreover, career information is not a one-time activity. As the educational and occupational scene changes, more information would be required. Therefore, a continuous collection of information is necessary

(b) As discussed earlier, one of the major services of a guidance programme is 'Pupil Information Service' where collection of information becomes a pre- requisite.

(c) To organise group guidance activities and also the individual guidance information is required. For example, if a guidance worker wants to organise career exhibition cum career conference, information is required to prepare posters and charts, career films etc.

Objectives of Career Information

Some of the basic objectives of collecting career information for a guidance programme are as follows:

- To help students in understanding, comparing and analysing various occupations and assessing their own potentials.
- To assist students in choosing a right field of education on the basis of the information
- To help in developing appropriate attitudes towards various kinds of occupations
- To provide a clear picture of various fields of occupations in terms of the actual working conditions, life style associated with each occupation, working hours, etc.
- To familiarise students about the various problems they may face in choosing an educational stream or a career.
- To analyse and provide information about the future trends and prospects of various careers.
- To provide information about the demands of various jobs and supply of people for the same and if there are any surplus or shortage categories of occupations.
- To give information about the financial aspects of pursuing a career.
- To assist the students in developing tentative career plans.
- To keep a watch on labour market changes and provide information to schools for modifications in course content as well as to students to amend their career plans, if necessary.

Sources of Information

There can be two types of sources of information. One can be the direct or primary source, *i.e.,* discussions with the employers, industries and collection of primary data, and, another the secondary source, *i.e.,* the published material. The information from secondary sources is available from:

1. *Career Publications*: A number of agencies – governmental as well as private are producing career literature. Some of these agencies are Central Institute for Research and Training in Employment Services (CIRTES), Employment Exchanges, State Directorates of Employment, National Council for Educational Research and Training, University Bureaus and private organisations like – YMCA, YWCA, Publishers, Newspapers, etc. Recently, many of the career publications of CIRTES have been placed on the official website of Ministry of Labour and can be accessed by anyone.

2. *Other Publications*: Other publications for career information include various magazines and journals such as Economic and Political Weekly, Yojana, magazines, Employment News, etc.
3. *Reports of Ministries and Other Departments*: Institute of Applied Manpower Research brings out a Manpower Profile which provides the overall statistics about labour market. Technical Manpower Bulletin of the Council of Scientific and Industrial Research, Reports from Ministry of Education, Ministry of Employment, UPSC, handbooks from Association of Indian Universities, Ministry of Health, Five Year Plan documents of reports of Planning Commissions, National Sample Survey Organisation and Directorate General of Employment & Training (DGE&T) provide information about various aspects of education & employment such as trades and courses in ITIs, polytechnics, apprenticeship training, competitive exams, statistics about education and employment, higher level courses and intake etc. The DGE&T also brings out a Bulletin on Job Opportunities.
4. *Prospectus of Institutes:* The prospectus of professional and technical institutions contains detailed information about courses available in the respective institutions, eligibility, seats, duration and prospects of the course, financial liabilities etc.
5. *Surveys:* Surveys conducted from time to time by various organisations provide a lot of information about employment market trends, prospects, shortage and surplus of vacancies, unfilled vacancies etc. Some of these surveys are Occupational Pattern surveys, Employment Exchange statistics, reports of the Employment Market Information (EMI) programme operated by DGE&T, Census, Industries Surveys and Census of Central Government Employees.
6. *Advertisements*: Various Vacancy and educational advertisements appearing in newspapers and their special job issues (like ASCENT of Times of India), internet, etc. provide a wealth of career information.
7. *Information from Computers:* A lot of information these days are available on various platforms and websites from computers which can be downloaded. Google provides information of various educational and vocational courses which can be very useful. But one must verify the information before using it as at some websites information can be fake. Students should be guided properly about which web sites are safe. Students should be sure about information before making payments on-line.

Primary Sources

1. *Interviews with People*: One way to collect the information directly from the source can be interviewing the experts in the field. For example, to collect information about self-employment opportunities, or loan facilities or on how to start self-employment ventures, interviews can be had with bank officials, personnel of District Industries Centres, persons who are already in the self- employment, or associations of small entrepreneurs.

2. *Mailing Questionnaires*: Another method of collecting the information from primary sources is to structure a questionnaire and mail it to the concerned department, industry or persons. For example, to collect the information about textile industry, a questionnaire has to be prepared on the items like, job- positions, nature of duties, hours of work, pay scales, perks, terms & conditions, annual vacancies at various levels, future prospects, skills required, method of recruitment, working conditions, health hazards in that industry. The questionnaire may then be mailed to the Personnel Managers of some of the textile industry units.
3. *Industry Visits*: This is yet another way to collect the information. It provides first-hand information about a field of occupation. One can visit some industry units and see for himself the job openings, the working atmosphere etc.
4. *Trade Unions and Employers' organisations*: Information can also be collected from the persons associated with trade unions and organisations of employers. In India apex employers' organisations such as Federation of Indian Chambers of Commerce and Industry (FICCI), Local chambers of commerce, Confederation of Indian Industries (CII) and trade unions such as Indian National Trade Union Congress (INDUC), Bhartiya Mazdoor Sangh (BMS), All India Trade Union Congress (AITUC), can provide information about future trends of employment. The local industries associations and plant level trade unions can provide first -hand information on specific occupations and industries.

Evaluating the Information

After collection of information, the following criteria should be followed to check the authenticity of the information. All the collected information may not be relevant. Some may be obsolete. Some may not be required. It is, therefore, necessary to sift and check the information collected from various sources to avoid duplication.

1. *When Published*: Year of publication of the information is important. Very old information may not be useful on most of the aspects, as eligibility conditions for a particular job change from time to time. On the other hand, analysing the trends in a particular occupation overtime using time series data may be useful.
2. *Who Published or Provided*: It has to be checked as to what is the source of the information. For example, the authentic person to provide data about ITI trades in a particular ITI may be the principal or a teacher of that particular ITI. If the material is in published form, the relevant question is who the author is. Is he providing his opinion or the facts? These aspects should be looked into.
3. *Where from the Information has been Brought:* This refers to the source. Was it a primary source or the secondary source? If it is from a secondary

source the question to look into is whether the published material provides authentic information, and if the source is primary, whether the person who collected the information from primary source could understand and note down the details properly or the person has provided the information without bias.

4. *Why:* Information has to be evaluated on the basis of the purpose of collection. Information should be sorted out on the basis of the purpose and irrelevant information should be scrapped.
5. *How:* The method of collection and dissemination of information is extremely important so that it is properly collated, checked and understood. To evaluate the authenticity of information, more than one method may be used. If the information has been collected through mailing the questionnaires, some interviews may be had with the experts to check the correctness, or it may be verified through a comparison with published material.

Information to be Collected by a Guidance Worker

1. *Educational Purposes*: Courses of various levels, directory of training institutions, eligibility and entry requirements, how to prepare, duration of courses, fees, content of the course, future prospects, scholarships, training opportunities at various levels, linkages with further education/ training/ employment, suitability of individuals to particular courses, hostel and other facilities, placement programmers, preparation for entrance examinations, institutions that assist for appearing in entrance examinations. *Narris et al* (1960) has summarised the educational information as "valid and usable data about all types of present ad probable future educational or training opportunities and requirements including curricular and co-curricular offerings, requirements for entrance and conditions and problems of student life."
2. *Vocational Purposes*: Nature of work, duties, service conditions, method of recruitment, pay packet, personal qualities required, promotional avenues, employment trends of various occupations, employing organisations, working environment, hours of working, perks and hazards, physical requirements, eligibility conditions, preparation for competitive examinations and sources of assistance, apprenticeship training, on-the-job training, preparation of CVs, assistance for appearing in interviews in terms of discussions with experts in the field who may like to help, employers' list, placement agencies, placement facilities, employers' requirements. Narris *et al.* (1960) defined occupational information as "valid and usable data about positions, jobs and occupations, including duties, requirements for entrance, conditions of work, rewards offered, advancement patterns, existing and predicted supply and demand of workers and sources for further information."

3. *Personal Guidance Purposes:* Information about the environment where the person is living, family background and culture, assisting agencies where the individual could be referred to for health problems, occupational experience through field visits, personal information about the person's needs, attitudes, potentials, experience, weaknesses, strengths are also required. The importance of personal information has got special focus in recent years in the field of occupational information as the personal information has to be collated with educational and occupational information. Without facilitating the personal matching with courses and jobs, help in vocational planning may turn out to be a useless affair. Norris *et al* defines social information and its uses as "valid and usable data about the opportunities and influences of the human and physical environment which bear on personal and inter-personal relations. It is that information about human beings which will help a student to understand himself better and to improve his relations with others."
4. *For Setting up Self-employment Ventures*: List of agencies involved in promotion of self-employment, market demand surveys for launching of self-employment ventures, availability of raw material, project profile preparation, samples of project profiles, credit and loan facilities and eligibility conditions, raw material sources, marketing outlets, personal qualities needed to start and continue with the ventures, experience in the field.

How to Collect Information

Need for Collection of Data in Guidance

Effective guidance requires that the counsellor/guidance worker is in possession of all relevant socio-economic and psychological facts about the individual or groups of individuals being guided. It also requires information that has to be given to the persons during the process of guidance.

On the other hand, information is needed about the educational facilities available, the information about world of work, the training options, the scholarships, etc. in a guidance programme.

While some of the information may be available from the existing records, a lot has to be collected from the individuals, orgnaisations, teachers, parents, peers and so on. There can be two basic approaches for collection of data. One is structured approach and another semi-structured approach. In the structured data collection approach, the information collected from various organizations, schools, colleges, employers, etc is uniform while semi-structured approach may vary from person to person. In Structured approach, the questionnaire method is generally followed while in semi-structured approach interview method is adopted. These two means of data collection for guidance purposes are basic tools for collection of data which can make the guidance programme a great success. Sometimes both the approaches are mixed up and a structured questionnaire is followed by interview. Interview method is useful when an in- depth understanding of experiences, description of a process, description of working conditions, etc. is to be collected. For example, to know in what condition a person has to work in a particular occupation, it is better to have an interview of the people who are already working in that particular occupation. This type of query can be made through structured questionnaire also but many people may not write in details the working conditions of an occupation. On the other hand, structured questionnaires are very useful where quantitative information has to be collected. For example, type of courses an institution is offering, eligibility criteria and other terms and conditions.

In a guidance programme both methods are used for collection and collation of data preparing a structured questionnaire is a bit difficult because questionnaires must be sequenced properly should be understandable and should be to the point. These should be self-explanatory. Many a times, the questionnaires are sent to the individuals for filling up the data. If questions are not clear and written language not simple the information thus collected may be wrong. On the other hand, interview method is relatively easy because it is a face-to-face communication. In case the respondent does not understand a question properly he may seek clarification. Moreover, there is also opportunity to seek more information from the person when needed. The interview method also needs some preparation because the purpose of the interview has to be defined and some probable list of questionnaires has to be drafted. Interviews are informal conversations and therefore, substantial qualitative data can be collected. Interview method has flexibility.

Advantages and Disadvantages of Questionnaire and Interview Methods

(a) Questionnaire Method

In the questionnaire method, a standardized questionnaire is sent to the individuals being surveyed calling for the required information. In this method

- The questionnaire is sent to the individuals through channels like Post, E-mail or Internet.
- The responses are received through the same channels.
- The questions have to be put with extreme care as the responses would depend on the clarity of the questions.
- Some times the data is collected in person on the structured questionnaires.

Advantages

- Questionnaire method is fast and cost-effective. Hence useful in situations where there are time or budget constraints.
- Large number of individuals can be covered in a short time.
- The individual can respond to the questionnaire at his/her convenience.
- As there is no facing of the interviewer, the respondent can be free in his responses.
- There is uniformity in data if collected from various organisations.

Disadvantages

- There is no face-to-face contact with the individuals.
- Responses depend upon the reading and writing skills and understanding of the individuals responding.
- No opportunity to discuss the responses with the individuals and clarify the questions.
- No opportunity to make an observation of body-responses while answering the questions.
- Questions of sensitive and confidential nature cannot be included.
- No opportunity to put any additional questions beyond what are covered by the standard questionnaire.
- Response may be inadequate and may depend on the nature of information sought.
- Response rate may be low.

(b) Interviews

In this method—

- Information is collected through personal interviews of the individuals from whom information is collected.
- The interviews may be in person or through telephones or internet chatting.
- There may be a questionnaire, but the interviewer may put additional questions.

Advantages

- Interviews can be conducted by trained interviewers.
- Rapport can be built with the respondents so that the responses are better.
- Observations can be made about the body language of the individuals.
- Additional questions may be put to seek clarifications on the responses.
- Attempts could be made to obtain responses to sensitive questions.
- This does not limit the responses.
- Allow clarifications.

Disadvantages

- Costly and time-consuming.
- Requires trained and skillful interviewers.
- Individual's privacy is affected.
- Interviews have to be fixed at the convenience of the individual Interviews cannot be too long.

These days substantial information is collected using mobile phones which restricts the information to those who have mobile phones. Moreover, certain information is lost which could be collected through cross questioning in face-to-face interviews. All information about guidance should be collected and used judiciously and after adequate verification.

20

Organising Guidance Programme: Career Resource Centre

Guidance can be imparted to students in an effective manner only if the guidance worker has a proper place to sit with sufficient privacy to enable discussion in confidence, and adequate space to organise, store and display the information, and students know where and how to meet the guidance worker. Thus, there is a need for a 'career corner' or a 'Career Resource Centre'. Professional services can be provided from this Centre. In a school, such a Centre should be established with the help of teachers. One room along with a hall may be sufficient for this purpose, where career information may be displayed, computers may be kept where students could come and explore the information. Group activities may be organised in the hall and individual counselling sessions may be held in the counsellor's room. The Career Resource Centre should be at a place, which is relatively noise-free and free from unnecessary movement of the students. For example, if it is near the canteen, too much noise or movement may interrupt the guidance activities. It is not that the guidance worker has to operate only from this Centre. He has to move out and interact with the students in the regular classes assigned for guidance activities to minimise the distance between himself and the students. Students would come to the Resource Centre only when they would feel that the guidance worker is a part of the school and their school life. Attractive display of material in the Resource Centre can catch the attention of the students. Career Resource Centre thus should be properly maintained, usable and reachable. Sometimes such Centre can be opened in one big school in the area that can cater to needs of other schools in the vicinity, as all the schools may not be having adequate resources.

To run a Career Resource Centre and meet the needs of the students, cooperation from Principal and teachers is imperative. They should understand the importance of these services. At many places where principals and teachers are not oriented properly, the feeling is that while teachers are given a regular time table with 20 classes a week plus other activities, the counsellor has no regular work to do. Besides orienting about the guidance activities, it is the duty of the counsellor to plan the guidance programme for the whole year with a number of activities. The programme should be shared with teachers and displayed properly.

There may be occasions where counsellor has to meet with the parents. Teachers and the individual student should be taken into confidence. Outcomes of the guidance activities performed from time to time should be shared with teachers and their assistance should be sought. Students should be asked to give their views and ideas to make the Career Resource Centre more effective and goal oriented. In preparing posters and charts students should be involved.

Such Career Resource Centres are of utmost importance even outside the school at community level. In some Employment Exchanges, such centres have been established but due to paucity of resources and negative attitudes, these are not very effective. In schools also, sometimes counsellors are asked to take subject classes instead of guidance activities. There are also private counsellors who have started guidance activities on their own and charge high fees, which most of the students may not be able to afford.

It is to mention here that due to COVID 19 situation, schools were closed and studies were going on using mobiles, computers etc. This has given a setback for guidance services. It is important that guidance is provided on-line like teaching of school subjects. Some private organisations have opened on-line portals for counselling of students in distress, but such initiative should also come from school and guidance workers.

Financial Budget for Guidance

Finances are required to initiate and implement a guidance programme- initially to acquire fixed assets (furniture, computer, display boards etc), to purchase psychological assessment tools and preparation of audio-visual aids, and later on for implementing the day-to-day guidance activities. The guidance worker should prepare a tentative budget for starting and implementing the activities for a year and communicate it to the principal. The guidance of the latter may be taken at this planning stage also. The staff required and the salaries to be paid out of the guidance budget should also be included in the guidance budget. Some indicative Heads of Expenditure in the guidance budget are discussed below:

- *Staff*: Besides counsellor himself at least two persons are required to assist him. The staff requirement would vary according to the number of children in the school to be attended to. In some schools, there is a prevision to train one of the subject teachers to help the counsellor in guidance activities. Such teachers are known as career masters. And they devote some of their fixed time for such activities. Special salary increments are admissible to such teachers. Staff requirements should be worked out taking into account the availability of such career masters.
- *Space and Equipment*: The tentative budget should provide estimates of expenditure on establishment of career resource centre, purchase of equipment like projector, lighting system, audio system, raw material

for preparing audio-visual aids and furniture and arrangement for group activities. Experience indicates that school administrations normally do not have enough resources to afford a large budget for the guidance activities. Therefore, planning and budgeting of guidance activities should be conservative with limited essentials to start with. If the programme is effective, school authorities may get motivated to invest larger sums for the purpose.

- *Guidance material*: Guidance material has to be collected, prepared and disseminated. The budget must provide for this. There are publications that are free of cost. Some more material can be acquired as complimentary if the guidance worker has good rapport with the agencies. Help of voluntary organisations can also be taken in the preparation of the material. Innovation can reduce the cost of guidance programme.
- Material required for the psychological assessment is costly but is essential. It is, however, one-time expenditure. Printing the answer sheets at local level can affect some saving. Record maintenance through computers may also limit the expenditure in the long run.
- Group activities: Some group activities such as organisation of career exhibitions or career conferences would require additional budget. Such activities may be planned and arranged for a cluster of schools wherever possible to optimise resources. It would be possible sometimes to get employers and voluntary agencies like Rotary clubs to sponsor such group activities.

In the pandemic like situation, it is necessary that online portals are opened up and resources provided for that.

Features of a Good Guidance Programme

A good guidance programme may be planned and executed only when the guidance worker understands the basic concepts underlying the guidance services, its principles and the processes. The objective of the guidance programme must be fully defined and understood, the target groups must be identified and accordingly a detailed programme should be drawn up. The following are the features of a good guidance programme.

1. The principle of the guidance programme is that it should be designed to serve all the people according to their needs in the process of their growth. That means, any programme, which is worked out, should have continuity and should address the needs of all. A good guidance programme will help each person to develop himself to his fullest capabilities. This full development of the individual should also be linked with the development of the society and individual should be able to help others. Here, it may be noted that some individuals might be having capabilities, which are

not socially desirable. These capabilities are to be channelised in the right direction so as to be beneficial to others and not harming anyone. The benefits to the society and others are relative which may vary according to the traditions and values of the society and culture.

2. Each person requires guidance services at some or the other time of his life. It could be during childhood, adolescence, adulthood or old age. A guidance programme should incorporate the services which may meet the needs of the individuals of all ages whenever they need them. In case the guidance programme being executed in the school is not incorporating the needs of the old people, the guidance worker should keep the information about the services available for this age group outside the school system.
3. Any guidance programme should be able to deal with varying kinds of problems. It is common to hear statements like 'he is a gone case', or 'nothing can be done for this child as he is totally mischievous' or 'he is not capable of doing anything'. In guidance services there is no scope for such statements. Each and every individual has his own strengths and limitations. Each child varies from the other in the manner of his expressions of his feelings. A guidance programme should accept each individual with his strengths and weaknesses and should be able to make an intervention programme that would lessen their weaknesses and develop their strength. The guidance worker should not keep any prejudices against any child.
4. There are cases where counsellors are in a hurry, as they have to cater to the needs of many. Group activities and guidance may not always be a substitute for individual attention. A guidance programme should be worked out in such a way that the counsellor is able to pay individual attention to the students, wherever required. The identification of needs and problems of the individuals is extremely essential. It should be a part of a good guidance programme.
5. A number of services have to be included in a good guidance programme. In most of the cases the guidance workers feel that educational and vocational guidance services is the major activity. But in the current socio-economic scenario, other services like placement, follow up, evaluation, counselling, etc., are equally important and should get a place in a good guidance programme.
6. The guidance programme should be based on the local requirements and the local resources available. The programme would vary according to the environment, the level of development and the nature of population in the local area.
7. A guidance programme should keep in mind that the services are not meant for helping the child for his immediate problem only. While providing the services, the counsellor should see the individual as a whole along with

his background and environment, and, the aim of guidance should be the overall development of the individual. The individual should be helped in such a way that he is able to solve his future problems also.

8. The guidance work is a team work. The help of all the persons who could contribute in the guidance services should be taken to make the program effective.
9. Education and guidance are complementary to each other. Both go hand in hand and neither of these two should hamper the development of the individual.
10. A guidance programme should help the individuals to make their own decisions. In most of the cases parents or friends decide for children what occupation they should choose in future. Sometimes, the guidance worker also persuades the child to choose a particular kind of occupational field. This is not the correct way of guidance. The counsellor should be able to provide the detailed information to the child and the options available to him, as well as to the parents and an atmosphere should be created where the child is able to take his own line of action.
11. In a good guidance programme, the choice of a good guidance worker is important. The guidance worker should be responsible, capable and fully trained. The qualities of a good guidance worker have been discussed. However, it is pertinent to mention that the guidance worker should follow professional ethics. He becomes a role model and, therefore, he should be totally unbiased as well as competent.
12. A guidance programme can be effective only when it is conceived well and implemented well. The basic guidelines for administration of a guidance programme are (Figure 20.1):

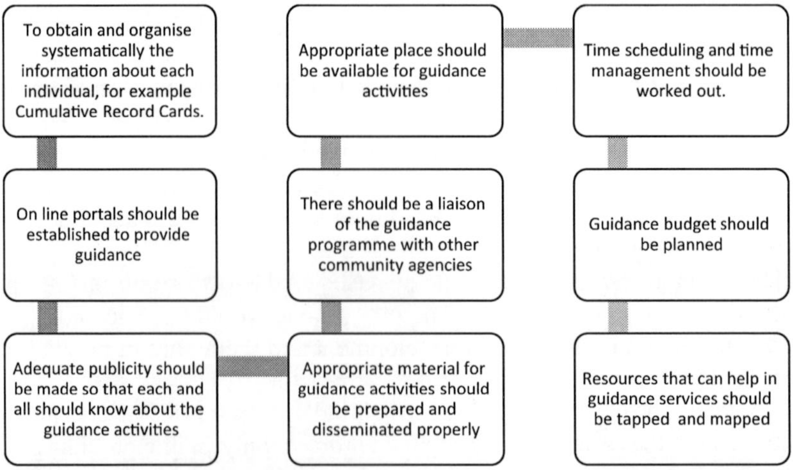

Figure 20.1: *Basic Guidance Programme*

An Action Plan

A tentative action plan for guidance services in schools is proposed as below:

- *Constitution of Guidance Committee*: Counsellor should constitute a Guidance Committee consisting of some members from the school and some from outside. From the school, the Committee may have the principal or his nominee, one teacher interested in guidance work, Officer from Employment Exchange, one or two representatives of Employers/Banks, one or two representatives from parents' group, representative of students and one or two other experts from the Community. The main policy issues and guidance services should be discussed during the meetings of this Committee. The number of members in the Committee should not be very large. The ideal number may between 6 to 10. The Quarterly or half-yearly meetings may be organised. Before organising such meeting, the agenda of the meeting, should be prepared and circulated to all members of the Committee in advance.
- *Setting up of a Career Resource Centre*: A Career Resource Centre should be set up by the counsellor using in-school as well as out- school resources. Counsellor should adopt participatory approach where the voluntary participation from the stakeholders and others should be sought. Career Resource Centre in the school is also named as Career Corner. Career Room, Guidance & Placement Centre. In the Centre, proper display about the guidance services, activities, objectives and its usefulness should be there.
- *Parent-Teacher Association Meetings*: Counsellor should make it a point to be a member of Parent-Teacher Association meetings. Parent-Teacher meet is organised in every school. This is where the counsellor can also interact with parents, orient the parents about guidance activities and seek the information about the individuals.
- *Plan Budget and Staff*: Yearly guidance activities according to the educational level to be planned in consultation with the Guidance-Committee. According to the activities planned a tentative budget should be worked out. The requisite staff should be assigned the specific duties.
- *Purchase of Assessment Tools*: After preparation of the guidance activity plan, purchases of psychological tests should be done. Tests should be purchased from authorised persons. Counsellor should ensure that the tests are applicable for the Indian population and norms are available for comparability and making decisions.
- *Record Maintenance*: Record maintenance is another important activity which is a must for the counsellor. Separate records should be maintained for each guidance activity/services. For example, for orientation services a register may be maintained detailing the activities organised, dates, the target group, the place, the outcome and the feedback. Similarly for other

services, separate files/registers should be maintained. Under counselling services detailed record of each counselling case with the dates of interviews should be kept. Such records may be maintained using Computers also.

Some Suggested Activities

1. *Elementary Level:*
   - Orientation of students with the school and guidance
   - Group activities to develop sense of cooperation and sharing, develop learning habits, adjustment with school and peers
   - Tips to give them a feel of occupations
   - Activities to develop their creativity
   - Identify problems of the students and take remedial measures
   - Help in developing the personalities of the students
2. *Educational Level and Activity*: Class VI:
   - Collection of information and preparation of Cumulative Record Card
   - Orientation of students about guidance activities and school
   - Orientation of parents about guidance services and school
   - Administration of Intelligence Test and preparation of results
   - Monitoring the academic progress according to the intelligence levels – Identification of slow-achievers and communicating this to teachers to organise special programmes for slow- achievers.

   Some Topics for Class Talks:
   - How to do homework
   - Choosing a leisure-time activity
   - How to improve study habits
   - Steps to improve 'Climate of learning'
   - Concept of occupations
   - Developing good habits

     Except class talks other group activities may be chosen
   - Counselling: Identified problem cases or those referred by teachers should be provided counselling.
   - Meetings with teachers and parents whenever necessary
3. *Class VII and VIII* may include Orientation of new students and their parents, introduction of concepts of self-understanding, field- trips for orienting the students towards technical courses may be organised. Potential dropouts may be identified and helped. Weak students to be identified and their remedial programmes may be organised.

   Topics for Talks/Discussion
   - Training Courses after VIII
   - How to develop self-confidence
   - Hobbies and their importance
   - How to prepare for Examinations
   - How to improve academic performance

4. *Class IX and X*:
    - Orientation of students and parents
    - Preparation of Cumulative Record Card if not already
    - available/updating of information
    - Administration of Psychological tests, preparation and
    - communication of results
    - Identification of under-achievers and potential dropouts
    - Counselling of problem cases
    - Meetings with parents whenever necessary
    - Discussions with teacher
    - Organisation of Career Exhibition and Career Conference
    - Field trips, Creativity activities
    - Educational & Vocational Information
    - Some suggested topics for Class/Career Talks
    - Educational options after X
    - Vocational options after X
    - Entrance Examinations
    - Technical Courses after X
    - Competitive examination for jobs and preparation
    - Importance of choosing a right career
    - How to improve decision making
    - How to contact and utilise the resources available
    - Financial Assistance
    - Importance of Self-employment
5. *Class XI and XII:*
    - Orientation of new students and their parents
    - Cumulative Record Card and Updating of information
    - Psychological testing programme, preparation and discussion of results
    - Remedial measures for weak students
    - Information about world of work, courses, skill development programmes
    - Organisation of Career Conference, Exhibition, field trips, film shows, interaction with successful candidates
    - Financial and other Community resources
    - Understanding, accepting and development of self
    - Counselling of problem cases
    - Parents guidance
    - Organisation of interactional programmes with employees/ Banks personnel etc.
    - Role of employment exchanges
    - Banks and credit institutions
    - How to match yourself with the world of work
    - Educational/Technical streams after XII

- Options after XII
- How to prepare for Competitive exams
- Time Management
- Learning habits
- Importance of choosing a right career
- How to appear in interviews
- Importance of physical fitness
- How to deal with failures

Time Scheduling

Orientation activity should be started immediately after opening of the school but after settling of the students. It may be planned during the first month of the school. Preparation of CRCs and assessment of students may be started from the second month. During this time individuals with specific problems should be identified. Other activities may be planned for the whole year according to the time availability, seeing the budget constraints and needs of the students.

Follow up and evaluation of the programme should be done on concurrent basis or after 6 months of implementation. Yearly assessment of the effectiveness of the services should also be done. Some services under guidance provides immediate results while some take time. Therefore, a schedule of evaluation should be decided in consultation with the guidance Committee.

Evaluation of Guidance Programme

To make any programme effective it is essential that its functioning should be evaluated from time to time. The evaluation of guidance services is necessary to see what kind of services are being rendered; whether these services are beneficial to the students or not and what are the areas where modifications are required?

The evaluation of the programme may be done in terms of its objectives, *i.e.,* whether the programme is meeting its objectives or not. The programme can also be evaluated in terms of the budget allocated for the services to see whether the services rendered are cost effective. Another basis of evaluation of the programme may be a time activity-planning schedule. whether the services planned during the specific period, and for the specific target groups have been rendered or not. Another basis could the outcomes of the programmes. In a guidance programme the outcome may be a number of students placed in jobs, the number of persons helped in solving their problems or the number of persons who could get educational streams of their choice, the number of persons who could be helped in assessing themselves and so on. The evaluation may be done having two groups – one group which was provided guidance and the other which was not given any services and the two groups may be compared.

It may be seen from the above that selection of criteria is an important element in the evaluation of guidance. Various criteria were adopted to evaluate the guidance programme and assess the effectiveness of the criteria by various research scholars but no one criteria has been considered as perfect. Some researches show that presence of certain services, material and activities, etc., lead to a successful guidance programme but absence of these activities does not lead to the conclusion that services are ineffective. Some of the criteria used relate to the ultimate vocational success and satisfaction. The appropriateness of the vocational choice had been another criterion for researchers. Stone studied the effect of counselling and instructions on vocational choices. The student's opinion has been used to determine the effectiveness of various school services and courses upon the vocational choices. Hoppock took the opinion of graduates and dropouts to determine their opinion about guidance programme when they were in the schools. Change in client's attitude before and after guidance has been studied by a number of scholars.

Williamson and Darley (1937) advocated four criteria on which the guidance services could be evaluated.

1. A case work method which involves the reading of case histories by competent counsellors, who make professional judgments of success in adjustment.
2. Scholastic adjustments in terms of both groups of students who leave college because of low scholastic aptitude, and those who are successful. The former group may achieve desirable outcomes of counselling 'by leaving,' if they become adjusted to the fact that they have little or no chance of college success (at that particular college) and act accordingly.
3. Students' satisfaction with counselling (their own judgment report).
4. Change and development of attitudes toward vocation or other problem. (As observed by the counsellor.)

Stoops and Wahlquist have given the following suggestions for giving the criteria for evaluation of the guidance programme

1. Evaluation should increase efficiency in the field appraised by determining how well the program's objectives are being achieved.
2. Measurement, research, interpretation, and analysis are indispensable.
3. The purposes of evaluation should be stated clearly in terms of desired changes.
4. Desired changes and purposes should be flexible and subject to review, re-evaluation, and restatement, as the needs of pupils and society changes.
5. Final decisions should be based upon factual data or upon valid judgments.
6. Results of measuring and counting, percentages and norms are not sufficient data from which to recommend changes. Other factors of a less tangible nature are also required.

7. All persons affected by the program should assist in arriving at the decisions made concerning the evaluation goals, procedures, and purposes to be achieved.
8. Evaluation programmes for guidance should be coordinated with, and be a continuous part of, the entire educational program of the schools.
9. Unique and experimental methods of evaluationin guidance should be encouraged, but adopted with caution.
10. All data and information submitted should be validated, studied, and weighed before they are used to effect program changes. Evaluation, wherever used, is concerned with both the means and the ends.
11. When changes in guidance have been proved desirable through evaluation, and agreed to, then all guidance workers should enthusiastically assist in revising the program.
12. Democratic procedure requires that all who are affected by a school policy, program, or decision should share both in its making and in its execution.

There can be any criterion for evaluation of the programme but the basic objectives of the evaluation are to see whether—

- The activities planned in the programme are covered.
- The needs of various kind of groups in the schools have been met.
- The programme has been successful in helping the students to solve their various problems.
- Various groups of students have been assessed adequately and results have been conveyed to the students in proper manner.
- Counselling has been effective in solving the individual problems.
- Students were able to improve their academic achievements through the guidance programme.
- Placement services have improved through guidance.
- Career information services rendered under the guidance programme have been effective.
- Guidance worker has been able to orient the principal, the teachers, the community, the parents and ultimately the students about the guidance services.
- Students feel the usefulness of guidance services rendered to them.
- Guidance helped students to prepare themselves for facing the competitive examinations, interviews, etc.

These are some of the points the guidance evaluation programme should look into.

Method of Collecting Information for Evaluation

The general method to collect the information for evaluating the services is survey method. The information may be collected from staff members, from parents, from friends of the person who has been rendered the guidance services and from the beneficiaries themselves to assess the effect of guidance upon the behaviours and adjustments in life of the beneficiaries. A follow up survey may also be done of the persons who have been provided guidance to see their activities status.

Another way of collecting the information is to conduct experimental research by having two groups controlled and experimental in which one group is provided services and the other is not. The changes in the two groups may be measured. This method has been used to study the effectiveness of counselling. To study the effectiveness of the guidance services through this experimental method, matching of the two groups on other variables, such as environmental factor, age, education, etc. is vital

Evaluation Technique

For collection of data, the most common method employed is the use of structured questionnaire. On the basis of the objectives of the evaluation as well as criteria adopted questionnaires are developed and sent to the persons from whom the information is to be collected. Another method is the interview method where people are personally interviewed. Interview is more personal and the information may be collected through probing. The problem in sending the questionnaire is that many people may not return the questionnaire or may not give their true opinion.

Attempts have been made to use the tests for evaluating the differences. Tests may be used on the student's pre and post guidance services. Pepinsky and others utilised socio-metro devices and observation methods. Some other scholars have used the rating scales.

All the techniques have some advantages and disadvantages. If more than one technique is followed the data may be more authentic and comparable. The suggestions may also be obtained from the students themselves. The ultimate aim of evaluation of guidance services is that the beneficiaries should be well adjusted in their lives and they should perform well when they are in schools and when in jobs.

Some Success Indicators

1. To what extent does the pupil work up to his level of ability?
2. To what extent is the school aiding the pupil who should stay in school and the pupil who should seek training and experiences outside the school? Again the criterion is based upon individual needs.
3. To what extent does the pupil learn to participate in group activities, such as expressing himself easily to others, tolerance toward the ideas of others, or willingness to help others in the group?
4. To what extent does a pupil learn to plan for himself?

5. To what extent does each pupil make educational and vocational plans that are compatible with reasonable expectations?
6. To what extent does the pupil learn to make friends and get along with others?
7. To what extent is the pupil able to establish heterosexual relationships?
8. To what extent is the pupil able to accept the responsibilities of citizenship in a school community?

Who should do the Evaluation?

Evaluation is a specialised work involving orientation for research; the schools may not be equipped with professional persons, who can evaluate the services. It is better to take the help from outside agencies or a cluster of the schools where services are available. An evaluation committee can be constituted comprising guidance professionals, experts in the field, schools, administrators, etc.

21

Use of ICT in Guidance and Counselling

Introduction

Recent decades have witnessed people in general, and youth in particular, getting increasingly technology-savvy and adept in the use of web-based applications. More and more people go and search internet web-sites for their day-to-day transactions and in quest of additional information and knowledge. In India, there were 624 million internet users (about half of the population) and 448 million (about a third of the population) active users of social media like Facebook, Twitter, etc. While internet users increased by about 8 per cent over 2020 level, users of social media jumped up by 21 per cent in the same period. Education and training programmes today lay great emphasis on advancement of digital knowledge. The National Educational Policy, 2020, for example, lists extensive use of technology in teaching and learning as one of the fundamental guiding principles for the education system. It is therefore to be expected that the preference of the youth to access digital platforms for their informational needs would rise by leaps and bounds in future.

As in almost all walks of life, influence and applications of modern technology has greatly impacted the field of guidance and counselling. For the purpose of this chapter, modern technology generally means computer-based and internet-based applications. While career guidance and counselling is basically a personalized and user-need-focused activity, it is necessary at the same time to find appropriate ways, resources, technology and tools to scale up the access to career information and guidance services for the ever increasing numbers of people seeking first or better jobs, or educational and training opportunities. Such expanded access to knowledge of career options and opportunities can be imbedded into guidance and counselling services through innovative application of Information Communication and Technology (ICT) tools. Apart from its ability to deal the complexity of providing services to a large number of people, use of technology helps in achieving considerably reduced time in providing services. Technological tools also help in quickly updating the information details in the system and allows the user to access the latest available information. It also helps in establishing self-service approach that enables the guidance-seekers access according to their own choice of what is to be explored, when, and in what detail. Against this background, it is no wonder that public and private employment service providers and individuals have in recent years been depending upon technology-driven guidance services, inter alia, in the fields of employment, education and training.

Technology-driven Applications

The common technology-driven tools that can be used in providing guidance services are:

- Online counselling
- Computerized data-bases of information on education, training, employment and related needs
- Software based search engines for specific search objectives
- Webinars
- Social media like Facebook, Twitter
- Computer-based psychological testing procedures

The advent of online communication facilitated remote career guidance services as opposed to in-person services. The transition from the latter to the former had to overcome some initial resistance but in recent decades the online mode of guidance is more readily accepted. In particular, after the incidence of Covid-19 pandemic and the social distancing norms that came into existence, online mode has become the preferred one. Guidance practice has expanded in scope and size due to adoption of online mode. Online procedures have removed the difficulties arising out of geographical distances and helped coverage of hard-to-reach sections of the population.

The most common application of ICT in career guidance is through the development and maintenance computer-based data bases on various career options, giving information on what is required to enter each career in terms of education, training and other preparations, job opportunities and career progression possibilities, jobs currently available in the data base and their details like remuneration, duration, etc. The data bases also provide information on educational and training opportunities, places where they can be availed of, preparatory requirements, etc. Such data bases, with easy access to the users, would be of great value to career and educational information seekers. Public Employment Services in many countries do maintain such data bases. The service providers need skills for assembling, collating, evaluating, organizing and presenting information. The most difficult aspect of this application is the maintenance of the data base up to date and ensure its security. The user must possess skills to identify the appropriate data base, and to retrieve and evaluate the information. Though it is possible to provide for interaction between the user and the counsellor through appropriate technological interfaces, so that the user is guided through the search, the process is generally self-guiding. Such data bases can be used by youth making educational choices, unemployed persons or those seeking change of jobs, guidance practitioners, or parents.

An example of such a data base from India is the National Career Service (NCS) Portal being maintained by the Ministry of Labour and Employment, Government of India. The portal provides for online search services for job-seekers, employers, placement organizations, counsellors, etc. as shown in the following table.

Table 21.1: *Services Provided through National Career Service Portal*

Type of user	*Services*
Job-seekers	• Registration • Find jobs • Find Counsellor • Find Career Center • Participate in job fairs • Career skill services (Digisaksham providing training in programmes like Python, Creation of job-seeker's video-profile, etc. • Services for differently- abled • Career information
Employers	• Registration • Post new jobs • Find candidates • Participate in job fairs
Placement agencies	• Registration • Post new jobs • Find candidates • Participate in job fairs
Counsellors	• Registration

Source: Ministry of Labour and Employment, Government of India, National Careere Services Portal https://www.ncs.gov.in/Pages/default.aspx

National Career Service (NCS) provides a host of career-related services such as dynamic job matching, career counselling, job notifications, vocational guidance, information on skill development courses, internships and alike. The national portal (www.ncs.gov.in) provides a nation-wide platform to connect job seekers and employers. As of March 2022, the Portal serviced about 14 million active job-seekers, 185 thousand active employers and 168 thousand active job vacancies.

In recent years a number of several digital applications and computer programs have been developed, designed for use in guidance processes, mainly for high school students or individuals who are about to make choices to begin a career. Such applications have the advantages of being easily accessible, are of low cost and allow the user freedom of choice. Most of them provide information and indications to the user, but may also contain aptitude tests and tools for the assessment of appropriated career choices.

There are, for example, online software systems, like CASCAiD, that provide (free or at a cost) guidance services. CASCAiD is a well-known and highly reputed software system owned by Loughborough University in United Kingdom that produces career-related tools such as its Online Careers Matching Tool, Adult Directions. Its systems are now available in a number of western countries. Sorprendo is a software developed for use in Italy on the model of CASCAiD to improve the quality of guidance eservices. It provides services to secondary school students, early school leavers, workers and the unemployed and is currently used in lower secondary schools as well as in public employment services in Italy. There are similarly software programmes guiding youth to prepare their resume, write out their job applications and provide templates for other preparatory needs in their job-quests.

Jobrapido, (https://in.jobrapido.com/), based in Milan (Italy), is one such digital bringing job offers close to job-aspirants, and is presently operating in 58 countries, including India. Within the portal there are over twenty million job offers per month. Jobrapido helps users to find a job among all the job offers on the web. The site collects and organizes systematically all the ads, inserted in thousands of websites, in job boards, in newspaper ads, or disseminated by associations, in the employment pages of individual companies such as in the "Work with us" sections of individuals. To identify offers on Jobrapido it is sufficient for the user to answer the questions: What job are you looking for? and Where? From this search, users get a description of the full text of the ad and are directed to the site from which it originated. In this way, Jobrapido users can directly submit their resume or application. The platform uses innovative job search technology with programmatic campaigns that combine Big Data, AI and Taxonomy.

There are other similar job search service providers like Indeed (https://in.indeed.com) one of the most popular job search sites, Monster (https://www.monsterindia.com) in operation for over two decades, Naukri (www.naukri.com/jobs-in-india) which is a popular job portal that offers exclusive job listings for both freshers and experienced professionals, TimesJobs (https://www.timesjobs.com)*, a leading job website in India*, Freshersworld (https://www.freshersworld.com), *Shine* (https://www.shine.com*) and* Smart (https://smartonlinework.com).

Webinars *or web-based seminars* are another possible means of disseminating career information or providing guidance services. These sessions can be used for providing information in general or may be focused on specific field of careers or educational streams or vocational training. During the last couple of years which witnessed extensive and extended lockdowns and other social distancing methods mposed to combat the Covid pandemic, webinars have been the main means of professional communication and spread of information. Webinars, unlike physical seminars, provide access to a larger number of participants, while like seminars allow exchange of information through Questions and Answers.

Social media like Facebook and Twitter or professional networks like Linkedin are another powerful means of providing career guidance to the youth or exchanging/disseminating career-related information among individuals who very frequently access such media. They have the advantages of power to connect counsellors and clients located far apart. Groups, chats and educational pages for career guidance help to stimulate career interventions. A good profile on LinkedIn is today an essential element in advancement of one's professional career.

Technology for Testing

Computerized procedures for testing and scoring individual's aptitudes are in vogue for some years. nTalents.ai ((https://ntalents.ai) is the flagship product of 'Ntalents Technology' launched in early 2018. The platform 'n TALENTS', for example, provides software for scientific and reliable assessments with AI (Artificial Intelligence) Enabled Pre-Employment Testing. It enables measurement of job-fitment using an assessment of soft skills, behavioural and psychometric traits, and creates a comprehensive cognitive and psychological profile of the candidate.

The Flipside

While the introduction of technology into guidance and counselling services has certainly helped guidance professionals to redesign and enhance the quality of their services, it must be remembered that there are certain limitations to extending ICT-based guidance services indiscriminately. In developing countries where availability of power and access to internet facilities is neither universal nor uniform, such extension would be ill-conceived and un-ethical as large sections of guidance seekers would stay out of access to the services. Not only that, personal communication between the counsellor and client is central in the counselling and guidance process, and cannot be easily and totally replaced by technology. The impact of the introduction of technology-based guidance practice should be assessed carefully considering the objectives of the guidance, the characteristics of the client and the physical infrastructure available. Moreover, technology-based procedures have the tendency to automatize the guidance process, whereas, the guidance seeker's needs vary from person to person and cannot always be straight-jacketed into a uniform pattern. For best results, the coming together of the guidance seeker and guidance provider is an essential element in the guidance process that enables totally objective interaction between the two, leading to a better assessment of the former's needs and how best the latter can help. Technological tools can and do help in the guidance process but they cannot totally replace personal interaction.

Artificial Intelligence (AI) in Guidance and Counselling

Artificial Intelligence (AI) is one of the important technologies with increasing applications in several fields today. AI computes systems that have the ability to perform tasks that are being done by human beings simulating their thought processes. AI's main aim is to teach machines to learn, think, and behave in a manner similar to humans and imitate human behaviours.

Career guidance in essence comprises four essential elements – gathering information on individual's abilities and aptitudes, information on jobs and careers (including external factors like the availability of jobs and the recruitment practices), decision-making on appropriate career options based on these two sets of information and a two-way communication between the counsellor and the counselled based on the options so reached. AI can help in fast and efficient processing of the ever-growing volumes of information and in decision-making, both by job-seekers and employers, and as well by the counsellors who help in bringing them together.

Now-a-days interviews for recruitment are being increasingly conducted with AI applications. The onset of Covid-19 pandemic, which inhibited traditional interview processes, has accelerated this trend. Apart from telephonic interviews, which are basically an~~d~~ extension of the physical mode, video-interviewing platforms like *Hireview* are finding place in the interview process. Once the candidates submit their responses in video mode, the employer may choose AI based methods in analysing the responses and in the selection process. AI can help in selecting candidates as per the characteristics, abilities and aptitudes desired by the employer through comparisons with the characteristics of their current employees. Counsellor's role in such situations will be to advise on how to face such video-interviewing with success, by familiarizing themselves with ~~the~~ employing company's requirements and preparing to answer generally expected questions.

One of the common uses of AI by employers in recruiting is in screening the job applications and resume/CV of candidates and selecting applications satisfy certain conditions laid down. Counsellor's job would be to assist the job-seekers in preparing a professional CV that is aligned to the job descriptions, and contains the key words/phrases mentioned in the advertisements.

AI can be used by employers to screen out candidates who exhibit undesirable participation or inappropriate behaviour in social media posts. The counsellor needs to advise the clients to be careful about their social media posts and how they engage with others.

AI can help employers to maintain databases on the talents and skills of candidates not selected in a particular recruitment for consideration at a future date.

Some of the good AI-enabled software used are *Arya, Hiretual, Turbohire, Fetcher, Humanly, Xor, Seekout, etc.* While all these assist in the recruitment process, each has its own specific use. For instance, Arya helps in hiring the best talent quickly, 'Seekout' helps in finding hard-to-find-talent. This can make it challenging for organizations to decide which solution is right for them, which is why many resort to customized artificial intelligence solutions.

Can Robots Deliver Counselling?

Another important task AI can play is provide company to those who feel lonely. Development of Robots is an upcoming trend who can understand people's emotions and can talk with them. Thus, AI can provide company to people. The time is not far when robots will provide personal counselling to those in stress.

A paper published in Journal of Medical Internet Research on the basis of a study conducted by the School of Psychology at University of Plymouth in the United Kingdom showed that a social robot can deliver a motivational interviewing that is helpful and enjoyable. Such counselling would be useful in inducing behavioral change.

Robotic software can support executive decisions and answer questions such as which training programmes are likely to improve a person's chances of advancing in one's career, or which jobs suit their skill-set best. A study of 14,600 HR managers conducted by researchers at Oracle and Workplace Intelligence indicated that 85 per cent of them wanted intelligent tools to help in their career progression. Three-fourths of the respondents were willing to be guided by recommendations from robots or AI equipped tools. The areas in which they expect help from the machines is in identifying skills critical to their success and in finding new learning methods.[1]

AI may not be able to replace the role of a human counsellor completely. It would be wise to remember Stephen Hawking's words of caution urging the need to "employ best practice and effective management" of artificial intelligence.

[1] *Humans are turning to robots for career advice* (Nov. 2, 2021) Rachel Ranosa in Peoplematters: News.

22

Emerging Trends in Counselling

Life in modern societies has been considerably impacted by developments in technological, socio-economic, cultural, education, employment and connected fields. In developing countries like India, the past few decades have witnessed immense changes in the way families are structured and the relationships within them, perspectives of youth and peer influences, education and career opportunities, influence of technology through use of computers and internet, and social media. All these factors have led not only to an increase in the need for educational counselling but also altered counselling landscape - the content and the way counselling is done. This chapter looks at some of the important developments of this nature.

Contemporary Issues Impacting Demand for Counselling

Current Shortage

Presently there is a huge shortage of professional counsellors in developing countries. In India, reports suggest that about 93 per cent of the schools in India do not have a professional counsellor, and the country needs 1.5 million counsellors for its 315 million students. "Apart from the usual pressures of competition, the increasing complexity of career choices and disruptive technologies in the volatile job market have made career choices a major challenge for both students and parents. A Mindler survey of career option awareness among Indian students has revealed that 93% of the students aged 14 to 21 were aware of just seven career options though there are more than 250 different types of job options available in India."[1] These numbers indicate the extent of shortage of counsellors in India at present.

Family Size and Structures

Families are becoming increasingly small in size, and often nuclear in structure, as opposed to joint families of the past, due to forces of urbanization, industrial and social development. The status of women in the family has been

---

[1] Times of India, May 06, 2019 accessed on 17.06.2022 from https://timesofindia.indiatimes.com/home/education/news/india-needs-15-lakh-counsellors-for-315-million-students/articleshow/69201566.cms#:~:text=India%20is%20perceived%20as%20a%20counselling-%20deficit%20sector,a%20major%20challenge%20for%20both%20students%20and%20parents. counsellors

undergoing change for the better. As a result of these changing patterns, the old system of decision-making power resting with the eldest male in the family has been yielding place to a more democratic form of collective decision-making. Counselling, or in fact ordering, children by parents and grandparents is increasingly becoming a rare practice. Where both parents work, they hardly find time to advise and guide the children. Due to increasing family income, the trend is to depend on outside professional counselling. With only one or two children at home, they are often given enormous amount of freedom of activities, parental control being voluntarily or voluntarily limited. Professional counselling often becomes a necessity. In a changed scenario, children also are developing dependency on outside counselling and other sources of guidance like friends specially in big cities and towns. Many times in well to do families, children are very demanding and parents also with little time to devote to their siblings fill the void with money and are treated like money givers.

Age-related Issues

Today, most countries in the world have ageing populations, with growing proportions of persons aged 60 or 70 and above. They may either continue to engage in gainful work or follow other pursuits or simply lead totally retired lives. In any case, guidance and counselling is important to help to lead happy and fruitful lives in the context of their activities and in relation to their families. Proper choice of occupations suited to their physical and mental abilities and aptitudes is important. Those without occupations or with no inclination towards work need guidance and counselling about alternative pursuits. With retirement, there is usually a change in the status of senior citizens in the family and they need to adjust their habits and style of living in consonance with the requirements of the younger and active members of the family. This adjustment may sometimes lead to frictions that counsellors can help in overcoming.

On the other side, children need to learn to co-living with elders. They should be sensitized about the needs, problems and issues of the elders. Some basic love and affection are needed from the side of children. Counselling from the very beginning about respecting and attending elderly in the family is a must.

Violence against Women

Women are coming out of their pre-determined spaces for education and work. Society not being used to such transformation indulging in various kinds of anti-social behaviours towards girls and women. Sexual violence, domestic violence and other types of unwarranted activities against women have become a growing phenomenon despite legislative and administrative action to prevent it. The victims, if they survive, have to put up with social stigma and shame, affecting their personal, social and economic lives. Counselling may alleviate their agony to a great extent and help in their eventual rehabilitation. Juveniles who are caught and punished in such shameful acts also need counselling to mend their behaviours in future.

In general, principles of gender equality and equity respect for women etc are to be inculcated in children from the very beginning starting from home, school and other social organisations. Counselling can go a long way in this endeavour.

Impact of Pandemics

Pandemics and natural calamities often leave indelible imprints on the psyche of the affected people. For example, the sweeping impact of Covid 19 on the physical and mental health of people is well-documented. A recent study has found that a quarter of the respondents told that they suffered anxiety (more females having anxiety than males). Again, 22 per cent of the people experienced fear in mind and about 19 per cent felt helplessness. The influence of lockdowns associated with the pandemic had unique impressions on behaviour changes in terms of time spent by the respondents on various activities. Over half of the respondents spent more time in household work, with family, social and electronic media. Eating out, shopping and outdoor activities (exercise, yoga, etc) have taken a beating due to lockdowns. Adjustment to such impact on mental health and induced behaviours becomes easier with proper counselling.

Children are facing specific problems due to COVID 19. Due to on-line studies, there communication skills got affected negatively. Many children have become introvert and not able to mingle with others and learn social skills. Those with lack of technological facilities are much behind in their studies in comparison to their counterparts leading to inferiority complex. Such and many more situations are to be dealt with cautious and care with the help of counselling.

Wide Choice of Careers

In olden days, and to an extent even now, children's career paths are determined by their initial educational choices, which are determined by the preferences of their parents. Usually, lawyers, doctors, engineers, politicians, public servants, and those who worked in armed forces, preferred their children to follow suit, and put them in the relevant educational streams. There could be eventual mismatches between preferences and opportunities leading to skewed career progressions in some cases, but the general pattern used to be that of sons following parental professions. Once the educational choice was made, career choice was automatic. It is no longer the case now. Today, there are enormous number of options at each stage and the linkages of one's career to his or her original educational choice are getting rather thin. A person trained for arts subjects in school can still change track and enter into computer education and pursue a technical occupation, NPE 2020 has opened more options. A person who pursued education in the field of psychology right up to the doctoral level can take up economics and sociology and pursue the profession of development evaluator. The possibilities are immense.

Technology

Today technology has permeated into almost all fields of human activity. Emergence of new technologies has led to emergence of new industries and activities, occupations, skills (including soft skills) and jobs with diverse specifications, and educational ladders that fit these job requirements. Developments in the fields of machine learning and artificial intelligence and in data analytics, for instance, have opened up an enormous variety of avenues of work. Computerization of almost all fields has revolutionized the job market. Access to internet and its use has been growing by leaps and bounds in all countries. Of the global population of nearly 7.9 billion (in 2021), there were 5.25 billion daily internet users, and this number is growing at 8.2 per cent per year. Over a billion in China and about 700 million in India are internet users. Over a third of the internet users are in the age group 25 to 34. Thus, a large proportion, that is increasing by the day, depends on internet-based information of all sorts, and web-based decision-making, including in the matter of career-choice. The availability of plenty of career options also poses a problem of choice and it is here that the role of a professional counsellor comes into play and assists the student in making a right choice.

Students today have access to several counselling and aptitude testing web-sites that provide career information. For example, Mindler, CareerGuide.com, mapmytalent.in, Univariety are some of the career guidance platforms[2]. A report cites 3RDiConsulting, AcmeCareers, Brain Checker, Brainwonders, Collegepond, Merittude, Momentsinbox Eduventures, Quest Systems, Tucareers and Tutelage as some of the top career counselling companies in India in 2019.[3] While they provide a vast canvas of information, internet-based counselling does not have that personal touch and element of trust between the counsellor and guidance seeker that is critical to counselling. Too much information could be confusing too.

Internet Addiction

While technology through internet has immensely enhanced range and speed of access to career information and even helps in occupational choice using aptitude tests, it has some negative impacts too. The most important is its addictive influence. Internet addiction disorder (IAD) is a type of behavioral

---

[2] Mindler (2017) Career Guidance Platforms in India – Comparison of Key Players, accessed on 17 June 2022 at lhttps://www.mindler.com/top-career-guidance-platforms-in-indiaatforms in India:

[3] https://education.siliconindia.com/engineering/ranking/career-counselling-companies-2019-rid-717.html, accessed on 17 June 2022.

addiction that makes people compulsive, uncontrolled users of the facility. This addiction may take the forms of online gambling, video games, pornography, use of social media, and the like. Use of mobiles too can lead to such addictive habits. While regular use of internet and mobiles is necessary in many walks of academic and occupational pursuits, and may be acceptable in social and recreational activities to an extent, uncontrollable use affects the addicts' personal and social life and drive them to undesirable habits. The problem is not a simple one that can be brushed aside. Compulsive Internet use is believed to be fairly common, affecting an estimated 1.5 to 8.2 percent of people in North America. This is where counsellors have a major role to play, in guiding internet and social media users to regulate their habits.

Social Networks

Social and professional networks (such as Linkedin) are another source of occupational and educational information, about 4.2 billion being daily users of one or the other social network in the world. And most children are addicted to extensively using social networks, which has its own good and bad impacts.

Social media addiction can affect the behaviour pattern and mental health of the users. The Displaced Behaviour Theory suggests that people who spend more time in sedentary activities like use of social media have less time for face-to-face social contact and communications that tend to be protective against mental disorders. The overuse of social media and its relation to the mental health of the users is a subject increasingly being studied by researchers. A systematic review of research work on the subject by Karim et al (2020) found that social media envy can affect the level of anxiety and depression in individuals. In a recent research paper titled 'Social Media and Mental Health', Bragheri et al (July 2022) dwelt on an extensive study conducted by them on the effects of Facebook use on the youth. Studying the hypothesis that 'The diffusion of social media coincided with a worsening of mental health conditions among adolescents and young adults in the United States, giving rise to speculation that social media might be detrimental to mental health', the authors' work found that a) the roll-out of Facebook at a college increased symptoms of poor mental health, especially depression, b) among students most susceptible to mental illness the introduction of the social media platform led to increased use of mental healthcare services, and c) after the introduction of the platform, students were more likely to report experiencing reduced academic performance resulting from poor mental health. Evidence presented by the authors also suggested that the results were due to the social media platform fostering unfavourable social comparisons. Individual counselling and behavioural therapy may benefit those addicted to overuse of social media. There is a growing need for guidance and counselling on the choice of proper social networks and on the right amount of usage of these networks.

Anti-social Habits

Socio-economic conditions, lack of discipline at home, failure or under-achievement in the educational pursuits and/or job-market, and exposure to wrong examples draws the youth into undesirable paths like drop out from schools, alcoholism and drug addiction, violent habits like road rage and gangsterism, and even indulging in terrorism. Such problems are much more rampant in the societies today than in the past. Counselling at an early stage is essential in such cases, but also is harder.

Diversity of Cultural Milieus

Today, the schools and societies, and even families, often present a mix of cultures. The students in a school come from varied backgrounds based on nationality and ethnicity, wealth, parental occupations, etc. These cultural differences could at times lead to frictions arising out of lack of understanding and tolerance. Counselling is required to ensure that these differences do not bring into play any element of intolerance and abuse.

Prevention versus Cure

Counselling in the past was more to spot a problem and attempt a solution to it. A physical or mental disability, or correcting a wrong step taken, used to trigger the need for counselling. Today, the emphasis is more on preventing the emergence of the problem by proper advice at the right time and guide the guidance-seeker into the correct path. This change in perspective considerably enlarges the counselling space.

These and several others point to the need for a growing need for professional counselling. Currently, over 93% of Indian schools do not have dedicated career counsellors. Schools, parents, and students are looking for various skill-based training opportunities and job profiles. Counselling has thus become more important than in the past.

Here it is also noteworthy that with the emerging new sets of problems, counselling techniques are also need to be innovative and evolving. Behaviour modification approaches with new methods like story analysis, art analysis, encouraging writings and ask the child to analyse her writings etc. can be some of the newer methods and can be very effective.

Changing Profile of a Counsellor

Changing requirements of guidance-seekers naturally call for changes in how the counsellor goes about his or her job. Therefore, the counsellor, today, has to be familiar with various possibilities at each stage of education to be able to provide effective guidance to the child. Immense increase is such possibilities requires that a counsellor keeps him/herself abreast of all developments in the education-employment matrix and is aware of the diverse alternative career paths appropriate to each education.

To be able to do that, the counsellor needs to be computer and internet savvy and must have a flair for exploring web-based career information, apart from using other sources. He/she has to go beyond the traditional way of depending upon just secondary sources of information and go about directly engaging the employers, academia and other relevant groups to learn about what is coming in future and be ready for providing advice appropriately. The counsellor needs to recognize that the guidance-seekers too have access to the internet-based career information and need guidance only to clear confusion in their minds. A counsellor has, therefore, to take into account this access to information to the clients from internet, from friends and other sources and decide what the clients want. He/she should also be aware of the aspirations, anxieties and approach to learning on the part of modern youth.

Technology has made the counsellor's job that much easy and that much difficult, easy because all the information that is needed has already been assembled and classified, and harder because the counsellor himself has to be familiar with the use of technology and then sift through the maze of information available to churn out details relevant to the guidance seeker. Technology has also made available avenues through online programmes to the counsellors for improving their own knowledge and skills. Today's counsellor can, in addition to the traditional aspects of work such as parent counselling, counselling in schools and in employment offices, also specialize in areas like profile-building and development of bio-data, studies abroad including choice of educational institutions, guidance in obtaining visas and related aspects, taking up self-employment and even resource mobilization. The counsellors need to be fully equipped with latest information, technology and tools in such fields. They need to anticipate changes in the educational and employment fields and be prepared to guide their clients accordingly.

In conclusion, it may be said that the current shortage of counsellors and the modern-day complexities in the right choice of careers indicate vast opportunities for professional counsellors with appropriate aptitudes, skills and initiatives.

23

Guidance for Entrepreneurship—Self-Employment

The need for being your own employer is growing as salaried jobs are shrinking. The mind set to have a salaried job is gradually changing but this change is very slow. A large majority of young still want a safe and secure salaried job that too with the government. Unemployment is growing with this type of mind set. People need to be educated to create their own employment. The idea is getting a momentum with various interventions in this area from the side of the government. But at the same time job- seekers need to be aware of their own potential to start their own enterprise, the gaps in their capabilities and information about how to start a business which could be sustainable and cost effective. The development of the mind set to be an entrepreneur has to be started at school level itself and guidance can play a vital role.

Importance of Self-Employment

Self-employment can provide huge space in job markets which will not only help in income generation but will also generate employment for many. It can bridge the gap between unemployment and employment opportunities. It also brings confidence and feeling of self -dependence. A person who starts an enterprise creates employment for others as well. One can implement his own ideas and he is the master of his own.

Opportunities of Self-Employment in various sectors:

Self- employment can be had in a large number of activities involving all the three sectors – primary, secondary and Tertiary sectors of the economy.

There are tremendous opportunities in all these three sectors for self-employment. The activities may range from large enterprises to a small roadside activities like selling. One can choose the activity as per choice resources and demand for a product. It is also noteworthy that if a product idea is good demand can be created.

There are certain common features of Self- employment.

- Risk: Self- employment involves risks of success and failure. As such risks are in every type of jobs; it is to be decided by the individual that which types of risk one can handle. There are market uncertainties as sometimes

Primary Sector	• Agriculture, forestry,fishing, metals, minerals etc.
Secondary Sector	• Relates to manufacturing or industrial sector such as textiles, automoboles etc. • This sector used produce of primaty sector as raw material
Tertiary Sector	• This sector includes all types of services like education, banking, finace sector, transportation, hospitality, tourism etc.

Figure 23.1: *Three sectors of economy having potential for Self-employment*

there is a demand of the product in the market, while sometimes there is no demand.

- Resources: Arranging resources like human resource, raw material, transportation etc everything is the responsibility of the entrepreneur. However, one can form a team for these arrangements.
- Competition: There is a tough competition and one has to decide how to survive in the market.
- Knowledge: One should have good knowledge of local situations, availability of resources nearby, cost effectiveness of the project, selling scheme etc.
- Requires certain personality traits: Be one's own employer requires certain traits which will be discussed later part of this chapter.
- Wide Choice: While salaried employment is limited, self- employment provides wider choices one can choose from as per the interest and aptitude.
- Higher Incomes: After the initial stage one can have higher incomes than the wage employment.
- Best use of skills: Self- employment provides opportunities for using one's own skills and abilities

Traits Needed for Entrepreneurship

There are certain traits needed to be an entrepreneur. These traits vary from business to business. For instance, if a person wants to start educational consultancy, he or she should have all sorts of information about educational streams, future prospects and so on. Similarly, if one wants to start a tourism office one should be fond of touring places, the communication skills should be good, politeness is needed for dealing with customers. Some of general traits can be:

- Self confidence
- Ability to foresee and plan
- Ability to take risks
- Ability for decision making
- Managerial and leadership abilities
- Creativity and innovation
- Ability to trap the opportunities
- Marketing skills, salesmanship
- Determination
- Ability to cope with failures or difficulties
- Proper education, training and experience in the field
- Ability to manage finances

Barriers in promotion of self-employment

As wrote earlier people want wage employment as it ensures regular and certain income while in self- employment activities such certainty may not be there. One day one may earn a high income by selling his products; on the other day, he may not be able to sell. In these circumstances he would not be sure of his earnings. Other barriers that hinder people to come forward are:

1. Social and psychological attitudes, bias towards salaried employment. Everybody wants a government job.
2. Educational training systems leading to no or non-marketable skills.
3. Lack of awareness about advantages and facilities available
4. Lack of resources
5. Institutional problems like procedures, delays, official attitudes, etc.
6. Pressure from parents to have a secure job.

Role of Guidance Person in dealing with Barriers

Guidance counsellor and other guidance personnel can play a very crucial role in changing the mindset among students and help in developing their skills to be entrepreneurs. They can also have interaction with parents and teachers and make a plan and activities that could motivate students to think about being self-employed. Some specific activities that can be performed by guidance personnel can be as below:

Steps in Self- Employment Promotion:

The major question is how to develop positive thinking among students about entrepreneurship who are set to take up salaried employment:

There are various steps a guidance worker should take

1. *Identify students with potential*
   Students who have some capabilities to be entrepreneurs should be identified as a first step. This can be done through psychological tests

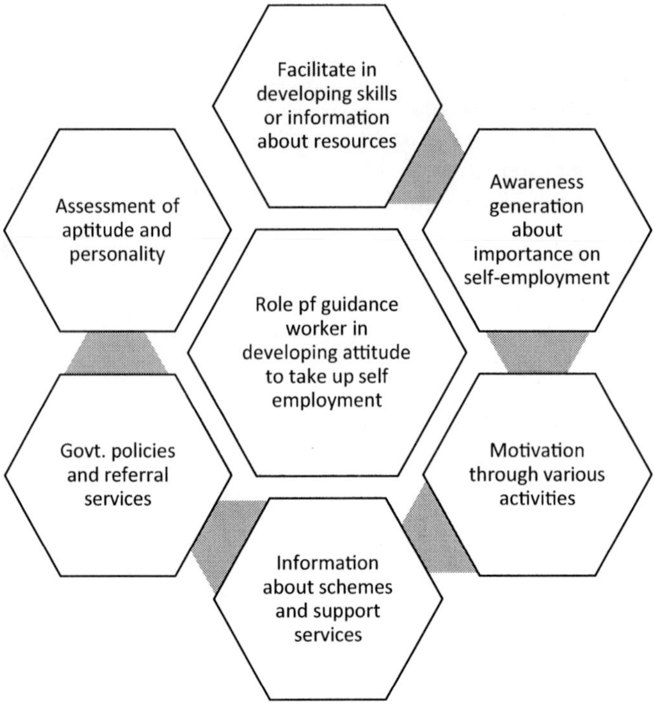

Figure 23.2: *Role of Guidance in Promoting Entrepreneurship*

by which one can the aptitude, interest and personality characteristics. Students who have some potential need to be nurtured.

2. *Motivate them towards self- employment*

   This requires large scale general awareness. Media like radio talks, class talks, messages through television, print media can be used for creating awareness about importance of being entrepreneurs. Demonstrations, visit to existing self- employment venture, discussions, distribution of print material, case studies etc. can be some good methods to motivate students. Guidance counsellor can also organise parent-teacher-student meetings.

   The content of message should include information about the labour market conditions, opportunities in self- employment, the schemes and facilities, the relative advantages of self- employment and so on. It is important that the client is not presented only one- sided picture. Guidance person should give both positive and negative aspects of pursuing self-employment and also risks involved.

3. *Develop leadership qualities and soft skills*

   It is important that those interested in being entrepreneurs should be provided needed skills like managerial skills, communication skills, social skills and so on from the very beginning. For this some programmes for development of soft skills can be introduced in the school itself. Opportunities must be provided in school to take up responsibilities, participation in debates and discussions etc.

4. *Provide information on possible avenues and service providers*
   Guidance worker should collect and provide information about possible lines of self- employment suitable to one's temperament and aptitude; rules and regulations such as registration, license, etc.; schemes of assistance; agencies providing various forms of assistance and services like finance, raw material training, technical advice, marketing, feasibility of a project in a certain area, procedures for availing of the assistance.
5. *Referral services*
   The guidance activity would comprise assisting in preparing a necessary document such as the project proposal, introducing to various service providers like banks, raw material providers, technical experts in the line chosen, referring to skill training in particular chosen area of venture where necessary, following up with the service providers and helping in getting the assistance required.

There could be post launch services also. The guidance services will have to continue even after a self- employment activity has been initiated by the individual or a group. It is necessary to organize periodic follow up to see that the activity is going on along the expected lines or if it is encountering any problem. In case of any problems proper counselling should be provided to overcome the same.

It may be noted here that many students go for higher studies after schooling and take up employment much later. Referral services are for those who want to enter in the job market after schooling. Some students keep in touch with the guidance worker even after the school. Guidance person may continue guiding such students. A basic motivation and information about entrepreneurship provides a bird's eye view about the employment market and the motivation can be used by the students at a later stage as well.

Emerging Areas for self-employment: (indicative list)

The list would help a guidance worker in providing guidance to the students may be like to have their own venture:

- Organic manure,
- Horticulture,
- Bio fuel and energy plantations
- Solar system
- Floriculture
- Fishing
- Medicinal plants,

- Mushrooms,
- Quality cotton,
- Oilseeds
- Silk production
- Poultry and egg production
- Beekeeping
- Cut Flowers
- Food processing
- Handicrafts with improved design
- Khadi and textiles
- New products and designs
- Jute and other bags
- Repair of domestic appliances, electric- electronic goods, tractor and pumpsets, repair of boats and Nets.
- Low- cost housing material.
- Parts for assembling for larger units.
- Tourism related services
- Adventure sports
- Restaurants and hospitality
- Value added services
- Transportation
- Storage of agricultural products
- Packaging of food
- Yoga, Indigenous Health practices
- Communication services- e-mail, fax, data related services, data entry, Internet, digital marketing,
- Ffinancial services, shares, bonds, insurance, mutual funds
- Beauty culture
- Domestic nursing
- Educational Consultancy- Project preparation, Thesis guidance, Costing etc.
- Innovative technology
- Infrastructure development and construction
- Fashion designing
- Event management
- Eco, friendly technology
- Production and processing of millets

Government Initiatives

Pradhan Mantri MUDRA Yojana (PMMY) is a scheme launched by the Hon'ble Prime Minister on April 8, 2015 for providing loans up to 10 lakh to the non-corporate, non-farm small/micro enterprises. These loans are given by Commercial Banks, RRBs, Small Finance Banks, MFIs and NBFCs. The portal www.udyamimitra.in . provides more information. Under the aegis of PMMY, MUDRA has created three products namely 'Shishu', 'Kishore' and 'Tarun' to signify the stage of growth / development and funding needs of the beneficiary micro unit / entrepreneur and also provide a reference point for the next phase of graduation / growth. This scheme is facilitating in 'Startups' and a large number of youth is attracted towards this scheme.

There are several other schemes like Prime Minister's Employment Generation Programme which is a credit linked subsidy programme implemented by Ministry of Micro, Small and Medium Enterprises. It helps in establishment of micro enterprises by organising artisans and other youth.

For Rural Youth Pt. Deen Dayal Upadhyaya Grameen Kaushalya Yojna which is linked to National Rural Livelihood Mission supports the government programmes such as Make in India, Start Up India etc. with focus on rural youth. Similarly, Aajeevika National Rural Livelihood Programme relates to Self Help Groups (SHGs).

These are some initiatives that highlight Government's intention to develop skilled India with focus on youth both rural and urban who have potential to become entrepreneurs.